Readings in the ANC Tradition

Volume I

UNDERSTANDING THE ANC TODAY

General Editor: Professor Ben Turok

Volume 1: The Historical Roots of the ANC

Volume 2: The ANC and the Turn to Armed Struggle

Volume 3: Readings in the ANC Tradition, I

Volume 4: Readings in the ANC Tradition, II

Volume 5: Development in a Divided Country

Volume 6: The Controversy about Economic Growth

Readings in the ANC Tradition
Volume I

Policy and Praxis

Edited by Ben Turok

Grateful thanks are due to the following organisations for allowing us to reproduce material in which they hold copyright: NB Publishers for permission to quote from Let My People Go *by Albert Luthuli (Tafelberg Publishers); and the ANC and SACP to quote from several of their documents.*

First published by Jacana Media (Pty) Ltd in 2011

10 Orange Street
Sunnyside
Auckland Park 2092
South Africa
+2711 628 3200
www.jacana.co.za

© 2011 Ben Turok (this selection)

All rights reserved.

ISBN 978-1-77009-969-2

Set in Minion 9.5/12pt
Printed and bound by Ultra Litho (Pty) Limited, Johannesburg
Job No. 001402

See a complete list of Jacana titles at www.jacana.co.za

Contents

Preface to the Series vii
Introduction ix

Part One: THE VISION
The Great Battle: The Story of African Resistance in 1879 (1979) 1
Pixley Seme, *The Regeneration of Africa* (1906) 9
Pixley Seme, *Native Union* (1911)................................ 14
Manifesto of the Communist Party of South Africa (1921) 17
Africans' Claims in South Africa (1943) 21
Women's Charter (1954)... 27
The Freedom Charter (1955) 32
Does the Freedom Charter Mean Socialism? (1957) 36
Albert Luthuli, 'The Defiance Campaign' from *Let
    My People Go* (1962) 40
*The Road to South African Freedom: The Programme
    of the South African Communist Party* (1962) 51

Part Two: THE ROAD TO POWER
Forward to Freedom: Strategy and Tactics of the ANC (1969) 97
Advance to People's Power! 75 Years of Struggle (1987)............... 116
*The Path to Power: Programme of the South African
    Communist Party* (1990) 135

Part Three: PREPARING TO GOVERN
The Reconstruction and Development Programme: Introduction (1994).. 153
*The Reconstruction and Development Programme: Building
    the Economy* (1994) 163
*Growth, Employment and Redistribution:
    A Macroeconomic Strategy* (1996)............................ 194
*Building a National Democratic Society: Strategy and
    Tactics of the ANC* (2007) 224

Preface to the series

As we go to press, the ANC is preparing to mark the centenary of its existence. This is a remarkable achievement for any political movement, with few precedents anywhere in the world. Even more remarkable is the fact that it has been the ruling party in South Africa for 16 years and remains the most powerful political force in the country, despite many shortcomings. The ANC may not rule forever, but it has made a huge impact on South Africa in every dimension of its existence, hence its history and present-day work merit special recognition.

This series 'Understanding the ANC Today' is an attempt to map in broad outlines the party's history, the external influences that shaped its policies and actions, the depth of the policy challenges it faced in the decades prior to its victory over apartheid, and the problems it is now confronting as a ruling party.

The scope of the whole series is vast. But the contributors are among the top thinkers in the ANC and they have not shirked exploring all these issues to the full. Since their writing deals with the realities facing all the people of the country, and shaping the future, the books should be of interest to the general public and not just members of the ANC and its allies.

It is our hope that the books will become standard texts in university courses and used in schools to broaden the understanding of our youth of where they come from and where the ANC would like to lead them. It is also our hope that the presentation of these books to the movement as a whole will encourage reading and study so that our cadres will be better prepared for the enormous but exciting tasks ahead as we plan for the new South Africa.

These books are not written in the spirit of propaganda. They are analytical and historical. They deal frankly and without reservation about the diverse influences on the ANC of many ideologies and historical experiences across the globe for over a century. At the same time the organic development of the movement as an indigenous force is also given its proper recognition.

Ben Turok

Introduction

ANC leaders frequently assert that the party is a 'broad church' encompassing members of diverse ideologies and social class. What is less frequently referred to is the diversity of influences on its policies and praxis, even while it retained a distinctive character as a liberation movement rooted in South African history.

In Volume 1 of this series, *The Historical Roots of the ANC*, the writers dealt with these diverse influences as actual experiences over a century.

The present volume provides the actual texts that constitute the backdrop of ideologies and experiences from around the world, which brought richness and depth to the evolution of ANC positions over the years.

Many of these documents are not easily available since they are buried in remote libraries without easy access. Yet they constitute the foundation of present thinking and culture of ANC political conduct.

In Part One, 'The Vision', we include essays by the founding fathers of the ANC, which give the flavour of their thinking. This is followed by a series of documents from the archives of the various components of the ANC and the Communist Party. Some of these are actual programmes of the day, which have huge historical interest as they reveal the changing balance of forces in the country and the maturing of the different sections of the movement.

Part Two, 'The Road to Power', provides documents of more immediate relevance to the ANC's approach to the transfer of power from apartheid to democracy. The key documents are the Strategy and Tactics tradition, which commenced in 1969 and which have been modified and brought up to date at each successive national conference of the ANC. The documents of the Communist Party contain some important theoretical material such as the concept of Colonialism of a Special Type, which has been adopted by the whole movement. There has also been significant analysis of the relation between class and race, and of the essence of African nationalism as an ideological construct in the movement.

Unfortunately, many of these subtle meanings have not been adequately conveyed to the present generation of ANC cadres. This may explain the weaknesses in political positions on such matters as the multiracial character of South African society, the persistence of race prejudice throughout the society, and the apparently fading belief that we can build a non-racial society. There is also a failure to analyse the roles of different classes and in particular the black business and middle strata.

Part Three, 'Preparing to Govern', provides the most important documents of the period just prior to the democratic transition in 1994 and of the immediate period after that. The historic Reconstruction and Development Programme (RDP) brought the nation together in a most unexpected way, and remains the most important vision statement of the movement second only to the Freedom Charter. However, it was displaced by the Growth, Employment and Redistribution (Gear) strategy document, which remains highly controversial. These two documents should be read side by side if we are to understand the issues that remain at the centre of debate even today.

We also include the most recent Strategy and Tactics document adopted at the critical 2007 Polokwane ANC national conference, at which Thabo Mbeki was replaced by Jacob Zuma as President of the ANC and of the country and which signalled a progressive shift in economy policy.

Part One

The Vision

The Great Battle: The Story of African Resistance in 1879

(From *Sechaba*, 30 February 1979)

'They were like lions and not afraid of death' – British soldier

It is indicative of imperialist and racist history books that the names Tshingwayo ka Mahoye and Mavumengwana are totally ignored. Yet these are the two generals – the former a spirited veteran of 70 years; the latter thirty years his junior – that led Cetshwayo's crack impis in a spectacular victory over British forces at Isandhlwana on January 22, 1879.

An Astonishing Victory
The battle – the centenary of which we are marking this year – is generally considered one of the most humiliating defeats suffered by an Imperial British Army in the annals of that country's blood-stained colonial history. It is difficult to exaggerate the astonishing nature of the British defeat. For this was a true David and Goliath situation; a 19th century counterpart to US imperialism's war on Vietnam. Mighty Britain, the world's leading industrial and colonial power, whose army was then the best trained and equipped in history, had launched a sudden, predatory war against a small African kingdom whose army fought with spears and shields and whose population numbered perhaps 300,000. Yet the fearless African warriors of that Zulu kingdom were able to overrun the main staging camp of the invading army despite the withering fire from the breech-loading rifles, cannons, rocket-tubes and Gatling machine-guns and, in ferocious hand-to-hand fighting, account for the lives of almost all the desperate defenders.

The British lost 858 men at Isandhlwana and an equal number of African levies of the so-called Natal Native Contingent. (Not for the first time in our history are the Pretoria Boers today attempting to use Africans to fight Africans!) The British casualties were colossal in a colonial war where the armed men on horseback expected to lose few of their number.

Yet at Isandhlwana 52 British officers lost their lives while at the battle of Waterloo 48 were killed! Six whole companies of the 24th Foot Regiment totalling 602 men, later known as the South Wales Borderers, were wiped out to a man.

News of the Imperial disaster shattered the confidence of Victorian Britain and colonial South Africa. The British Prime Minister, Disraeli, stated that the 'evil consequences' for his country were 'incalculable' and indeed as a result of the rumpus he soon lost office. The arrogant British general, Lord Chelmsford, was disgraced and chided as follows in the Durban *Daily News*: 'You will have seen of our great disaster at Isandhlwana, only a short distance from the border where every man was butchered … it is evident that our general was out-generalled by the Zulus.' No less an authority than Frederick Engels, a military expert in has own right, was later to write: 'The Zulus did what no European army can do. Armed only with lances and spears, without any firearms, they advanced under a hail of bullets from breechloaders up to the bayonets of the English infantry – the best in the world for fighting in closed ranks – and threw them into confusion more than once, yea, ever forced them to retreat in spite of the immense disparity of weapons.'

At this time when much racist superficiality and academic claptrap will be written and said both in Britain and South Africa about Isandhlwana, we must ask ourselves what are the important lessons to be learnt from this notable victory, and indeed subsequent defeat of Cetshwayo's kingdom, and the relevance today.

An Unjust, Colonial War
To start with, let us examine the cause of the war which lasted from January to July, and masquerades in colonial history books under the title of the Zulu War. A cursory glance at events in South Africa in the 1870s and 1880s shows that in this short period Great Britain launched, one after another, violent and sudden wars on our people, who were then organised into small and separate national entities and chiefdoms. For example, wars to the finish were launched on the Hlubi in 1873, the Gcaleka and Pedi in 1877, the Ngqika, Thembu, Pondo, Griqua and Rolong in 1878, the Sotho in 1880, and the Ndebele in 1893. For centuries Dutch, British and Boer had by degrees been dispossessing our people of their land and birthright. This was part of the world-wide process of colonial conquest that had begun in the 15th century. By the last third of the 19th century the 'Scramble for Africa' between the rival colonial powers was intense and Britain was determined to finally bring the whole of Southern Africa under her control. It is no

coincidence that the discovery of diamonds at Kimberley in 1870 excited Britain's insatiable greed and haste. This was the great dividing period in South African history where the basis for dramatic and far-reaching socio-economic transformation was laid and mine and factory were soon to compete with farming estate for cheap labour. As has been pointed out before now, South Africa's industrial era was baptised in the blood of our people. Aptly summing up the economic requirements of the time, Shepstone, then Native Administrator in Natal, had remarked at the time of Cetshwayo's coronation in 1872 that there was a pressing need to transform the Zulu warriors into 'labourers working for wages'.

Spearpoint of Leadership
By the beginning of 1879, having completed the bloody repression of the Ngqika under chief Sandile and the Gcaleka under Hintsa's son Kreli, the British were free to turn their attention on Cetshwayo. Clearly the independence and military power of the kingdom founded by the great Shaka represented a formidable obstacle to Britain's imperial designs. Indeed, it was generally held that 'Cetshwayo was the source of disaffection among most of the tribes of South Africa, to whom he sent emissaries and who looked to the warriors of Zululand as the spearpoint of aggressive leadership' (Frank Emery, *The Red Soldier*). The British even regarded Sekhukhune, who was giving them and the Transvaal Boers a great deal of trouble, as 'Cetshwayo's cat's paw'. But Cetshwayo had always steered a cautious and friendly diplomatic course with the British and their Natal Colony. It was the Transvaal Boers and particularly those in the disputed border lands of the Blood River who were the Zulus' traditional enemy. The British had also cultivated a pacific relationship with Cetshwayo. Now when it suited them he was suddenly depicted as the 'apostle of darkness and evil' and his people described as a 'barbaric and unruly race, unfit to govern their country and a constant menace to the white civilisation of Natal'. It was not hard to find a trifling incident as the occasion on which to declare war – in this case Zulu justice meted out to an adulteress who had sought refuge in Natal – and by January 11, when Chelmsford's ultimatum to Cetshwayo to disband the regiments and lay down arms had been ignored, a British army of 18,000 troops, cavalry and hundreds of wagon trains loaded with food, weapons and equipment, crossed the Tugela River and invaded Zululand.

Bloody Repression
Thus we see that the cause of the war lay entirely at the door of the British, as was the case with all wars of colonial conquest. The troops and officers who

were waging an unjust, bloody war of repression against the Zulu were the very troops fresh from the most recent wars against the Ngqika and Gcaleka and the other people of our country; indeed hardened campaigners from colonial repression in the Gold Coast and Ethiopia, India and Afghanistan! Not for the first time in history were the people who were being invaded, whose land was being stolen and plundered, blamed as the blood-thirsty war-mongers. We see the same racist mythology working today with regard to Zimbabwe, Namibia and our own liberation struggle.

Neither did the British wage war as though it was a game of cricket. This was total war. Kraals and huts were put to the flame; cattle were seized; crops were destroyed; non- combatants tortured for information; the wounded were shot out of hand; after Isandhlwana no prisoners were taken alive. Whether it be the terrorism of Ian Smith or of the Americans in Vietnam, the methods of imperialism have little changed through the ages! The British was the army which, in the words of the historian H. Lawson, 'brought calamities compared to which the cattle raids of the Boers had been mere flea bites'. He has written: 'The British way was not composed of cowardly cattle thieves but of ruthless and dehumanised mercenaries whose profession was destruction. Moreover, they appeared in their thousands, where the Boers had mustered only a few hundred. When they attacked the African people, the damage they were able to inflict was tremendous.'

Formula for Victory
How then did Cetshwayo's impis manage to inflict such a devastating defeat on the British army at Isandhlwana? It is said that the necessity of any successful army is high morale, superior tactics and excellent weapons. The Zulu success is all the more remarkable given the immense disparity of weapons. They made up for this through many superb qualities bred into every warrior from the time of Shaka. These included superb physical fitness, high mobility and speed, iron discipline and above all a fighting determination and fearlessness that provoked total awe in the enemy. Armed with the knobkerrie and short stabbing assegai devised by Shaka, the Zulu warrior was a formidable foe at in-fighting. Confidence in his own ability, with a proud combat record to emulate, helped create the conditions for high morale. Fighting a just war in defence of king and country against the alien invader made for a razor-sharp morale at Isandhlwana. Cetshwayo had addressed 12 of his regiments numbering 20,000 warriors destined for the attack on the British camp with the words: 'I am sending you against the Whitemen who have invaded Zululand and driven away our cattle.' The problem for generals Tshingwayo and Mavumengwana

and regimental indunas such as Zibhebhu, Sigcwelegcwele and the King's brother Dabulamanzi was how to overcome the superior firepower of the enemy and get to close quarters with the defenders of the camp. The way this was achieved is a testament to the ability of Cetshwayo's generals and the discipline and training of the warriors. It led a British survivor to complain: 'The way our camp was taken could not be more cleverly taken by any of our Generals.'

Spies, Decoys and Surprise Attack
Once they had invaded Zululand the British task was to locate the impis. No matter how far and wide they scouted, they failed to achieve this. By the skilful use of decoys Tshingwayo and Mavumengwana drew the British reconnaissance parties up all manner of blind alleys. On the other hand the Zulu intelligence system – based on spies and scouting parties – was extremely efficient and the position and strength of the various British invading columns were well known. By the dawn of January 22, Chelmsford had left his main camp in search of the elusive enemy. Isandhlwana was down to half its strength; that is 2,000 men. While Chelmsford and the other half of the camp's contingent were chasing round the countryside, the Zulu force of 20,000 warriors was resting in a steep ravine only four miles from the camp. It was an amazing and brilliant achievement to move an army of this size so close to the British position through countryside which was not exactly covered in forests and which was alive with British scouting parties. One can only marvel at the ability of the commanders; the stealth and discipline of the regiments. Undoubtedly this was the basis for the famous victory, for the attack was launched with great speed and surprise, enabling the traditional Zulu 'horns' to encircle the camp while the main body – the 'chest' – charged at the weakest point. For half an hour the British poured out a desperate fire, cutting down many warriors. Displaying great valour and determination the impis kept charging the lines of redcoats until they were able to come to close quarters with infantrymen Engels described as 'the best in the world for fighting at close quarters'. On this occasion the assegais of African warriors proved too much for English bayonets and, after a battle that lasted little more than an hour, there were very few survivors on the British side to tell the tale. Two thousand Zulu warriors had died in defence of their country and Cetshwayo remarked that 'an assegai has been thrust into the belly of the nation'.

Generalship and Fighting Ability
The imperialist history books explain away the British disaster through

the ineptitude of Chelmsford; the unreliability of the African levies; the shortage of ammunition. This is all arrant nonsense designed to obscure the superior Zulu generalship and fighting ability which had won the battle for Cetshwayo and for African posterity. Chelmsford was simply out-generalled; the African levies were a minor appendage to the British infantrymen and cavalry, who were the main fighting force, and were not the only soldiers to run when the warriors broke through the defending lines; and as far as the ammunition was concerned there was a quarter of a million rounds in the camp. The fact that runners from the quartermaster's store could apparently not keep supplies flowing as fast as became necessary at the peak of the Zulu assault was as much the result of the ferocity of the attack as it was owing to the general disorganisation. And that of course is why a surprise attack is so advantageous to the attacker! That Isandhlwana was not a flash in the pan is evidenced by further Zulu victories at the Intombi River on March 12 and at Hlobane on March 28. The British lost 100 men at the former and 80 men at the latter engagements; in both cases they were taken by surprise.

British Power, Boer Power
As crushing a defeat as Isandhlwana was, it could only be a temporary reverse for an enemy with the resources of Britain. Thousands of reinforcements arrived in Natal during the ensuing months and by June Chelmsford had at his disposal an army of over 30,000 troops. The arrogant British general had anticipated defeating Cetshwayo – in a matter of weeks; in the event it took him six months. Superior firepower finally won the day at the Battle of Ulundi in July. Zulu power was broken. Cetshwayo was dethroned; the kingdom was split into 13 separate units; the chiefs were subordinated to white magistrates; the disputed territory handed to the Boers and two-thirds of the farmlands given to the settlers. By 1897 what remained of Zululand was made a part of Natal. All of which makes it perfectly clear that the subjugation of all our people took place because of the power of Britain. The Boers on their own did not have the capacity or the resources to carry out this design and were often put to flight by the warriors of Moshoeshoe, Sekhukhune and Dingane and in the hundred years' engagements on the Cape frontiers. Incidentally the victory at Isandhlwana makes utter nonsense of the Boer claim and racist-mongering every December 16 that they had crushed Zulu power once and for all at Blood River in 1838.

It is interesting and important to note that just as it was impossible for the colonial settlers alone to impose their authority on our people, so the Pretoria Boers and racists like Smith are today incapable of ruling without the enormous support they receive from Britain, the US and other Western countries.

Divide and Rule
Following another historic link through to the present, we see how carefully the British followed their strategy of divide and rule. In the first place they made certain of quelling the resistance of Sandile and Kreli in what is today the Transkei and then, after dethroning Cetshwayo, fostered numerous rival claimants such as the traitor Zibhebhu so as to destroy the kingdom from within. The policy of isolating centres of resistance and of playing one group against another is imperialism's cardinal rule to this day. It is not hard to see the tap-root from which Afrikanerdom's Bantustan schemes spring. Our people in the 19th century well understood the need for unity and co-ordination; perhaps more so than is generally understood, as the British description of Sekhukhune as Cetshwayo's 'cat's paw' indicates. It is clear that an understanding along these lines existed between Moshoeshoe's Southern Sotho kingdom, Sekhukhune and Cetshwayo. There is plenty of evidence of British casualties from Zulu marksmen during the war of 1879 and it is said that they received some training from Moshoeshoe's expert riflemen. British and settler anxiety about a united front of the Africans is evidenced from a letter from one of Chelmsford's officers, who wrote during the campaign against Sandile: 'It is said that a general simultaneous rising against the white people was only spoilt by the quarrel between the Gcalekas and Fingoes bringing on the Kaffir War prematurely.' Clearly the objective conditions did not then exist for the national unity which the African National Congress dedicated itself to forging from its historic inception in 1912; just as the conditions for the Balkanisation of South Africa are today a thing of the past and are doomed to failure.

Unity the Key
The broad unity of all our people laying claim to an indivisible South Africa on the basis of the Freedom Charter and under the leadership of the ANC is the indispensable condition for our liberation. That is the recurrent lessons of our history and experience of centuries of struggle against colonial conquest, national oppression, racist tyranny and vicious economic exploitation.

The threads of that struggle of Africans, Indians, Coloureds and democrats of all races are intimately related. In celebrating the centenary of the Battle of Isandhlwana we salute an historic landmark in the more than three centuries' resistance of our people. Although the nature of the times were such that actions were generally uncoordinated, the many wars our people fought form an indivisible chain that links that era of epic resistance with the national liberation struggle today. The traditions and heritage of that heroic era live on, fiercely burning in the hearts of our people. The names of Hintsa, Makana, Moshoeshoe, Adam Kok, Dingane and Cetshwayo serve as the great landmarks of those epic struggles.

Fearlessness and Determination
The significance of Isandhlwana is that it epitomises the fearless and determined fighting spirit of that whole era of resistance wars. The battle serves as a clarion call to all our freedom-loving people, inspiring them to spare no effort in the continuing war to liberate every inch of our beloved country. Just as the victory of the Vietnamese people over US imperialism inspires oppressed people everywhere in the knowledge that it is possible to defeat a mighty power, so the victory of Isandhlwana reminds us of our warrior heritage and our people's ability to fearlessly face and overcome a military giant.

Today we fight with different methods and under different circumstances when the tide of history is running against imperialism, racism and reaction. With the unity of our people; with the determination of our ancestors; with the correct theory and leadership of the ANC; with international support and with Umkhonto spearheading a People's War, we will win many victories as astonishing as Isandhlwana until the nation is free.

Isandhlwana is a challenge!

Isandhlwana is a clarion call to People's War!

Pixley Seme
The Regeneration of Africa
(From *The African Abroad*, 5 April 1906)

I have chosen to speak to you on this occasion upon 'The Regeneration of Africa'. I am an African, and I set my pride in my race over against a hostile public opinion. Men have tried to compare races on the basis of some equality. In all the works of nature, equality, if by it we mean identity, is an impossible dream! Search the universe! You will find no two units alike. The scientists tell us there are no two cells, no two atoms, identical. Nature has bestowed upon each a peculiar individuality, an exclusive patent, from the great giants of the forest to the tenderest blade. Catch in your hand, if you please, the gentle flakes of snow. Each is a perfect gem, a new creation; it shines in its own glory – a work of art different from all of its aerial companions. Man, the crowning achievement of nature, defies analysis. He is a mystery through all ages and for all time. The races of mankind are composed of free and unique individuals. An attempt to compare them on the basis of equality can never be finally satisfactory. Each is self. My thesis stands on this truth; time has proved it. In all races, genius is like a spark, which, concealed in the bosom of a flint, bursts forth at the summoning stroke. It may arise anywhere and in any race.

I would ask you not to compare Africa to Europe or to any other continent. I make this request not from any fear that such comparison might bring humiliation upon Africa. The reason I have stated: a common standard is impossible! Come with me to the ancient capital of Egypt, Thebes, the city of one hundred gates. The grandeur of its venerable ruins and the gigantic proportions of its architecture reduce to insignificance the boasted monuments of other nations. The pyramids of Egypt are structures to which the world presents nothing comparable. The mighty monuments seem to look with disdain on every other work of human art and to vie with nature herself. All the glory of Egypt belongs to Africa and her people. These monuments are the indestructible memorials of their great and original genius. it is not through Egypt alone that Africa claims such unrivalled historic achievements. I could have spoken of the pyramids of Ethiopia, which, though inferior in size to those of Egypt, far surpass them in architectural beauty; their sepulchres which evince the highest purity of taste, and of many prehistoric ruins in other parts of Africa. In such ruins Africa is like the golden sun, that, having sunk beneath the western horizon, still plays upon the world which he sustained and enlightened in his career.

Justly the world now demands:
'Whither is fled the visionary gleam,
Where is it now, the glory and the dream?'

Oh, for that historian who, with the open pen of truth, will bring to Africa's claim the strength of written proof. He will tell of a race whose onward tide was often swelled with tears, but in whose heart bondage has not quenched the fire of former years. He will write that in these later days when Earth's noble ones are named, she has a roll of honor too, of whom she is not ashamed. The giant is awakening! From the four corners of the earth Africa's sons, who have been proved through fire and sword, are marching to the future's golden door bearing the records of deeds of valor done.

Mr Calhoun, I believe, was the most philosophical of all the slaveholders. He said once that if he could find a black man who could understand the Greek syntax, he would then consider their race human, and his attitude toward enslaving them would therefore change. What might have been the sensation kindled by the Greek syntax in the mind of the famous Southerner, I have so far been unable to discover; but oh, I envy the moment that was lost! And woe to the tongues that refused to tell the truth! If any such were among the now living, I could show him among black men of pure African blood those who could repeat the Koran from memory, skilled in Latin, Greek and Hebrew, Arabic and Chaldaic – men great in wisdom and profound knowledge – one professor of philosophy in a celebrated German university; one corresponding member of the French Academy of Sciences, who regularly transmitted to that society meteorological observations, and hydrographical journals and papers on botany and geology; another whom many ages call 'The Wise', whose authority Mahomet himself frequently appealed to in the Koran in support of his own opinion; men of wealth and active benevolence, those whose distinguished talents and reputation have made them famous in the cabinet and in the field, officers of artillery in the great armies of Europe, generals and lieutenant-generals in the armies of Peter the Great in Russia and Napoleon in France, presidents of free republics, kings of independent nations which have burst their way to liberty by their own vigor. There are many other Africans who have shown marks of genius and high character sufficient to redeem their race from the charges which I am now considering.

Ladies and gentlemen, the day of great exploring expeditions in Africa is over! Man knows his home now in a sense never known before. Many great and holy men have evinced a passion for the day you are now witnessing, their prophetic vision shot through many unborn centuries to this very hour. 'Men shall run to and fro,' said Daniel, 'and knowledge shall increase upon the earth.' Oh, how true! See the triumph of human genius to-day! Science has searched out the deep things of nature, surprised the secrets of the most distant stars, disentombed the memorials of everlasting hills, taught the lightning to speak, the vapors to toil and the winds to worship-spanned the sweeping rivers, tunneled the longest mountain range, made the world a vast whispering gallery, and has brought foreign nations into one civilized family. This all-powerful contact says even to the most backward race, you cannot remain where you are, you cannot fall back, you must advance! A great century has come upon us. No race possessing the inherent capacity to survive can resist and remain unaffected by this influence of contact and intercourse, the backward with the advanced. This influence constitutes the very essence of efficient progress and of civilization.

From these heights of the twentieth century I again ask you to cast your eyes south of the Desert of Sahara. If you could go with me to the oppressed Congos and ask, What does it mean, that now, for liberty, they fight like men and die like martyrs; if you would go with me to Bechuanaland, face their council of headmen and ask what motives caused them recently to decree so emphatically that alcoholic drinks shall not enter their country; visit their king, Khama, ask for what cause he leaves the gold and ivory palace of his ancestors, its mountain strongholds and all its august ceremony, to wander daily from village to village through all his kingdom, without a guard or any decoration of his rank, a preacher of industry and education, and an apostle of the new order of things; if you would ask Menelik what means this that Abyssinia is now looking across the ocean; oh, if you could read the letters that come to us from Zululand – you too would be convinced that the elevation of the African race is evidently a part of the new order of things that belong to this new and powerful period.

The African already recognizes his anomalous position and desires a change. The brighter day is rising upon Africa. Already I seem to see her chains dissolved, her desert plains red with harvest, her Abyssinia and her Zululand the seats of science and religion, reflecting the glory of the rising sun from the spires of their churches and universities, her Congo and her Gambia whitened with commerce, her crowded cities sending forth the hum of business, and all her sons employed in advancing the victories of peace, greater and more abiding than the spoils of war.

Yes, the regeneration of Africa belongs to this new and powerful period! By this term regeneration I wish to be understood to mean the entrance into a new life, embracing the diverse phases of a higher, complex existence. The basic factor which assures their regeneration resides in the awakened race-consciousness. This gives them a clear perception of their elemental needs and of their undeveloped powers. It therefore must lead them to the attainment of that higher and advanced standard of life.

The African people, although not a strictly homogeneous race, possess a common fundamental sentiment which is everywhere manifest, crystallizing itself into one common controlling idea. Conflicts and strife are rapidly disappearing before the fusing force of this enlightened perception of the true intertribal relation, which relation should subsist among a people with a common destiny. Agencies of a social, economic and religious advance tell of a new spirit which, acting as a leavening ferment, shall raise the anxious and aspiring mass to the level of their ancient glory. The ancestral greatness, the unimpaired genius, and the recuperative power of the race, its irrepressibility, which assures its permanence, constitute the African's greatest source of inspiration. He has refused to camp forever on the borders of the industrial world; having learned that knowledge is power, he is educating his children. You find them in Edinburgh, in Cambridge, and in the great schools of Germany. These return to their country like arrows, to drive darkness from the land. I hold that his industrial and educational initiative, and his untiring devotion to these activities, must be regarded as positive evidences of this process of his regeneration.

The regeneration of Africa means that a new and unique civilization is soon to be added to the world. The African is not a proletarian in the world of science and art. He has precious creations of his own, of ivory, of copper and of gold, fine plated willow-ware and weapons of superior workmanship. Civilization resembles an organic being in its development: it is born, it perishes, and it can propagate itself. More particularly, it resembles a plant, it takes root in the teeming earth, and when the seeds fall in other soils, new varieties sprout up. The most essential departure of this new civilization is that it shall be thoroughly spiritual and humanistic, indeed a regeneration moral and eternal!

O Africa!
Like some great century plant that shall bloom
In ages hence, we watch thee; in our dream
See in thy swamps the Prospero of our stream;
Thy doors unlocked, where knowledge in her tomb
Hath lain innumerable years in gloom.
Then shalt thou, walking with that morning gleam,
Shine as thy sister lands with equal beam.

Pixley Seme
Native Union
(From *Imvo Zabantsundu*, 24 October 1911)

I have been requested by several Natives, Leaders and Chiefs, to write a full and concise statement on the subject of the South African Native Congress, so called. I feel, however, that I shall better meet their desire as well as more properly treat this subject if I disregard the pretentious title and write on the simple subject of Native Union, for after all, this is what the Congress shall be.

There is to-day among all races and men a general desire for progress, and for co-operation, because co-operation will facilitate and secure that progress. This spirit is due no doubt to the great triumph of Christianity which teaches men everywhere that in this world they have a common duty to perform both towards God and towards one another. It is natural, therefore, that there should arise even within and among us this striving, this self-conscious movement, and sighing for Union. We are the last among all the nations of the earth to discover the priceless jewels of co-operation, and for this reason the great gifts of civilisation are least known among us today. I repeat, co-operation is the key and the watchword which opens the door, the everlasting door which leads into progress and all national success. The greatest success shall come when man shall have learned to cooperate, not only with his own kith and kin but with all peoples and with all life.

The South African Native Congress is the voice in the wilderness bidding all the dark races of this sub-continent to come together once or twice a year in order to review the past and reject therein all those things which have retarded our progress, the things which poison the springs of our national life and virtue; to label and distinguish the sins of civilisation, and as members of one household to talk and think loudly on our home problems and the solution of them.

Such national Conferences of the people are bound to give a wide publication of the Natives' own views on the questions which primarily concern him to-morrow and to-day. Through this Congress the Native

Senators in the Union House of Parliament will be able to live in close touch with the Natives of the whole country whose interest each Senator is supposed to represent. The Government also will find a direct and independent channel of informing itself as to the things uppermost in Natives' mind from time to time, and this will make it easier for the Union Government to deal with the Natives of the whole of South Africa. If we wish to convince the Government that it is possible to have a uniform Native policy for the whole of South Africa than let us form this Congress. Again, it is conclusively urgent that this Congress should meet this year, because a matter which is so vitally important to our progress and welfare should not be unnecessarily postponed by reason of personal differences and selfishness of our leaders. The demon of racialism, the aberrations of the Xosa–Fingo feud, the animosity that exists between the Zulus and the Tongas, between the Basutos and every other Native, must be buried and forgotten; it has shed among us sufficient blood! We are one people. These divisions, these jealousies, are the cause of all our woes and of all our backwardness and ignorance to-day. A great Paramount Chief accepting that his name be included in the honourable list of Native princes who endorse and support this movement, writes that 'He however wishes to point out that whilst the objects and the aims of a Congress appear to be good and reasonable, much of the success depends upon the attitude of the members. There should be among other things a firm resolve on the part of every member to eliminate factors which have in the past proved fatal to the continued existence of such Societies. They should set their faces strongly against the jargon of racial feeling, the ebullition of the Xosa–Fingo element, and the excessive display of political partisanship.'

In conclusion, I do not feel that it is at all necessary that I should preach Union even in this article. The Natives everywhere now and to-day know that a South African Native Congress such as is proposed in these columns, will give them the only effective means whereby they will be able to make their grievances properly known and considered both by the Government and by the people of South Africa at large. Through this Congress the Natives will have the opportunity and means with which to influence the public opinion of this country and to greatly assist the South African Statesmen who are working for the peace, prosperity, and the development of this land.

The Executive Committee, which is simply a Committee elected by a part of the people, is busy performing the thankless task of organising this movement. As one of the Committee, I am pleased to say that we have been greatly encouraged by the support which we have received from all the great sections of our country. Today this movement is known, and in a great measure is openly supported, by nearly all the leaders and the greater Chiefs of at least three Provinces and all the Protectorates. The Committee, therefore, intends to summon the first sitting of the Congress in the early part of December. This will certainly be an important day in the annals of our Native history; we shall have come together to bury forever the greatest block to our security, happiness, progress and prosperity as a people. We shall have come together truly, as we are, the children of one household to discuss our home problems and the solution of them.

This is a general announcement sent to all the Native leaders, Societies and Editors asking them to explain this important news to the people at large, and to advise them to arrange for the sending of delegates so that every section of the people shall be represented in that Conference of the races.

Manifesto of the Communist Party of South Africa (1921)
(Adopted at the inaugural conference of the CPSA, Cape Town, 30 July 1921)

The Communist Party of South Africa, which has been formed by the union of the former International Socialist League (S.A.), Social Democratic Federation of Capetown, Communist Party of Capetown, Jewish Socialist Society of Capetown, Jewish Socialist Society (Poalei Zion) of Johannesburg, Marxian Club of Durban, and other Socialist bodies and individuals, and which expects shortly to be affiliated to the World Communist International, makes its appeal to all South African workers, organised and unorganised, white and black, to join in promoting the overthrow of the capitalist system and outlawry of the capitalist class, and the establishment of a Commonwealth of Workers throughout the World.

What does this mean?

All recorded history is the history of class struggles and consequent evolutionary changes in the form of society; the class divisions and institutions varying from age to age according to the current economic basis, and each form being superseded by another when its mission is fulfilled. Today this is more true than ever. Under the form of society dictated by modern capitalist production, the means of life are concentrated in the hands of a small privileged class, which exploits the propertyless working masses, appropriates all the product of their labour, reduces them to the lowest and most servile level of existence that will permit them to continue working and reproducing their kind, and in addition obtains, by virtue of that economic supremacy, control of the entire State Power. This regime of contradiction between 'social production' and 'individual appropriation', of irreconcilable antagonism between masters and man, employers and employed, property owners and proletarians – the class struggle of today – has brought mankind into unprecedented conflict, misery and chaos – a veritable abomination of desolation and terror. But it is fast approaching a crisis entailing its overthrow by the revolting masses in favour of a New Order, the transition to which will be masterfully controlled by a politically victorious working class, but the eventual outcome of which will be an emancipated world, a society of economic and social equals wherein class divisions, privileges and disabilities will for the first time in history be impossible; a system of social ownership of the means of production industrially administered by the workers on an organised and harmonious plan, ensuring from every man according to his capacity and to every man according to his needs, under the motto 'All for each and each for All'.

This Social Revolution is the essential objective of the Labour Movement, the end towards which every step it takes must directly tend. The task is no mere pastime; it is a fight, a grim, often a dangerous, sometimes a mortal fight. It is idle to deny the war between the classes, or to pretend it can somehow be composed by a drawn battle or an armistice. So elemental a conflict – which a defeat of Labour obviously only prolongs – can be solved by nothing short of the world-wide destruction of the capitalist power; and it is in that direction that the world is actually evolving, for Russia is only the first country where the working class has realised in practical fashion that industry needs no exploiters, and agriculture no landlords, by locking them out. That pioneer victory has set the pace for the politics of the whole world today; everyone feels that others are bound to follow the Russian lead. The governments representing the bourgeois power, having strained every nerve to strangle that young Workers' Republic, are now all the more determined to prevent its example from spreading, and are ready to adopt every method to that end, from diplomatic chicanery, false propaganda in press, school, pulpit and platform, economic pressure and intimidation, artificial trade depression, hypocritical appeals to snobbery, patriotism, religious prejudice and racial fear or pride, to the brute force of the Mailed Fist and the Iron Heel wherever they dare. Lately they have instituted a determined campaign all over the world to reduce wages. They are criminally conspiring to maintain as long as they can their decadent, outworn, slave-grinding system with its political expression, the so-called democratic state, notwithstanding that, as a glance at any day's newspaper will show, it has not only failed to fulfil a single one of the promises still held out for it, but, by crushing the workers with the perpetual dread or actuality of unemployment, starvation, repression, massacre and war, it is driving mankind ever deeper into the abyss.

It is time for the Labour Movement in South Africa too to hearken to the call of the times to discard its futile reformism, its misleaders' careerism, its petty middle class opportunism, its subservient snobbery and cowardice, of the past – all typical of the 'social patriotic' Second International which failed the workers so miserably at the outbreak of the great war, and which is even now being rehashed as the '2½ International'. It is time to recognise the historic and titanic nature of the fight, and to unite all our forces in countering the enemy's palpable activity with an even more active Red forward movement, political and industrial, of all the workers; a Great Push so militant, well organised and unified by solidarity as to deliver, in co-operation with the advanced Labour Movement of the rest of the world, the knockout blow to a hated class and system. To this standard the United Communist Party of S.A. bids all class-conscious workers rally, whether previously adherents of any other party or not.

For the immediate future, indeed, the main duty of the party and of every member of it is to establish the widest and closest possible contact with workers of all ranks and races and to propagate the Communist gospel among them, in the first instance among the industrial masses, who must provide the 'storm troops' of the Revolution, and secondly among the rural toilers. Even that path will not be smooth. Immediate repression in the form of raids, prosecutions, mob attacks and bloodshed by 'Black (and Tan) Hundreds' or 'White Guards' may be looked for as the propaganda is seen to be working among the submissive helot races whose enlightenment and organisation the ruling class dreads above all. The Communists will therefore proceed neither timorously nor tactlessly, losing no opportunity of demonstrating that, inasmuch as the cheap docile labour is what attracts the world capitalist investor to South Africa, so its understanding of and conscious entry into the working class movement is the most deadly blow South Africa can deal to world capitalism.

But propaganda 'is not enough' in these days of rapid change and action, and the party will be alert to turn to the advantage of the Labour Movement wherever possible any phase of discontent or disaffection, any opposition to imperialism, any indignation at the accepted 'skiet skiet' native policy, any genuine revolt of the masses against tyranny; striving always to hasten, sharpen and shorten the inevitable conflict, to guide and inspire the struggling workers in times of stress and trial like the present, and generally to act as the revolutionary vanguard of the Labour army of South Africa.

In any sacrifices it may be called upon to undergo the party will derive great strength and inspiration from its connection with the World Communist International, at present headed by the Russian Communist Party, with which is also closely identified the Red Trade Union International; besides which circumstances will bring it from time to time into specially close touch with the movement in Britain, where the struggle of the miners has recently disclosed unexampled heroism and endurance. Heartened by this sense of solidarity and support, and by the exhilarating comradeship known only to fellow workers in a militant movement, we advance to do battle with the capitalist Goliath, confident that if we play our part unfalteringly we shall in our lifetime see the robber and butcher class brought low and the workers' 'Soviets' in power. We hold aloft the glistening banner of the World Commune to be, when the class war shall have been for ever stamped out, when mankind shall no longer cower under the bludgeon of the oppressor, when the necessaries and amenities of life, the comfort and the culture, the honour and the power, shall be to him who toils, not him who exploits, when none shall be called master and none servant, but all shall be fellow workers in common.

Down with the Capitalist System!
Up with the Workers' Commune!
Speed the Social Revolution!

Africans' Claims in South Africa
(Adopted by the annual conference of the ANC,
Bloemfontein, 16 December 1943)

BILL OF RIGHTS

Full Citizen Rights and Demands
We, the African people in the Union of South Africa, urgently demand the granting of full citizenship rights such as are enjoyed by all Europeans in South Africa. We demand:
1. Abolition of political discrimination based on race, such as the Cape 'Native' franchise and the Native Representative Council under Representation of Natives Act, and the extension to all adults, regardless of race, of the right to vote and be elected to parliament, provincial councils and other representative institutions.
2. The right to equal justice in courts of law, including nomination to juries and appointment as judges, magistrates, and other court officials.
3. Freedom of residence and the repeal of laws such as the Natives (Urban Areas) Act, Native Land Act and the Natives Law Amendment Act that restrict this freedom.
4. Freedom of movement, and the repeal of the pass laws, Natives (Urban Areas) Act, Natives Laws Amendment Act and similar legislation.
5. Right of freedom of the press.
6. Recognition of the sanctity or inviolability of the home as a right of every family, and the prohibition of police raids on citizens in their homes for tax or liquor or other purposes.
7. The right to own, buy, hire or lease and occupy land and all other forms of immovable as well as movable property, and the repeal of restrictions on this right in the Native Land Act, the Native Trust and Land Act, the Natives (Urban Areas) Act and the Natives Laws Amendment Act.
8. The right to engage in all forms of lawful occupations, trades and professions, on the same terms and conditions as members of other

sections of the population.
9. The right to be appointed to and hold office in the civil service and in all branches of public employment on the same terms and conditions as Europeans.
10. The right of every child to free and compulsory education and of admission to technical schools, universities, and other institutions of higher education.
11. Equality of treatment and any other section of the population in the State social services, and the inclusion on an equal basis with Europeans in any scheme of Social Security.

Land

We demand the right to an equal share in all the material resources of the country, and we urge:

1. That the present allocation of 12% of the surface area to 7,000,000 Africans as against 87% to about 2,000,000 Europeans is unjust and contrary to the interest of South Africa, and therefore demand a fair redistribution of the land as a prerequisite for a just settlement of the land problem.
2. That the right to own, buy, hire or lease and occupy land individually or collectively, both in rural and in urban areas, is a fundamental right of citizenship, and therefore demand the repeal of the Native Land Act, the Native Trust and Land Act, the Natives Laws Amendment Act, and the Natives (Urban Areas) Act in so far as these laws abrogate that right.
3. That African farmers require no less assistance from the State than that which is provided to European farmers, and therefore demand the same Land Bank facilities, State subsidies, and other privileges as are enjoyed by Europeans.

Industry and Labour

We demand for the Africans

1. equal opportunity to engage in any occupation, trade or industry; in order that this objective might be realised to the fullest extent, facilities must be provided for technical and university education of Africans so as to enable them to enter skilled, semi-skilled occupations, professions, government service and other spheres of employment;
2. equal pay for equal work, as well as equal opportunity for all work; and for the unskilled workers in both rural and urban areas such minimum wages as shall enable the workers to live in health, happiness, decency and comfort;

3. the removal of the Colour Bar in industry, and other occupations;
4. the statutory recognition of the right of the African worker to collective bargaining under the Industrial Conciliation Act.
5. that the African worker shall be insured against sickness, unemployment, accidents, old age and for all other physical disabilities arising from the nature of their work; the contributions to such insurance should be borne entirely by the government and the employers;
6. the extension of all industrial welfare legislation to Africans engaged in agriculture, domestic service and in public institutions or bodies.

Commerce
1. We protest very strongly against all practices that impede the obtaining of trading licences by Africans in urban and rural areas, and we equally condemn the confinement of African economic enterprise to segregated areas and localities.
2. We demand the recognition of the right of the Africans to freedom of trading.

Education
1. The education of the African is matter of national importance requiring State effort for its proper realisation. The magnitude of the task places it beyond the limits of the resources of the missionary or private endeavour. The right of the African child to education, like children of other sections, must be recognised as a State duty and responsibility. We, therefore, demand that
   a. the state must provide full facilities for all types of education for African children.
   b. Education of the African must be financed from General Revenue on a per caput basis.
   c. The State must provide enough properly built and equipped schools for all African children of school-going age and institute free compulsory primary education.
   d. The State must provide adequate facilities for secondary, professional, technical and university education.
2. We reject the conception that there is any need of a special type of education for Africans as such, and therefore we demand that the African must be given the type of education which will enable him to meet on equal terms with other peoples the conditions of the modern world.
3. We demand equal pay for equal educational qualifications and equal

grade of work for all teachers irrespective of their race or colour. We also urge that pensions, conditions of service, and other privileges which are enjoyed by European teachers should be extended to African teachers on equal terms.
4. We claim that the direction of the educational system of the African must fall more and more largely into the hands of the Africans themselves, and therefore we demand increased and direct representation in all bodies such as Education Advisory Boards, School Committees, Governing Councils, etc., which are responsible for the management and the shaping of policy in African schools, institutions and colleges and/or adequate representation in all bodies moulding and directing the country's educational policy.

Public Health and Medical Services

1. We regard it as the duty of the State to provide adequate medical and health facilities for the entire population of the country. We deplore and deprecate he fact that the State has not carried out its duty to the African in this regard, and has left this important duty to philanthropic and voluntary agencies. As a result of this gross neglect the general health of the entire African population has deteriorated to an alarming extent. We consider that the factors which contribute to this state of affairs are these:
   a. the low economic position of the African which is responsible for the present gross malnutrition, general overcrowding, high mortality and morbidity rates;
   b. the shortage of land resulting in the congestion in the reserves and in consequence the bad state of the African's health and the deterioration of his physique;
   c. the slum conditions in the urban areas;
   d. neglect of the health and the general education of the Africans;
   e. neglect of the provision of water supplies, proper sanitary and other conveniences in areas occupied by Africans both in urban and rural areas.
2. To remedy this state of affairs we urge and demand:
   a. a substantial and immediate improvement in the economic position of the African;
   b. a drastic overhauling and reorganisation of the health services of the country with due emphasis on preventive medicine with all that implies in modern public health sense.
3. We strongly urge the adoption of the following measures to meet the

health needs of the African population:
a. the establishment of free medical and health services for all sections of he population;
b. the establishment of a system of School Medical Service with a full staff of medical practitioners, nurses and other health visitors;
c. increased hospital and clinic facilities both in the rural and in urban areas;
d. increased facilities for the training of African doctors, dentists, nurses, sanitary inspectors, health visitors, etc.;
e. the co-ordinated control of finance of health services for the whole Union;
f. the creation of a proper system of vital statistics for the whole population including Africans;
g. the appointment of district surgeons in rural areas with a large African population.

Discriminatory Legislation

1. We, the African people, regard as fundamental to the establishment of a new order in South Africa the abolition of all enactments which discriminate against the African on grounds of race and colour. We condemn and reject the policy of segregation in all aspects of our national life inasmuch as this policy is designed to keep the African in a state of perpetual tutelage and militates against his normal development.
2. We protest strongly against discourteous, harsh and inconsiderate treatment meted out to Africans by officials in all State and other public offices and institutions. Such obnoxious practices are irreconcilable with Christian, democratic and civilised standards and are contrary to human decency. We, therefore, demand:
    a. the repeal of all colour-bar and/or discriminatory clauses in the Union's Constitution, that is the South Africa Act 1909;
    b. the repeal of the Representation of Natives Act 1936;
    c. the repeal of the Natives Land Act 1913 and the Native Trust and Land Act 1936;
    d. the repeal of the Pass Laws, Natives (Urban Areas) Acts as amended, the Natives Administration Act 1927;
    e. the repeal of the 'Colour Bar' Act or Mines and Works Act 1926, Natives Service Contract Act, Masters and Servants Act, the Natives Labour Regulation Act and the amendment of all discriminatory and disabling clauses against African workers contained in the Industrial Conciliation Act.

In short, we demand the repeal of any and all laws as well as the abandonment of any policy and all practices that discriminate against the African in any way whatsoever on the basis of race, creed or colour in the Union of South Africa.

Women's Charter
(Adopted by the first national conference of the Federation of South African Women, Johannesburg, 17 April 1954)

Preamble
We, the women of South Africa, wives and mothers, working women and housewives. Africans, Indians, European and Coloured, hereby declare our aim of striving for the removal of all laws, regulations, conventions and customs that discriminate against us as women, and that deprive us in any way of our inherent right to the advantages, responsibilities and opportunities that society offers to any one section of the population.

A Single Society
We women do not form a society separate from the men. There is only one society, and it is made up of both women and men. As women we share the problems and anxieties of our men, and join hands with them to remove social evils and obstacles to progress.

Within this common society, however, are laws and practices that discriminate against women. While we struggle against the social evils that affect men and women alike, we are determined to struggle no less purposefully against the things that work to the disadvantage of our sex.

Test of civilisation
The level of civilisation which any society has reached can be measured by the degree of freedom that its members enjoy. The status of women is a test of civilisation. Measured by that standard, South Africa must be considered low in the scale of civilised nations.

Women's lot
We women share with our menfolk the cares and anxieties imposed by poverty and its evils. As wives and mothers, it falls upon us to make small wages stretch a long way. It is we who feel the cries of our children when

they are hungry and sick. It is our lot to keep and care for homes that are too small, broken and dirty to be kept clean. We know the burden of looking after children and land when our husbands are away in the mines, on the farms, and in the towns earning our daily bread.

We know what it is to keep family life going in pondokkies and shanties, or in over-crowded one-room apartments. We know the bitterness of children taken to lawless ways, of daughters becoming unmarried mothers whilst still at school, of boys and girls growing up without education, training or jobs at a living wage.

Poor and Rich

These are evils that need not exist. They exist because the society in which we live is divided into poor and rich, into non-European and European. They exist because there are privileges for the few, discrimination and harsh treatment for the many. We women have stood and will stand shoulder to shoulder with our menfolk in a common struggle against poverty, race and class discrimination, and the evils of the colour bar.

National Liberation

As members of the National Liberatory movements and Trade Unions, in and through our various organisations, we march forward with our men in the struggle for liberation and the defence of the working people. We pledge ourselves to keep high the banner of equality, fraternity and liberty. As women there rests upon us also the burden of removing from our society all the social differences developed in past times between men and women, which have the effect of keeping our sex in a position of inferiority and subordination.

Equality for Women

We resolve to struggle for the removal of laws and customs that deny African women the right to own, inherit or alienate property. We resolve to work for a change in the laws of marriage such as are found amongst our African, Malay and Indian people, which have the effect of placing wives in the position of legal subjection to husbands, and giving husbands the power to dispose of wives' property and earnings, and dictate to them in all matters affecting them and their children.

We recognise that women are treated as minors by these marriage and property laws because of ancient and revered traditions and customs which had their origin in the antiquity of the people and no doubt served purposes of great value in bygone times.

There was a time in the African society when every woman reaching marriageable stage was assured of a husband, home, land and security.

Then husbands and wives with their children belonged to families and clans that supplied most of their own material needs and were largely self-sufficient. Men and women were partners in a compact and closely integrated family unit.

Women Who Labour
Those conditions have gone. The tribal and kinship society to which they belonged has been destroyed as a result of the loss of tribal lands, migration of men away from their tribal home, the growth of towns and industries and the rise of a great body of wage-earners on the farms and in the urban areas, who depend wholly or mainly on wages for a livelihood.

Thousands of African women, like Indian, Coloured and European women, are employed today in factories, homes, shops, offices; on farms and in professions as nurses, teachers and the like. As unmarried women, widows or divorcees they have to fend for themselves, often without the assistance of a male relative. Many of them are responsible not only for their own livelihood but also that of their children.

Large numbers of women today are in fact the sole breadwinners and heads of their families

Forever Minors
Nevertheless, the laws and practices derived from an earlier and different state of society are still applied to them. They are responsible for their own person and their children. Yet the law seeks to enforce upon them the status of a minor.

Not only are African, Coloured and Indian women denied political rights, but they are also in many parts of the Union denied the same status as men in such matters as the right to enter into contracts, to own and dispose of property, and to exercise guardianship over their children.

Obstacles to Progress
The law has lagged behind the development of society; it no longer corresponds to the actual social and economic position of women. The law has become an obstacle to progress of the women, and therefore a brake on the whole of society.

This intolerable condition would not be allowed to continue were it not for the refusal of a large section of our menfolk to concede to us women the rights and privileges which they demand for themselves.

We shall teach the men that they cannot hope to liberate themselves from the evils of discrimination and prejudice as long as they fail to extend to women complete and unqualified equality in law and in practice.

Need for Education
We also recognise that large numbers of our womenfolk continue to be bound by traditional practices and conventions, and fail to realise that these have become obsolete and a brake on progress. It is our duty and privilege to enlist all women in our struggle for emancipation and bring to them all realisation of the intimate relationship that exists between their status of inferiority as women and the inferior status to which their people are subjected by discriminatory laws and colour prejudices.

It is our intention to carry out a nation-wide programme of education that will bring home to the men and women of all national groups the realisation that freedom cannot be won for any section or for the people as a whole as long as we women are kept in bondage.

An Appeal
We appeal to all progressive organisations, to members of the great National liberatory movements, to the trade unions and working class organisations, to the churches, educational and welfare organisations, to all progressive men and women who have the interests of the people at heart, to join with us in this great and noble endeavour.

Our Aims
We declare the following aims:

This organisation is formed for the purpose of uniting women in common action for the removal of all political, legal, economic and social disabilities. We shall strive for women to obtain:

- The right to vote and to be elected to all State bodies, without restriction or discrimination.
- The right to full opportunities for employment with equal pay and possibilities of promotion in all spheres of work.
- Equal rights with men in relation to property, marriage and children, and for the removal of all laws and customs that deny women such equal rights.
- For the development of every child through free compulsory education for all; for the protection of mother and child through maternity homes,

welfare clinics, crèches and nursery schools, in countryside and towns; through proper homes for all; and through the provision of water, light, transport, sanitation and other amenities of modem civilisation.
- For the removal of all laws that restrict free movement, that prevent or hinder the right of free association and activity in democratic organisations, and the right to participate in the work of these organisations.
- To build and strengthen women's sections in the National liberatory movements, the organisation of women in trade unions, and through the people's varied organisations.
- To co-operate with all other organisations that have similar aims in South Africa as well as throughout the world.
- To strive for permanent peace throughout the world.

The Freedom Charter
(Adopted at the Congress of the People, Kliptown, 1955)

We, the People of South Africa, declare for all our country and the world to know:
    that South Africa belongs to all who live in it, black and white, and that no government can justly claim authority unless it is based on the will of all the people;
    that our people have been robbed of their birthright to land, liberty and peace by a form of government founded on injustice and inequality;
    that our country will never be prosperous or free until all our people live in brotherhood, enjoying equal rights and opportunities;
    that only a democratic state, based on the will of all the people, can secure to all their birthright without distinction of colour, race, sex or belief;
    And therefore, we, the people of South Africa, black and white together equals, countrymen and brothers, adopt this Freedom Charter;
    And we pledge ourselves to strive together, sparing neither strength nor courage, until the democratic changes here set out have been won.

The People Shall Govern!
    Every man and woman shall have the right to vote for and to stand as a candidate for all bodies which make laws;
    All people shall be entitled to take part in the administration of the country;
    The rights of the people shall be the same, regardless of race, colour or sex;
    All bodies of minority rule, advisory boards, councils and authorities shall be replaced by democratic organs of self-government.

All National Groups Shall Have Equal Rights!
    There shall be equal status in the bodies of state, in the courts and in the schools for all national groups and races;

All people shall have equal right to use their own languages, and to develop their own folk culture and customs;

All national groups shall be protected by law against insults to their race and national pride;

The preaching and practice of national, race or colour discrimination and contempt shall be a punishable crime;

All apartheid laws and practices shall be set aside.

The People Shall Share in the Country's Wealth!

The national wealth of our country, the heritage of South Africans, shall be restored to the people;

The mineral wealth beneath the soil, the banks and monopoly industry shall be transferred to the ownership of the people as a whole;

All other industry and trade shall be controlled to assist the wellbeing of the people;

All people shall have equal rights to trade where they choose, to manufacture and to enter all trades, crafts and professions.

The Land Shall Be Shared among Those Who Work It!

Restrictions of land ownership on a racial basis shall be ended, and all the land re-divided amongst those who work it to banish famine and land hunger;

The state shall help the peasants with implements, seed, tractors and dams to save the soil and assist the tillers;

Freedom of movement shall be guaranteed to all who work on the land;

All shall have the right to occupy land wherever they choose;

People shall not be robbed of their cattle, and forced labour and farm prisons shall be abolished.

All Shall Be Equal before the Law!

No-one shall be imprisoned, deported or restricted without a fair trial; no-one shall be condemned by the order of any Government official;

The courts shall be representative of all the people;

Imprisonment shall be only for serious crimes against the people, and shall aim at re-education, not vengeance;

The police force and army shall be open to all on an equal basis and shall be the helpers and protectors of the people;

All laws which discriminate on grounds of race, colour or belief shall be repealed.

All Shall Enjoy Equal Human Rights!

The law shall guarantee to all their right to speak, to organise, to meet together, to publish, to preach, to worship and to educate their children;

The privacy of the house from police raids shall be protected by law;

All shall be free to travel without restriction from countryside to town, from province to province, and from South Africa abroad;

Pass Laws, permits and all other laws restricting these freedoms shall be abolished.

There Shall Be Work and Security!

All who work shall be free to form trade unions, to elect their officers and to make wage agreements with their employers;

The state shall recognise the right and duty of all to work, and to draw full unemployment benefits;

Men and women of all races shall receive equal pay for equal work;

There shall be a forty-hour working week, a national minimum wage, paid annual leave, and sick leave for all workers, and maternity leave on full pay for all working mothers;

Miners, domestic workers, farm workers and civil servants shall have the same rights as all others who work;

Child labour, compound labour, the tot system and contract labour shall be abolished.

The Doors of Learning and Culture Shall Be Opened!

The government shall discover, develop and encourage national talent for the enhancement of our cultural life;

All the cultural treasures of mankind shall be open to all, by free exchange of books, ideas and contact with other lands;

The aim of education shall be to teach the youth to love their people and their culture, to honour human brotherhood, liberty and peace;

Education shall be free, compulsory, universal and equal for all children; Higher education and technical training shall be opened to all by means of state allowances and scholarships awarded on the basis of merit;

Adult illiteracy shall be ended by a mass state education plan;

Teachers shall have all the rights of other citizens;

The colour bar in cultural life, in sport and in education shall be abolished.

There Shall Be Houses, Security and Comfort!

All people shall have the right to live where they choose, be decently housed, and to bring up their families in comfort and security;

Unused housing space to be made available to the people;

Rent and prices shall be lowered, food plentiful and no-one shall go hungry;

A preventive health scheme shall be run by the state;

Free medical care and hospitalisation shall be provided for all, with special care for mothers and young children;

Slums shall be demolished, and new suburbs built where all have transport, roads, lighting, playing fields, creches and social centres;

The aged, the orphans, the disabled and the sick shall be cared for by the state;

Rest, leisure and recreation shall be the right of all:

Fenced locations and ghettoes shall be abolished, and laws which break up families shall be repealed.

There Shall Be Peace and Friendship!

South Africa shall be a fully independent state which respects the rights and sovereignty of all nations;

South Africa shall strive to maintain world peace and the settlement of all international disputes by negotiation – not war;

Peace and friendship amongst all our people shall be secured by upholding the equal rights, opportunities and status of all;

The people of the protectorates Basutoland, Bechuanaland and Swaziland shall be free to decide for themselves their own future;

The right of all peoples of Africa to independence and self-government shall be recognised, and shall be the basis of close co-operation.

Let all people who love their people and their country now say, as we say here:

These freedoms we will fight for, side by side, throughout our lives, until we have won our liberty.

Does the Freedom Charter Mean Socialism?
(From *New Age*, 17 November 1957)

The Freedom Charter, adopted four months ago at the Congress of the People, is a stirring document, embodying all the deepest and most pressing needs of the people and charting a new course for a free South Africa. The programme is not a sectarian one, the property of any single political party or movement. In its phrases and demands the Charter is as old as the people's struggle in South Africa. Its calls for security, an end to discrimination, for work, housing and education re-echo the demands of the many hard battles the people have waged on all these fronts.

Yet the Charter is unique. It differs from all previous political documents of the liberatory movements in its completeness and all-embracing nature. Above all, it not only exposes all that is rotten, decaying and oppressive in the present system, but it unfolds the vision and the shape of the new life that will replace it.

The Charter is unique, too, in that it was adopted not at some restricted leaders' or delegates' conference, but by the people themselves after over a year of prolonged and intensive discussion. The Charter thus is of the people and belongs to them.

Yet the Charter is more than a document. It is a political programme, and political programmes which are not a guide to action are like a paralysed limb. The people have entrusted the Charter to their organisations who had the courage to call into being the Congress of the People, and a great campaign is now under way to get the Charter endorsed with a million signatures.

Enthusiasm for the Charter must be born not of blind obedience to its aims, but of the understanding that, taken together, these aims are the only possible way out of the present impasse and towards the formation of a people's government founded on justice and equality.

Doubts

Everywhere the people have received the Charter with enthusiasm. Yet, in some quarters there have been doubts expressed about aspects of the Charter. Some of our most respected leaders have expressed genuine misgivings about that section of the Charter which reads:

'*The People Shall Share in the Country's Wealth. The national wealth of our country, the heritage of all South Africans, shall be restored to the people. The mineral wealth beneath the soil, the banks and monopoly industry shall be transferred to the ownership of the people as a whole. All other industry and trade shall be controlled to assist the well-being of the people. All people shall have equal rights to trade where they choose, to manufacture and to enter all trades, crafts and professions.*'

The Charter does not propose merely a reform of the present system, a patching-up of its worst evils, an amelioration of some of its conditions. This Charter proclaims that only a complete change of state form can result in the people achieving their aims. Some groups, like the Liberals, have the illusion that real democracy can be achieved within the existing constitutional set-up. They believe that the repeal of certain laws on the statute book is sufficient. Such a purely reformist attitude is unrealistic and takes no note of history.

Every state form has been moulded to serve a particular set-up and through the centuries, as one order made way for another, the emergent ruling group had to erect quite new state forms to consolidate its power. It had to do more than that. It had to break the stranglehold which the old regime had on the economy of the country and, through the economy, on the state apparatus. It would, for instance, have been impossible to do away with serfdom and feudal social relations without breaking the economic power of the land barons.

The Colour Bar

Why the system of colour discrimination in South Africa? Is it some natural inhumanity of Whites towards Non-Whites? Is it just re-education in the spirit of justice, and a change of heart that is needed among the Whites?

No. The system of White supremacy has its roots in the cheap labour need of the major economic groups of the country. South Africa's economy is dominated by giant monopolies in the gold mining industry linked with big financial and farming interests, whose tentacles reach also into secondary industry. These groups have been responsible for the Reserve system, migratory labour, the low wage policy. These groups own and control the national wealth of our country and determine the basic structure of the South African state. It would be a dream to pretend that the changes of the Charter could be realisable if their economic grip were not loosened. Super-profits are incompatible with a sharing by the people in the wealth of the country. Migratory labour and the compound system cannot go hand in hand with the right of the worker to receive equal pay for equal work, his right to organise in trade unions, and so on.

There is another aspect. The mere acknowledgement in a phrase that the people shall have the right to own the land and to manufacture is of little value. The *right* to do these things is one thing: the *opportunity* is another. Over 300 years the system of White supremacy has resulted in the concentration of wealth in the hands of the present power group. To allow this wealth to remain in the hands of the monopolies is to condone the past, to perpetuate the lower economic status of the Non-Europeans.

First Tasks
Immediately after political changes have resulted in the establishment of the sort of government envisaged by the Charter, those in power will be faced with the major problem of raising the economic status of the Non-European and of doing away with the basic inequality of wealth which is part and parcel of the present system. White supremacy is not only an ideological catchphrase. In terms of the real lives of the mass of the people it has resulted in the accumulation of the basic wealth of the land in the hands of a small section of the White caste. As long as this balance remains undisturbed, the inferior status of the Non-European cannot be radically altered.

If tomorrow every discriminatory law on the statute book were repealed, but the mineral wealth, monopoly industry and financial empires were not transferred to the ownership of the people as a whole, the system of White superiority would in its basic essential be perpetuated for many generations. The wealth of South Africa cannot be created by law. It is there. If it is left in the hands of the present dominant groups the new state will, with a great deal of justification, be able to say it cannot 'afford' to provide education, to do away with slum conditions, and so on.

Not Socialism
Some are concerned that this solution is in advance of what should be the programme of a national liberatory struggle and that it might commit the national movements to a socialist aim.

Whatever one's views might be as to the desirability of establishing a socialist system in South Africa, the immediate aim of the liberatory movement is not and cannot be the establishment of socialism.

Does it therefore follow that the liberatory movement must automatically reject any part of a programme which happens to coincide with a section of that of socialists? If this were so then 'votes for all' and all the other basic aims of the liberatory movement would have to be scrapped. It is obvious that the sole test for the acceptability of an aim must be: Is it possible to implement the programme without the inclusion of this aim? In any event, socialism and the nationalisation of the basic wealth of a country are not synonymous terms. In South Africa today the railways are nationalised and serve the interests of the dominant group.

The Charter does not advocate the abolition of private enterprise, nor is it suggested that all industries be nationalised or that all trade be controlled by the state.

'All people shall have the right to trade where they choose, to manufacture and to enter all trades, crafts and professions,' says the Charter. The right to do these things would remain a dead letter without the restoration of the basic wealth of the country to the people, and without that the building of a democratic state is inconceivable.

Albert Luthuli
'The Defiance Campaign' *from* Let My People Go
(First published by Collins, London, 1962)

10. THE PROGRAMME OF ACTION

When the whites of South Africa went to the polls in 1948, I doubt whether anybody realised how significant the election was to be. General Smuts's United Party, feeling that it had done well by white ex-servicemen, appeared confident of victory. Malan's 'Purified' Nationalists hoped for gains.

As usual, but this time even more extremely than before, the election campaigns were fought over the Africans. The United Party feebly tried to introduce bread-and-butter issues, but these gained them very little support. The 1948 General Election was the apartheid election. Malan's claim to have an answer to South Africa's race difficulties, the fear of the Black Peril which his party had instilled into the white electorate, and the obvious bankruptcy of the party in power in all directions, influenced the outcome of the voting far more than anybody had predicted. It was the end of Smuts. When the votes were counted, not only were the Nationalists in power, but Smuts had been defeated in his own constituency by a little-known opponent.

It was not the end of an era. There is a tendency nowadays to look back to the Smuts regime as a day of restraint and just government. In point of fact, however, the General did not once exert his undoubted influence to extend a helping hand on the masses who groaned under their disabilities, and it was he who gave Hertzog the power to disenfranchise the few African voters.

What he failed to do as a politician was to recognise that white South Africa was ready to go further than he along the road to discrimination which he himself trod. In 1946, when he introduced the Asiatic Land Tenure Act, he was still sensitive to his electorate and quick to carry out their cruel bidding. By 1948 he had been left behind, while white South Africa had entered its next logical phase. The white voter was more eager than he was aware to continue the dismemberment of justice and morality displayed so boldly in the Hertzog-Smuts Bills. And, with the usual handful of exceptions, even those who were not eager were either quite ready to connive or to remain colourlessly neutral. It has always seemed to me a pity that a man as gifted as Smuts should have gone into eclipse, not because of adherence to any principle, but because of political obtuseness. Yet, since he did not at home ever stand on principle, perhaps that was just.

For most of us Africans, bandied about on the field while the game was in progress and then kicked to one side when the game was won, the election seemed largely irrelevant. We had endured Botha, Hertzog and Smuts. It did not seem of much importance whether the whites gave us more Smuts or switched to Malan. Our lot had grown steadily harder, and no election seemed likely to alter the direction in which we were being forced.

Fundamentally, of course, we were right. The Nationalist win did not either surprise nor extremely interest us, though we did realise that there would probably be an intensification of the hardships and indignities which had always come our way. Nevertheless, I think it is true that very few (if any) of us understood how swift the deterioration was destined to be. I doubt, too, whether many of us realised at the time that the very intensity of Nationalist oppression would do what we had so far failed to achieve – awake the mass of Africans to political awareness, goad us finally out of resigned endurance, and so advance the day of our liberation.

It seems hard to recognise at the moment that the Nationalists more than anybody have given force and insistence to African demands. Now we are caught in the agony and struggle which must precede freedom in a country such as South Africa. But for the Nationalist victory in 1948 we might have had to wait and organise for years to produce widespread refusal to accept the white yoke.

Malan, Strijdom and Verwoerd have done an important part of our work for us. They have demonstrated unambiguously to the African people what it is that the Congress movement is pledged to resist. And at last the African people have responded unambiguously. No longer do a few Congress voices oppose each new measure. Now the voice of the African people says, 'We do not consent.'

The Nationalist regime must take at least some credit for this. A good measure of the work of Congress has simply consisted of co-ordinating, and giving direction and nonviolent expression to the anger and repudiation which they have aroused. By intensifying our experience of serfdom, they have given us a deeper thirst for freedom. It was coming anyway, but Nationalist rule has appreciably shortened the day of white tyranny.

Although members of Congress did not foresee the speed with which the Nationalists would set about depriving us of the few shreds of humanity and opportunity which remained, yet we were not this time caught on the wrong foot. We had already seen the writing on the wall, in the Hertzog Bills and in the Smuts about-face, once our men were no longer required as drivers and potato-peelers in his army. The founding of the Congress Youth League had met a longstanding need, giving to young men a sphere of action, and assurance that the days of polite, unheeded complaint were over. We were already girding ourselves against the Smuts regime when Malan took his place.

Some index of the earnestness of the younger element, and of the rapid change which they worked on Congress thought is given by the eclipse of Dr. Xuma. When Xuma took over the national leadership, he was at the spearhead, and the contribution which he made to the organisation of the movement should not be forgotten. But by the time Malan came to power, Congress rank and file in general, and the Youth League in particular, were in advance of him.

Congress was more than fortunate in the quality of the men who were the moving spirits in the Youth League. At their head was a forceful and gifted Roman Catholic, Anton Lembede, and with him was a group of men such as Mandela, the younger Matthews, Walter Sisulu, Mda, Yengwa, Dr. Conco and Oliver Tambo.

It was not long before they found that, while all were agreed about the work of organising the movement, Dr. Xuma hung back over the question of what to do with the organisation once it was there. Congress was urgent, Xuma cautious. The younger members looked around for an alternative leader, and found one in Dr. James Moroka.

In 1949, under Moroka, newly-elected President-General of Congress, the movement met and evolved its Programme of Action. This Programme of Action is a milestone in Congress history. It represents a fundamental change of policy and method. Underlying it was the refusal to be content for ever with leavings from white South Africa's table – stated uncompromisingly and finally.

The challenge was to be on fundamentals, we were no longer interested in ameliorations and petty adjustments. There was no longer any doubt in our mind that without the vote we are helpless. Without the vote there is no way for us to realise ourselves in our own land, or even to be heard: Without the vote our future would be that decreed by a minority of whites, as our past has been. The whites always insist that they know what is best for us, and that this is what we *really* want – only we are too foolish and backward to know it. The whites are an interested party in this controversy:

they invariably hand out what is best for them – passes, crippling industrial laws, African poverty, but never land and never the smallest measure of self-determination. Never human dignity, never opportunity.

The Programme of Action adopted in 1949 stressed new methods. Representations were done with. Demonstrations on a countrywide scale, strike action, and civil disobedience were to replace words. Influenced by the combined action of the Indian community after the passing of the Ghetto Act, we agreed to concentrate mainly on non-violent disobedience. This disobedience was not directed against law. It was directed against all those particular discriminatory laws, from the Act of Union onwards, which were not informed by morality.

Once Congress as a whole had thrashed out our new approach, the matter was placed in the hands of the National Executive. They were to apply the general principles to specific occasions, to work out the details, and to issue the calls for action to the provinces, who would then relay them to local branches.

During 1950 there was a major demonstration on 26th June. Its immediate purpose was to protest against the Group Areas Bill and the Suppression of Communism Bill. It took the form of a one-day stay-at-home, and was most successful in Johannesburg and Port Elizabeth, and in Durban. In the minds of the organisers (Africans, Indians, and Coloureds participated) one purpose was that those who stayed at home should fittingly mourn the many people – many Africans – who had up to that time lost their lives in the struggle for liberation. There has for many years been a steady loss of life of demonstrators at the hands of the police. It is seldom sensational enough to attract attention – it is simply a feature of South African life. It was high time we mourned our dead – they number thousands.

In May, 1951, there was an effective protest strike of Coloured people, supported by Africans and Indians, in Port Elizabeth and the South Western Cape. This was directed against the Nationalist intention to remove Coloureds from the Common Electoral Roll.

These were first steps, the early outcome of the Programme of Action.

In July, 1951, the National executives of the Congresses met together. A Joint Planning Council was appointed to organise co-operation between the different non-white groups – this, indeed, was a major step forward.

The significance of the Joint Planning Council should not be missed. The very fact that it was able to be formed and to function was a sign that all but the white races in South Africa were beginning to think and act across barriers of race. The desire to shed apartheid could now at last be translated into outward expression. The joint organisation of the Defiance Campaign took us one step nearer to a South Africa where race will be of incidental importance.

In Natal we were placed at a disadvantage. We were, on the whole, very much in line with the Programme of Action. But by this time A.W.G. Champion was beginning to have his doubts. He did not voice them, he did not openly oppose the new policy. He simply held his peace, when he returned from meetings of the National Executive, over what had passed there. The result was that we inevitably fell behind, knowing little of what was being discussed and planned in the rest of the country.

At this time, because Champion insisted upon reverting to the practice (which had prevailed in earlier Congress days) of appointing his own Executive, I declined to serve under him – his action seemed retrograde, undemocratic, and it was unconstitutional. I remained on friendly terms with him. My status was that of an ordinary Congress member, and in view of the personal clashes which now began to appear within the Executive, this did not distress me.

The Press brought the clash into the open, and the conflict between the Natal leaders came to a head at the Annual General Meeting of 1951. The meeting was held in Pietermaritzburg, but it adjourned to Durban, for the election office bearers. It turned out to be a 'packed' meeting. Champion overrode the objections of those of us who objected to the unconstitutional presence of non-members. Rather than break up the meeting, we submitted.

Just before the resumption of Durban – the only outstanding business was the annual election – I had been approached by a group of Youth League men who asked me to stand for the Natal Presidency. Knowing that Msimang, the excellent Congress secretary in Natal, had been approached, I refused. But the younger men were insistent. 'If we are to save Natal for Congress,' they declared, 'there must be a change in the leadership.'

In the end, I agreed, but on one condition. I wished to remain quite clear of squabbles for position and of the personal conflicts within the movement. I told the younger men that my name could go forward only if Msimang agreed to this. So we talked it over with him, and his view was that his name should be withdrawn and that 1 should stand against Champion.

When nominations were called for only Champion's name and mine went forward. The irregularly constituted meeting recorded its votes, and by a modest majority I was elected to replace Champion at the head of Congress affairs in Natal. Since I had no intention of appointing my Executive, we proceeded to elect other office bearers.

But we were in a quandary. We knew full well that the meeting was, unconstitutional. At the same time we knew that if we did not function, the A.N.C. would disintegrate in Natal. For the moment we felt that we had to act as a sort of caretaker Executive, so that the work of Congress might not lapse.

At the earliest possible opportunity we convened a special general meeting, where we explained our odd position to the delegates. The meeting decided that, rather than spend time on a fresh election, it would simply ratify what had been done at the unconstitutional meeting.

At the end of the year (1951) a National Conference of A.N.C. was held in Bloemfontein. Shortly before I was due to depart, the Natal headquarters were sent material relating to this conference. To my astonishment, this included suggestions and resolutions about a campaign of civil defiance. The National Executive and other provinces had been considering this for some time – but here was Natal's first hint of it!

It was already too late to summon my Executive. Our only opportunity for discussion was in the car on the way to Bloemfontein. We decided that we would agree in principle to the Defiance Campaign, but that we would have to plead, because the matter had not so much as been raised in Natal, for postponement of the proposed date (6th April, 1952). We could not commit Natal to something so momentous while it was still in ignorance of the whole issue. Nor could we get Natal ready in time.

At Bloemfontein the President-General, Dr. Moroka, asked me to take the chair for the conference. I left it only when the time came for me to present Natal's views on the proposed campaign of civil disobedience.

This was no easy matter – my audience was unsympathetic. I well remember the interjection of one woman delegate when I tried to argue for a later date:

'Coward! Coward!' she shouted at me.

'It is better far me to express my cowardice here,' I retorted, 'than that I should keep silent and then go away and play the coward outside.'

The truth was, however, that the other provinces were geared to launch the campaign in the second quarter of 1952. The only concession made to Natal was that it was agreed that if we were not ready in time, we should came in as soon as we were ready, and later in the same year.

Outside the conference hall, however, some members from other provinces did confide in me that they were fearful that the campaign might suffer from preparation that was too hurried. This contradiction expresses a real dilemma. We have continually needed to act and act urgently. At the same time, ill-prepared action can be worse than none. The Congress movement cannot rely on occasional spontaneous demonstrations – too often these, coming at a time when patience has snapped for the moment, develop into violence. The people need to be briefed with clarity and care, and they must be given the opportunity to signify their willingness and readiness to participate.

Had Congress ever been an organisation which placed reliance on bloodshed and violence, things would have been simpler. What we have aimed to do in South Africa is to bring the white man to his senses, not slaughter him. Our desire has been that he should co-operate with us, and we with him.

At first we argued far a change of heart which would permit this. Then, with the Programme of Action and the years that have followed, we have tried to demonstrate the realities in a less academic way; we have tried to show what the realities are in the hope that the whites could see the imperative need to conform to them. A few have seen this need – some Congress of Democrats, Liberals, maybe some Progressives. A few have known of it all along; and have acted on their knowledge. But the vast majority, like Pharaoh, have hardened their hearts.

It has naturally crossed our minds to wonder whether anything but indiscriminate bloodshed and violence will make any impression; so impervious do they seem. It will do neither them nor us any goad, and if they get it, it will not be from Congress. It will be simply the result of unendurable provocation, of trading far too long on a patience which has its limits. If the whites continue as at present, nobody will give the signal for mass violence. Nobody will need to.

The Natal delegation returned from Bloemfontein to face an attack upon our proposed. action in the Press, both white and white-owned 'African'. But at the general meeting which we immediately called, we found no disaffection in our own ranks.

The meeting, publicised by adverse Press comment, was well attended. The main paints at issue were the question of co-operation with other organisations and the Defiance Campaign. At Bloemfontein we had endorsed the earlier decision to undertake the Defiance Campaign in conjunction with the Indian Congress movement, and with any others who cared to join in. But among Natal Africans there was a degree of anti-Indian feeling, and it was not difficult for those who opposed the Campaign far other reasons to exploit this form of racialism. Malcontents represented the policy of co-operation as the invention of the new leaders in Natal.

But it was not difficult to reply to this, since the 'new policy' of Congress co-operation had in fact been firmly established before Moroka took over the National leadership from Xuma, and before I had replaced Champion in Natal. The meeting endorsed the Defiance Campaign, and stated Natal's desire to be included in it. The details and the date of Natal's entry were left to the executive, working in conjunction with the other congresses.

It is perhaps worth underlining here one of the great strengths of the African National Congress. It has displayed the power to adapt itself. Who would have predicted, at the time of the Durban riots of 1949, when Africans and Indians were involved in terrible mutual hostility, that within three years Africans and Indians in Durban itself would be acting together to demonstrate their repudiation of injustice, cruelty and tyranny?

Step by step along our difficult road, Congress has adapted itself to the real needs of the situation. This has not always been easy, but it has happened. And with each adaptation, we have brought ourselves and our country nearer to the vision of a homeland where men may eventually live at peace with neighbours of all races – because they really are neighbours, not white masters and other-race servants.

11. DEFIANCE AND DEPOSITION

Preparations for the Defiance Campaign went forward. June 26th was chosen for the launching of open disobedience, but the earlier date, 6th April, did not go unused. It turned into a warm-up for the Campaign proper. Large meetings were held in the main centres at the same time as the whites were, in their way, observing the three-hundredth anniversary of the landing of Jan van Riebeeck at the Cape.

To put it simply, while they celebrated three hundred years of white domination, we looked back over three hundred years of black subjection. While the whites were jubilant over what they said God had given them, we contemplated what they had taken from us, and the land which they refuse to share with us though they cannot work it without us.

Speaking to a crowd of over five thousand people of all races in Freedom Square, Sophiatown, Dr. Moroka said: 'In Capetown to-day the Van Riebeeck celebrations have reached an unprecedented climax ... The white man's cup of joy is overflowing. The Europeans have every reason to display their joy on this colossal scale ... Taken man for man, the Europeans of this land are some of the richest people in the world ... But we Africans also look back over that period of three hundred years. We see a record of sadness ... I wish to remind the Europeans of this country that in taking stock of the past three hundred years they cannot escape the fact that whatever page they turn in the history of South Africa, they find it red with the blood of the fallen, they find ill-will and insecurity written plainly across the pages. I appeal to them to weigh and consider.'

In Capetown, Port Elizabeth, East London, Pretoria and Durban, crowds of up to ten thousand attended mass meetings and demonstrated their support of the coming Defiance Campaign. These were the main centres, but satisfactory preparation was going ahead in smaller places too. Such meetings were not confined to 6th April – during the first half of 1952 there were gatherings at different times throughout the country.

At this time there was a fruitless interchange of letters between the Congresses and the authorities. I say 'interchange'. It was not exactly that. Our letters were sometimes completely ignored, though there was an answer or two from 'the office of the Prime Minister'.

But the white rulers, at least, were left in no doubt about what we intended or why we intended it. When they did reply, it was to scold us for sending our letters to the wrong person, to assure us that we have 'no inherent right' and will not get any, and to threaten us with 'full use of the machinery at its (the Government's) disposal to quell any disturbances, and thereafter deal adequately with those responsible for initiating subversive activities of any nature whatsoever'.

One thing which this correspondence did underline was that there is not really even a common language in which to discuss our agonising problems. The Nationalist rulers cannot speak to Africans except in the restricted vocabulary of white *baasskap*. They cannot discuss. They know, and they then proceed to arrange and give orders.

For our part, we cannot employ the phrases of supplication and subservience, we cannot take up the unreal posture of 'good native boys' towards good, all-knowing, and all-beneficent white rulers. Our whole protest and resistance is based on our claim to human dignity. With those who recognise it we are at one. We cannot discard it in our dealings with those who deny it.

We made it abundantly clear long before the Campaign was launched that it was a system, not a race, which we were opposing: 'The struggle which the national organisations of the non-European people are conducting is not directed against any race or national group, but against the unjust laws which keep in perpetual subjection and misery vast sections of the population.'

The target of the Campaign was unjust, oppressive laws. The intention was to disobey these laws, suffering arrest, assault, and penalty if need be, without violence. The method was to send in groups of carefully trained 'volunteers' to disobey publicly.

The fact that the African and Indian Congresses were participating jointly, and that we were joined by, some coloured organisations – the coloured people had no national organisation – limited the scope of what we could jointly defy. Different laws oppress different non-white groups. What we all had in common, however, was the humiliation of discrimination in public places. For this reason the main force of the Defiance Campaign was directed against the national motto of white South Africa, EUROPEANS ONLY, which is found over the length and breadth of the country. Railway stations, waiting-rooms, post offices, public seats, train accommodation, all bear this legend. The volunteers were to abandon the 'separate but unequal' facilities set aside for us, and to make challenging use of the alternative white facilities. In addition to this, the flouting of curfew and pass regulations was determined upon.

With Natal and Capetown postponing defiance until they were ready, the rest of the country went into action on 26th June as planned. Whenever possible, the authorities were forewarned of the detailed intentions of each batch of volunteers – in some cases full lists of the names of the volunteers involved were politely handed in. In July the two Natal Congresses joined in. During the following three months the Defiance Campaign gathered momentum. October, with 2354 resisters, was the peak month of this part of the Campaign. There is no doubt at all that a profoundly successful movement was under way, and was accumulating support as it went along. The Defiance Campaign will go down as the first major breach in the defences of White Supremacy.

Even the white Press took note, reporting almost daily on the progress of the Campaign. Before the late forties the whites were hardly aware (except at election time) of the nine or ten million Africans who surround them and carry them on their backs. Now they were forced at least to register our presence. A number of them even began to consider seriously the implication of our existence, and a few have been thinking ever since.

But it cannot be said that the Press was helpful. They provided pictures, and stated the number of arrests. The Afrikaans Press was, as might be expected, nearly hysterical. The English Press signally failed to acquaint its readers with our side of the case, repeatedly put to the courts which tried the volunteers.

Throughout, the discipline of the volunteers was excellent. I will not say that they were ever subdued – the new militancy was clearly discernible. But they were restrained and well behaved, and no detachment of volunteers ever got out of hand. At no time was there even the suggestion of violence or disorder. The Eastern Cape (Port Elizabeth and East London) organised brilliantly well, and the Reef kept up its pressure. Natal fell behind in execution. The mass meetings were successful enough, but the enlistment of volunteers was not as high as the enthusiasm of the meetings led us to expect. It was a salutary lesson.

In Durban it became our practice to send groups of volunteers, Indians and Africans, only after giving them some instruction on what to do and how to behave. We invariably informed· the police in advance, before a batch was sent out. The local traffic police were certainly taxed to the limit – indeed, they came to rely on our help. On one occasion they were caught unawares and we had to see to traffic control ourselves. Yet not once was the public discipline less than impressive. Our greatest problem was not the volunteers but the crowds of bystanders.

The Durban Corporation quickly introduced and passed a by-law giving themselves additional powers to control meeting and processions. As soon as we heard of it, we challenged it. We wrote to the municipality and announced our next meeting in 'Red Square'. The Special Branch duly arrested Dr. Naicker and me and others, but their difficulty was to get the vast crowd to disperse. From under arrest we did the job for them, and then went along to the central charge office where, to our surprise, we found the place thick with heavily armed police. (We were charged. We appeared. The case was adjourned. As far as I know, it still is.)

We had some trouble with the police, not of the usual kind. They were obviously reluctant to arrest us. My Natal Chairman, Dr. Wilson Conco, had to spend three nights leading his group in law-breaking before the police would arrest them, and other groups suffered a similar fate. The police tended to keep watch out of the corner of the eye.

On the whole, as South African police go, the Durban and Natal men were not over-aggressive. There was, however, one foolish incident. A crowd of spectators left the magistrate's court together. That they were together was an accident – they had all left the court at the same time. An over-eager white constable rushed up and put everybody in sight under arrest for 'forming a procession'. The crowd accepted the situation and followed along. A senior man rushed up and ordered the crowd to disperse. It began to do this, but not in time to avoid a baton charge. A woman dressed as a diviner was arrested – she refused to part with her equipment. A male bystander was arrested .for saying, 'Why are you manhandling that woman?' Both were later discharged.

But these, I emphasise, were not yet the days when South Africa bristled from end to end with heavily armed police and troops ...

The Road to South African Freedom: The Programme of the South African Communist Party

(Adopted by the fifth national conference of the South African Communist Party, 1962)

1
Introduction
Our country, South Africa, is known throughout the world because of its system of White domination, a special form of colonialism which has been carried to extremes under the Nationalist Party policy of apartheid. Nowhere else is national and racial oppression practised so nakedly and shamelessly, with such systematic brutality and disregard of human rights and dignity.

The three million Whites hold a monopoly of political rights and economic opportunities. They alone can vote for and be elected to Parliament and other governing bodies. They are fortified behind a wall of privilege in the civil service, in jobs and professions, in educational opportunities and a hundred other fields. 87 per cent of the land is reserved for White ownership, and White capitalists own and control the mines, factories and banks and most of commerce. Their government inculcates a lying and insulting doctrine of race superiority.

The eleven million Africans, two-thirds of the population, suffer ruthless national oppression. They have been robbed of their ancestral lands. The thirteen per cent of land set aside for African occupation – the so-called Reserves, or 'homelands' – are grossly overcrowded and the soil exhausted. Hunger and the network of pass laws and special taxes drive Africans to work in mines, industries and farms, where they are terribly exploited and underpaid. African languages are despised and undeveloped. The growth of national cultures is stifled. Africans are doomed from birth to little or no education, to the status of 'hewers of wood and drawers of water'.

The other non-White groups – one and a half million Coloured people and a half million South African Indians – are but little better off. Indeed the advantages they once enjoyed over Africans are one by one being removed. They have no vote or say in making the laws. Apartheid means gross national oppression for all non-Whites.

This system of race domination and oppression has its origins far back in South African history. However, it has developed into its present, extreme form with the development of capitalism and especially of the great diamond and gold-mining monopolies. Capitalism everywhere cultivates and plays upon race and national antagonisms. These are to the advantage of the capitalists because they are a weapon in the competition between capitalists of different nationalities, and because they are a means of dividing and weakening the working class. In the highest, imperialist phase of capitalism the West European monopoly capitalists developed vicious racial theories to justify their subjection of African, Asian and Latin American peoples to colonial slavery. The South African and foreign monopoly capitalists and large-scale landowners, who, together, are the real rulers of this country, have cultivated racial differences and prejudices as their most effective instrument in their insatiable drive for cheap labour and high profits. The colonial status of the African people facilitates the maximum exploitation of their labour. The privileges extended to White businessmen, farmers, professional people and workers are a means of maintaining their support for the ruling capitalist class and for the South African colonialist system.

Since 1948 the Nationalist Party government has intensified this system to an unendurable degree at the very time when racialist and colonialist theories and practices have been discredited and condemned throughout the world, and when hundreds of millions of people of Africa and Asia have gained independence and self-government. To maintain this system the Nationalists rely more and more on suppression, force and violence. Almost every channel of legal protest is closed. The main organs of people's resistance have been driven underground, South Africa is being turned into an armed camp. The State moves increasingly towards the pattern of fascism: an open, terrorist dictatorship of the most reactionary and racialist section of capitalists.

One of the first attacks of the Nationalist government on the people's rights was the Suppression of Communism Act of 1950. The Communist Party of South Africa which for twenty-eight years had marched at the head of the freedom struggles of the workers and oppressed peoples, was outlawed. The Act laid down heavy penalties for defending or advocating Communist ideas. It was no accident that the Nationalist Government made this Party and these ideas their first target, and sought to destroy them as the main obstacle to their plan of subjugating the people. Communism stands for the direct opposite of the theories and practices of the Nationalist Party. Communism stands for the rights of the workers and oppressed people – against all forms of racialism, privilege, colonialism and exploitation of man. Communism stands for peace, freedom, democracy and national independence.

Laws and force cannot destroy the ideas of Communism, of Marxism-Leninism, because these ideas are true and answer the needs and aspirations of the people. They correctly explain the world we live in and show mankind the way forward to a better world: a world without wars and racialism, without poverty and exploitation.

In this Programme, the South African Communist Party states its fundamental principles. It surveys the vast changes which are transforming the world and the continent we live in. It analyses the historical roots and the underlying realities of South African society. It puts forward its answers to the problems facing the people of our country today.

As its immediate and foremost task, the South African Communist Party works for a united front of national liberation. It strives to unite all sections and classes of oppressed and democratic people for a national democratic revolution to destroy White domination. The main content of this Revolution will be the national liberation of the African people. Carried to its fulfilment, this revolution will at the same time put an end to every sort of race discrimination and privilege. The revolution will restore the land and the wealth of the country to the people, and guarantee democracy, freedom and equality of rights, and opportunities to all. The Communist Party has no interests separate from those of the working people. The Communists are sons and daughters of the people, and share with them the over-riding necessity to put an end to the suffering and humiliation of apartheid. The destruction of colonialism and the winning of national freedom is the essential condition and the key for future advance to the supreme aim of the Communist Party: the establishment of a socialist South Africa, laying the foundations of a classless, communist society

2
Communism the Vital Force of Our Time

Communism – Marxism-Leninism – is the dynamic social and political force of our times. Already, under the leading banner of the Marxist parties, one-third of mankind has chosen the road to socialism. Already, in the Union of Socialist Soviet Republics, the gradual transition has begun to Communism, the highest form of human society. The world over millions of men and women, inspired by the Parties of Communism, are struggling for peace, socialism, democracy and national independence.

Karl Marx, the great 19th Century thinker and revolutionary who, together with his comrade Frederick Engels, was the founder of the modern Communist movement, laid bare the basic laws which determine change in the universe and in human society. The Marxist world outlook, dialectical materialism, enables us to understand the laws of change. It enables us to understand the world as it really is – and how to change it. All progress and development comes through inner conflict and contradictions: the conflict between what is new and struggling to be born, and what is outworn and dying. Like everything in nature, human society develops from lower to higher stages, according to the development of the productive forces at each stage. Feudalism is a higher stage than slavery. Capitalism is still higher, and Socialism and Communism the highest of all. Social progress has always come about through class struggles; struggles between slaves and slave-owners, between feudal lords and their serfs, and today between the two main classes of society, the capitalists and the working class.

Marx analysed the capitalist system of production. He exposed how it rests on the basis of the exploitation of man by man. All value comes from labour. Because they own the means of production, the capitalists hold the whip-hand over the workers. They do not own them, as a slave-owner owned his slaves. They pay them wages. But the wages are not equal to the real value produced by the worker. The worker works only part of the day to earn his wages. The rest is free labour for the boss. This is surplus value, out of which the capitalists make their profit and accumulate wealth. Because of their great economic power and wealth, the owners of the means of production dominate in every capitalist country. They run parliament and the press; their ideas prevail in educational and religious institutions. The laws are made to suit their interests. The State, the army, the police and the courts, defend, in the first place, their property. However democratic it may appear on the surface, every capitalist state is in reality a dictatorship of the capitalist class.

Imperialism

The genius of Vladimir Lenin, recognised leader of the workers and oppressed people of all countries, threw a bright light on the further development of 20th Century capitalism into its highest and last stage – Imperialism. As capitalism develops, more and more the control of wealth passes to fewer and fewer hands. Big firms eat up small ones. Huge monopolies grow, both national and international, and a few giant firms dominate whole branches of the national economy. Banks and other financial institutions buy shares in industrial concerns, and the 'kings of industry' acquire controlling interests in the banks. So the two kinds of monopoly capital, financial and industrial, merge with one another. The imperialists export capital to the sources of raw material and cheap labour, to the countries which are less developed economically. Economic penetration is followed by political domination. A handful of West European powers, Japan and the United States of America, seeking higher profits, dominated the whole of Africa, Asia and Latin America, mercilessly looted their natural resources and exploited their people. The colonial system of imperialism did incalculable damage to these peoples. It held back and stifled their independent economic, political, social and cultural development. In extreme cases it resulted in the wholesale massacre and near-extermination of indigenous peoples. Imperialism produced disgusting and utterly false theories and practices of so-called 'superior' and 'inferior' races, which culminated in Hitler's Germany and Verwoerd's South Africa

Imperialism breeds war, on a scale and of a frightfulness previously unknown in human history. Following the 'scramble for Africa' towards the end of the 19th Century, the entire world was partitioned between the imperialist powers. Powerful new capitalist states arose, and demanded their 'right' to own colonies. But all the colonial territories had already been grabbed by the older imperialists. The desperate conflict between the rival imperialists for the re-partition of the world, erupted in the terrible world war of 1914–18, which shook the foundations of imperialism and exposed its true nature to the masses.

Capitalism, in its time, was a progressive social system. With all its defects it represented an advance over feudalism, higher production, greater liberties. But, in the world of today, capitalism is no longer progressive. Modem production is a great and complicated process, arising from a highly organised society. But the means of production remain in private hands, and the fruits are appropriated by the few. This deep contradiction between social production and private appropriation leads to great conflicts in society: between the masses of the people and the group of monopoly capitalists who control their destinies, between rival capitalist countries, between colonial peoples seeking national freedom and their imperialist masters, between the working class as a whole and the capitalist class. These conflicts cannot be resolved within the framework of the capitalist system. They are leading to the breakdown of that system. Symptoms of this breakdown are the ever-recurring crises of overproduction; the turning of the ruling classes towards fascism; the gigantic expenditure on armaments; the ceaseless drive towards aggression and war.

Capitalism is obsolete. It is giving way to the new and higher social order of socialism and communism. Socialism puts an end to the contradictions of capitalism by abolishing private ownership of the main means of production and placing them under public ownership. It replaces the dictatorship of the capitalists with that of the workers, thus for the first time ensuring genuine democracy for the masses. It overcomes the class and national conflicts inherent in capitalism by abolishing the exploiting classes and the exploitation of man by man; by guaranteeing equality and national rights to all peoples. Socialism aims to meet the growing material and cultural needs of the people by overall planning, by steadily developing and improving social production. It develops socialist consciousness and labour enthusiasm among the working people by applying the principle: 'From each according to his ability, to each according to his work'. The great development of the productive forces under socialism, and in the rise in the socialist consciousness of the masses, enables the gradual development towards a still higher stage of human society: communism. Communism is a classless social system, with one form of public ownership of the means of production. All members of communist society will enjoy full social equality. The all-round development of the people, accompanied by the growth of the productive forces sufficient to ensure abundance of goods, enables the principle to be applied: 'From each according to his ability, to each according to his needs'. Under communism – a highly organised society of free, socially-conscious people enjoying public self-government – labour will cease to be a burden. Everyone will recognise that to work for the benefit of the people is a necessity willingly performed as life's first need.

The October Revolution
A new era in human history opened with the great October Socialist Revolution of 1917 when, led by the Communist Party, and inspired by the great teachings of Marx and Lenin, the workers and peasants of Russia and the former Tsarist Empire overthrew capitalist class rule and established, over a vast territory, the dictatorship of the proletariat The heroic victories of the Soviet workers and peasants against counter-revolutions and foreign intervention, their triumph over famines and backwardness, their great achievements in the building of socialism, inspired millions of working people in many parts of the world. Powerful Communist Parties arose in many countries. In the areas of the greatest population, the colonies of imperialism in Asia, Africa and Latin America, the October Revolution aroused hundreds of millions to fight for national liberation.

Following the historic victory of the Soviet Union in the second world war and the defeat of fascism on an international scale, the people's cause made a further leap ahead. Led by the Communist Party, the great Chinese nation of 750 million put an end to domination by imperialism and its agents and took the road to socialism. In a number of European and Asian countries the people rose against capitalist and landlord rule and laid the basis for socialism. These countries have joined the Soviet Union in the socialist camp, comprising no less than one third of the human race bound together by firm fraternal and equal relations among themselves, advancing the people's living standards by leaps and bounds, and providing a powerful safeguard for peace, national liberation, democracy and progress for all the peoples of the world.

The colonial system of imperialism is crumbling. The peoples of practically the whole Continent of Asia have within an astonishingly short space of time liberated themselves from direct colonial rule. The tide of national liberation has advanced with equally dramatic swiftness throughout the continent of Africa and the great majority of our fellow-Africans today enjoy formal political independence. The inspiring example of Cuba has called forth a great wave throughout Latin America of resistance to the economic enslavement by United States imperialism. Determined to win a place of equality in the world, and to overcome the evil heritage of imperialism, the peoples of the colonial and formerly colonial countries are conducting vigorous and mounting struggles against imperialism and its agents in their midst. They fight against feudalism and other forms of local reaction. They are striving to build states of national democracy, which will move forward from formal independence and break all imperialist financial, economic, political and military entanglements. They seek rapidly to put an end to the chaos and economic backwardness which imperialism has left behind it. They aim to overcome the crippling lack of equipment, communications, and trained and skilled personnel; and to conquer illiteracy, mass poverty, disease and ignorance. They aim to catch up with the most advanced countries in industrial and agricultural development, in living standards and conditions, in educational, cultural and scientific achievement. Only thus can true equality, independence and democracy be established for the hundreds of millions of people in the former colonies of imperialism.

More and more the masses of people in Africa and other formerly colonial countries are coming to understand that capitalist forms of production, based on private ownership, can never enable them to accomplish this gigantic task. Led by the small, but growing, working class, in close alliance with the masses of rural people, they are striving to achieve non-capitalist forms of development, leading towards socialism. They are demanding a vast process of agrarian reform, enabling the African, Asian and Latin American farmer, for the first time in history, to have sufficient land at his disposal for a decent life. To place the control of their countries firmly in the hands of the people, they are fighting for genuine democracy, guaranteeing freedom of speech, of the press and organisation, and enabling masses of workers and peasants to play a full part in public life. The newly independent countries no longer constitute a reliable reserve of imperialism. They are moving more and more out of the sphere of influence of imperialism, and becoming a powerful factor for peace, against imperialist war.

The greatest threat to the aspirations and the future of the peoples of all countries lies in the aggressive plans of international imperialism against socialism and national independence. Should the imperialists succeed in triggering off a nuclear world conflict it would destroy a great part of humanity and man's greatest achievements. Imperialism has not changed its character. Mobilised and organised by the leaders of world reaction, the United States monopoly capitalists, the imperialists are intensifying the armaments race and the cold war, they commit continuous fresh acts of intervention and aggression, attempting to check and reverse the world tide towards national independence and socialism. They threaten the world with nuclear destruction. But because of the tremendous strength, economic, social and military, of the Socialist countries, attracting the powerful support of hundreds of millions of people in the newly liberated and the capitalist countries, the power of the imperialists to impose colonialism, or to start wars, has been checked; their wings have been clipped.

Powerful peace movements, embracing millions of people of varying political beliefs, have grown up in many countries. The forces of national liberation and of the labour movement everywhere are insistently demanding an end to the cold war and the observance of the principles of peaceful co-existence of states with different social systems. All these forces are rallying to demand universal and complete disarmament. This crucial policy, advanced by the Soviet Union, crystallises the longings of our generation for peace and security, for life itself. Universal disarmament would lift a crushing burden of taxes from the shoulders of the people. It would make available the huge resources and quantities of manpower now diverted to arms production for useful production to raise the people's living standards. It would greatly assist the cause of national liberation by striking the weapons from the hands of the colonialists. It would free the world from the nightmare of nuclear war. Unity of all the forces demanding peace is capable of enforcing this demand. Even though imperialism still rules in powerful countries, such as the United States, the countries of Western Europe and Japan, and even though the war danger is still acute, the possibility already exists of achieving universal disarmament and eliminating war, providing the people struggle resolutely to assert their will for peace.

It is no longer the imperialists, but the international working class and its proudest creation, the world socialist system, which determine the main characteristics and trends of our times. We live in an epoch of struggle between two opposing social systems, an epoch of socialist and national liberation revolutions, of the breakdown of imperialism and the abolition of the colonial system. It is an epoch of the transition of more and more peoples to the socialist path and the triumph of socialism and communism on a world-wide scale. These vast changes in the world spell the doom of capitalism and imperialism. The victory of socialism and communism will ensure the eradication of all types of exploitation and oppression, a future of peace, friendship, well-being, and unlimited advance for all peoples of the earth. Idlers and parasites will no longer exist, for 'he who does not work, neither shall he eat'. Selfishness, ignorance, superstition and other evils of the acquisitive society will disappear. Mankind will enter upon a greater freedom, in terms of the principles of Communism.

But this great change will not come about of its own accord, or by persuading the capitalist ruling classes that change is reasonable and desirable. No ruling class in history ever bowed itself gracefully off the stage. The defeat of capitalism and the transition to socialism can only come about through struggles of the masses of the people, headed by the most advanced, resolute and revolutionary class, the working class. In their fight against exploitation and capitalist class domination, the weapon of the working class is organisation. The workers organise trade unions to fight for higher wages, better conditions and shorter working hours. They build mass political organisations to oppose and protest against the injustices of capitalist class rule. Answering Marx's great call: 'Workers of all countries, unite!' the workers of each country strengthen brotherly ties between themselves and those of other countries beyond their borders, on a regional, continental and international basis.

Due to differences of history and national tradition, which the Communist Parties take into account, the precise path to socialism will differ from one country to another. But international experiences show that certain basic laws apply to all countries. Headed by the Marxist-Leninist Party and in alliance with most of the peasants and other working people, the working class must destroy the state of dictatorship of the capitalists, and replace it with the dictatorship of the working class, offering the widest democracy to the great majority of the people. Attempts at counter-revolution by the reactionary classes and groups must be suppressed. Private ownership of the main means of production must be abolished, and public ownership must be established in its place. The land must be in the hands of those who till it, and agriculture gradually transformed on a socialist basis. The national economy must be planned, to raise the people's living standards and build socialism and communism. Capitalist influence must be rooted out in the fields of ideology and culture, and a new type of intellectual must be trained, devoted to the welfare of the people and to socialism. All forms of racial and national discrimination and oppression must be wiped out, complete equality of rights and opportunities and brotherly friendship must be an unvarying principle governing all relations between people of different national groups. The achievements of socialism must be defended against enemies inside and outside the country. Working class internationalism – close ties between the workers of all lands – is essential for the building of socialism in any country.

The highest form of working class organisation is the Marxist-Leninist Party, the most advanced, conscious and determined section of the class. This Party, the Communist Party, is a voluntary association of the best, most militant and devoted fighters for the cause of the workers, peasants and all oppressed people. All Party members enjoy equal rights irrespective of race or nationality. All members pledge themselves to maintain the highest standards of discipline, political training, loyalty and courage. Led by the Party, the working class aims, not merely at reforms of the capitalist system, but at the revolutionary overthrow of the system itself and its replacement by socialism.

3
The African Revolution
For centuries the peoples of Africa were subjected to exploitation and robbery by the capitalist maritime nations of Western Europe and other marauders. Millions of sons and daughters of Africa were transported as slaves to far-away countries. In the words of Karl Marx, Africa was 'a warren for the commercial hunting of black skins'. The invaders destroyed Africa's ancient civilisations. They seized and laid waste her natural wealth. By the end of the 19th Century almost the whole of Africa had been conquered - by trickery or the force of superior arms – and brought beneath the alien yoke of a handful of European powers – Britain, France, Portugal, Belgium, Germany and Spain. Her peoples were deprived of self-government,

alienated from their ancestral lands and driven to work as forced labourers on white-owned plantations, mines and other enterprises. Africa's normal economic and political development was arrested and set back. Vast fortunes were accumulated in Europe and North America out of African resources and African labour. But the people of our Continent remained the most poverty-stricken in the world, with the highest death rate and the lowest expectancy of life. The colonialists proclaimed that their mission was altruistic and civilising. But now when they are being driven from Africa, they leave behind them a crippling heritage of illiteracy, ignorance, economic stagnation, starvation and disease.

As a result of the heroic struggles of the African peoples, all over the Continent, and also of the break-up of the colonial system of imperialism which was inaugurated by the great October Socialist Revolution, the peoples of Africa have swept forward to win freedom and independence. At the end of the second world war, only Ethiopia and Liberia could claim to be African states governed by Africans. By 1962 the whole picture had been transformed. Only Angola, Mozambique and a few other scattered territories remained under the direct colonial rule of European powers, and in the Republic of South Africa, South-West Africa and the Rhodesias, White minorities continued to dominate. The area of formal political independence had spread to almost the entire continent. This sweeping process – the return of Africa to the rule of the African people themselves – is a great victory for the African people and the cause of freedom. It must be pressed forward and completed as soon as possible. It is the essential basis for all future advance. The working class, and its most advanced leaders, the Communists, are intimately concerned with this great movement for political independence; they form its spearhead and its most determined and uncompromising defenders.

But, formal political independence alone will not ensure the genuine independence of the African peoples, and their equality amongst the nations of the world. The former colonies remain tied by a thousand bonds to their former owners. Through the 'British Commonwealth' and the 'French Community' powerful pressures are exerted to influence them and ensure their continued adherence to political, diplomatic, military and economic systems of Western imperialism. There is a new 'scramble for Africa' in which United States, West German and Japanese finance capitalists are vying with the older imperialists to extend their investments and their economic stranglehold over African territories and resources. The imperialists all strive to retard the development of national economies and national industries in the African countries. Through such instruments as the European Common Market they strive to keep them backward, in a position of suppliers of raw material and cheap labour for imperialism. These plans of neo-colonialism are the greatest threat to the real independence and development of the newly emerged African States.

The young African states need to abolish illiteracy, backwardness and economic dependence. They need to 'Africanise' their civil services and administrations, rapidly to train personnel from amongst their own people to administer and develop their countries. They need radical land reform, to transform and improve African agriculture and greatly raise the desperately low living standards of the masses. They need rapid industrialisation and economic development, in order to overcome the terrible heritage left behind by colonialism, and to catch up with the advanced countries of the world. In these aims the young African Republics are tremendously assisted by the generous and unconditional aid extended to them by the Soviet Union and other countries of the socialist world system. Such aid is rendered upon the principles of strict equality and true brotherly friendship. It aims to lay the basis for the industrialisation of undeveloped countries – the foundation stone of true independence and equality – and to train competent specialists in the hundred fields which the new Africa so urgently requires.

Only if they can achieve a social transformation, a fast rate of economic and social development, can the African countries ensure genuine independence and equality in the world family of nations, and higher standards of life, health and culture for their people. In their drive towards these goals the African peoples are faced with the choice between capitalist and socialist paths. More and more, the revolutionary workers and peasants, the radical intellectual youth of Africa are turning towards the socialist path. They have seen the evils of capitalism at work in their midst, its greed and wastefulness of life and resources; its ruthless contempt for the dignity and value of the human being. They have learnt of the tremendous rate of development which socialism has made possible especially in the Asian Republics of the Soviet Union, in People's China and other formerly colonial countries which, under workers' rule and socialism, have advanced with giant's strides. Non-capitalist forms of development, aimed at the building of socialism, are the only way in which Africa can rapidly liquidate racialism, feudalism, tribalism, poverty, backwardness and disease, and the exploitation of man by man.

The South African Communist Party regards as a dogmatic distortion of Marxism, the concept that African countries which are in a precapitalist stage of development must necessarily pass through a period of capitalism before achieving socialism. We are living in the epoch of the transition, on a world scale, from capitalism to socialism. The experience of the Soviet Asian Republics, of People's China, Vietnam, the People's Republic of Korea, and People's Mongolia, show that in our epoch it is possible for the people of colonial countries to advance along non-capitalist lines towards the building of socialism.

Recognising the tremendous attraction of socialist ideas in Africa, various leaders have advanced the concept of a special kind of 'African Socialism' different from Marxism-Leninism. These concepts are mistaken. It is true that the precise paths of the African peoples towards socialism will differ from those of peoples of other continents, due to differences of national tradition and history, to the long period of colonialist domination which, amongst other factors, has prevented the development of African societies along the same lines as those in Europe and Asia. But the whole of international experience has proved beyond any shadow of doubt, that the main truths of Marxism-Leninism are fully applicable to countries in every stage of social development. The only road towards a socialist and communist future is that indicated by Marxism. The innumerable attempts, in many parts of the world, to propound or practise non-Marxist socialism, or to 'revise', 'modify' and 'improve' Marxism-Leninism, have one and all ended in disaster and betrayal of the working class.

National Democracy

The countries of Africa are in various stages of historical and social development. In some areas, such as the Republic of South Africa and the Congo, there is a relatively high degree of industrial development, of powerful monopoly capitalism and a numerically strong working class. Other areas have hardly been touched at all by capitalist development. There is little or no commodity production and exchange, and modern nations have not developed. Feudal and pre-feudal societies prevail. There is thus no common solution which would answer the needs of all the territories of Africa; each area needs to be studied specifically in the light of its own actual conditions. But, in most parts of Africa, the needs of the people will best be met at the present time by the formation of states of national democracy, as a transitional stage to socialism. The minimum essentials for a state of national democracy as indicated in the declaration of 81 Marxist Parties in December 1960, are that it: 'consistently upholds its political and economic independence, fights against imperialism and its military blocs, against military bases on its territory; fights against the new forms of colonialism and the penetration of imperialist capital; rejects dictatorial and despotic methods of government; ensures the people broad democratic rights and freedoms (freedom of the press, speech, assembly, demonstration, establishment of political parties and social organisations) and the opportunity of working for the enactment of agrarian reform and other domestic and social changes, and for participation in shaping government policy'. The basis of a national democracy is a leading alliance of workers and rural people. Such a state will provide the most favourable conditions for advance, along non-capitalist lines, to socialism.

In their advance towards national independence, democracy, unity and socialism the African peoples are seriously handicapped by the lack of understanding of socialist ideology – largely a result of the imperialists' censorship and distortion of Communist ideas – and by the absence in most parts of our Continent of independent Marxist-Leninist parties of the working class. Socialism cannot effectively be built without socialist organisation guided by socialist theory. The development and growth of such parties, devoted to the people's struggle for freedom and independence, and building and forming part of the united front of all patriotic classes for national liberation, would be an important contribution to the cause of Africa. By making a profound study of scientific socialist theory and creatively applying it to the solution of the problems of their own countries, such Parties can play an indispensable role in carrying the African Revolution forward uninterruptedly to its consummation: the crowning of national independence with deep-reaching social revolution and the full emancipation of the African peoples from bondage.

The common struggle of the peoples of Africa against imperialism and colonialism in all its forms has brought the peoples of Africa closer together than ever before. The African countries which have already achieved independence render fraternal assistance to the freedom struggle of their brothers who still suffer under foreign or White minority domination. A powerful urge towards closer ties and solidarity exists among all Africans based upon the understanding that unity can best enable the African people to maintain and consolidate independence, overcome their grave social and economic problems, develop the resources of the Continent and raise their living standards. This urge finds its expression in the historic All-African People's Conferences and in regional groupings such as the Pan-African Freedom Movement of East, Central and Southern Africa; in the formation of the All-African Trade Union Federation; in joint economic and defence plans; in actual or projected regional Federations aimed at the ultimate establishment of a United African Commonwealth. This movement is progressive and anti-imperialist in character, reflecting the essential unity of the African Revolution. The frontiers of Africa were drawn by the imperialists. For the most part they record past conflicts and settlements among the colonialists. They do not reflect African interests, nor do they demarcate natural geographical, linguistic or other divisions. Progressive elements in Africa will seek to re-draw these frontiers, to create larger and more viable communities, leading to a fraternal commonwealth of Africa as a whole. Because they are achieving independence in the epoch of the world transition to socialism, it is not inevitable that the African nations should follow the path of other continents by developing antagonistic nation states, each jealously guarding its frontiers. Such states are the product of capitalism. Provided all the African countries follow non-capitalist forms of development the achievement of a united Africa will become practical and desirable. But if this great historical process is to be effected without sowing the seeds of new conflicts, it must be based on consent and persuasion, not upon force.

Communists recognise the right of all peoples and national groups to self-determination. They respect the languages and progressive traditions of all African peoples, and their right to independent development of their culture. While recognising the progressive elements in African nationalism and the movement for Pan-African unity, South African communists remain true to the principles of working class internationalism. They will fight against all expressions of racialism, isolationism, and the glorification and perpetuation of reactionary traditions, which have their roots in capitalist, tribal and feudalist outlooks.

The struggle of the peoples of the rest of Africa and those of South Africa, against colonialism and for freedom are one and indivisible. White colonialism in the Republic of South Africa threatens the independence, peace and progress of the whole of Africa. It is a stronghold and refuge of reaction and imperialism threatening the gains of the African revolution; a breeding ground for plots and activities designed to restore colonialism throughout the Continent. A poor and backward Africa profits the South African monopoly capitalists, enabling them to exploit cheap African labour, both in their heavy investments in many parts of the Continent and by importing workers from other territories to mines and other enterprises in the Republic itself. The South African state and its military forces collaborate with those of the Portuguese, Rhodesian and other colonialists. In fighting against White supremacy, for the democratic revolution in South Africa, the people of our country are fighting for the cause of the African Revolution as a whole. In this fight they are greatly heartened by the victories of their brothers and sisters beyond their borders, and by their actions of solidarity with South Africa. They welcome the decisions for the complete diplomatic and economic isolation of the Republic, the boycott of South African goods and the withdrawal of migrant labour from this country, and call for the strict implementation of these decisions. The liberated South Africa of the future will build ties of the closest fraternity and mutual assistance, based upon equal friendly relations, with all peoples of Africa. Its wealth, experience and skills will be a source of strength to the new Africa.

3
Colonialism of a Special Type

The White ruling classes, and especially the leaders of the Nationalist Party have manufactured a version of the past and present of this country which they systematically attempt to impose everywhere, from the schoolroom to international opinion. According to this picture, the early White settlers penetrated peacefully into a virtually unoccupied country. The African population, who are depicted as savage barbarians without culture, achievements or history, are represented as relative newcomers who entered the country at about the same time as the Whites, and conducted aggressive wars and raids against them. The impression is given that African occupation was always more or less confined to the present Reserves – the 'Bantu Homelands'. This version of South Africa's past is entirely false.

From the time of the first White settlement, established by the Dutch East India Company 300 years ago, the pattern was set for the ruthless colonial exploitation of the non-White peoples of our country, the expropriation of their lands and the enforced harnessing of their labour power. The Dutch made war on the people of the Cape, whom they contemptuously called 'Hottentots', and rejected their appeals for peace and friendship. The so-called 'Bushmen' were all but exterminated. Slaves were imported from Malaya and elsewhere. White settlers gradually penetrated into the interior. They drove the indigenous people from the best farm lands and seized their cattle. They subdued them by armed conquest and forced them into their service – at first through direct slavery, later through a harsh system of pass laws and taxation.

This pattern was not basically changed by the seizure of the Cape Colony from Holland by Britain in 1806. The British colonialists conducted a savage series of wars of conquest against the AmaXhosa people in the Eastern Cape and the Zulu people in Natal. They imported more White settlers from Britain, and greatly extended the area of White domination. Through the agency of missionaries, traders, or armed bands of adventurers, they extended British sovereignty or 'Protectorates' through Bechuanaland and

Basutoland, and beyond the Limpopo River in Mashonaland, Barotseland, and other territories to the north, which they have named after the infamous adventurer and multi-millionaire Cecil Rhodes.

The beginnings of the pass system were introduced under British rule. However, as the foremost capitalist country at that time, Britain was opposed to direct chattel slavery. In 1836 a law was passed abolishing slavery in the Cape Colony. In protest against this law, and to get away from British rule, large parties of Boers left the Cape and crossed into Natal, the Orange Free State and the Transvaal. In the course of this Great Trek, the Boers conducted continuous aggressive wars against the African tribes whom they found in possession everywhere. They usurped their lands, exploited their labour and even practised forms of slavery. They established new Republics founded on White domination and the racialist principle 'No equality in Church or State'.

Colonialist propaganda has emphasised the negative features of traditional African society: the relatively low development of productive techniques; the illiteracy, inter-tribal conflicts and wars, superstitions and poverty. It is true that such features existed in traditional African society just as they did among all peoples at the period of simple tribal economy. But hostile propaganda has presented a distorted image. Prior to the European conquest of Southern Africa, the indigenous peoples had developed their own independent culture and civilisation. They mined and smelted iron, copper and other metals and fashioned them into useful implements. They had developed a number of handicrafts. Their system of extensive agriculture and livestock breeding was well-suited to the type of country and the tools at their disposal. It produced a surplus sufficient to maintain full-time specialist workers, smiths, doctors and others. Their system of government, though simple, was essentially democratic and popular in character. The hereditary chiefs were assisted in their functions as law-givers and judges by the senior people of the tribe, and important decisions affecting the whole tribe were always referred to a general meeting of the people – the Tswana and Sotho Pitso, the Xhosa and Zulu Imbizo. Private property in land was unknown, and food and shelter were freely shared, even with strangers.

When Whites first appeared they were welcomed courteously. But when the colonists began their ceaseless acts of armed aggression, the African people resisted bravely to defend their cattle and their land from robbery and their people from enslavement. They took up spear and assegai against the bullets of the invader with his horses and wagons. The Xhosa people, under leaders such as Nqgika, Ndlambe, Hintsa and Makana, the Zulus using Chaka's battle tactics, under Dingane, Cetywayo and Bambata, the Basotho under Moshoeshoe, and in the North, the Tswana, Pedi and other African peoples, fought back bravely against the Boer and British invaders. The Coloured people, too, struggled valiantly. Revolts took place and the Coloured community, led by the great Adam Kok, established their own independent Griqua Republic. But, tribal society and a rural economy could not provide the material basis for successful warfare against an enemy with a more advanced economy and more destructive weapons. The impact and penetration of White missionaries and traders paved the way for military conquest. Disunity amongst the various African peoples prevented the development of a common front of resistance. The farsighted vision of Moshoeshoe did indeed encompass this idea, and he sent emissaries to the Zulu and Xhosa people, and to Adam Kok, to propose such a united front. But Moshoeshoe's idea of a grand alliance came before its time. Time and again in their wars of conquest against African peoples, the British and Boer imperialists were able to play off one tribe against another and to enrol African auxiliaries.

The discovery of diamond fields at Kimberley and goldfields on the Witwatersrand had profound and far-reaching consequences. Foreigners flocked into South Africa. Great British and European finance houses exported vast sums of investment capital to South Africa. To seize complete control over the gold of the Transvaal, British imperialism invaded the two Republics, and after a cruel war, in which the Boers defended themselves with great heroism and resourcefulness, brought them within the British Empire. One of the pretexts for Britain's aggression had been the oppression of the African people under the Republics. Yet, following the British victory, the colonial status and subjugation of the indigenous peoples was continued and even intensified. The goldmining interests were now the true rulers of the country. They had only one interest in the African – to force him into labour on the mines at minimum rates of pay. They found the harsh colonial policy of the Republics admirably suited to this purpose. The poll tax and pass systems were intensified. Dispossession of the Africans from the land was speeded up. Not a single move was made to introduce into the northern colonies even the minimum citizen rights which had been conceded to the non-Whites in the Cape In the oppression, dispossession and exploitation of the non-Whites, British imperialism and Afrikaner nationalism found common ground. This was the basis for the establishment of the Union of South Africa in 1910

Dominating the all-White parliament, the representatives of the wealthy Boer farmers and the imperialist mine-owners joined in an unholy alliance to squeeze the last drop of cheap labour out of the African people. The Land Act of 1913 ended African land ownership or tenancy except in the Reserves which were deliberately designed to be insufficient to support the population, so that the menfolk would be driven forth by hunger to work in White-owned enterprises. The state developed the contract system of migrant labour, separating the wage-earner from his family, so that the employer would not have to pay for the maintenance of the worker's wife and children. The democratic, co-operative basis of tribal society was broken down, and the entire African people turned into a rightless community of impoverished peasants and underpaid forced labourers in White-controlled farms, mines and factories.

South Africa is not a colony but an independent state. Yet masses of our people enjoy neither independence nor freedom. The conceding of independence to South Africa by Britain, in 1910, was not a victory over the forces of colonialism and imperialism. It was designed in the interests of imperialism. Power was transferred not into the hands of the masses of people of South Africa, but into the hands of the White minority alone. The evils of colonialism, insofar as the non-White majority was concerned, were perpetuated and reinforced. A new type of colonialism was developed, in which the oppressing White nation occupied the same territory as the oppressed people themselves and lived side by side with them.

A rapid process of industrialisation was set in train, especially during the two world wars. South African heavy industry and secondary industry grew to occupy first place on the Continent. This process had profound effects on the country's social structure. It concentrated great wealth and profits in the hands of the upper strata of the White population. It revolutionised the economy, transforming it from a predominantly agricultural into an industrial-agricultural economy, with an urban working class, mainly non-White, which is the largest in Africa. But no commensurate benefits of this industrialisation have been enjoyed by the masses of non-White people.

Two South Africas
On one level, that of 'White South Africa', there are all the features of an advanced capitalist state in its final stage of imperialism. There are highly developed industrial monopolies, and the merging of industrial and finance capital. The land is farmed along capitalist lines, employing wage labour, and producing cash crops for the local and export markets. The South African monopoly capitalists, who are closely linked with British, United States and other foreign imperialist interests, export capital abroad, especially in Africa. Greedy for expansion, South African imperialism reaches out to

incorporate other territories – South West Africa and the Protectorates.

But on another level, that of 'Non-White South Africa', there are all the features of a colony. The indigenous population is subjected to extreme national oppression, poverty and exploitation, lack of all democratic rights and political domination by a group which does everything it can to emphasise and perpetuate its alien 'European' character. The African Reserves show the complete lack of industry, communications, transport and power resources which are characteristic of African territories under colonial rule throughout the Continent. Typical, too, of imperialist rule, is the reliance by the state upon brute force and terror, and upon the most backward tribal elements and institutions which are deliberately and artificially preserved. Non-White South Africa is the colony of White South Africa itself.

It is this combination of the worst features both of imperialism and of colonialism, within a single national frontier, which determines the special nature of the South African system, and has brought upon its rulers the justified hatred and contempt of progressive and democratic people throughout the world.

All Whites enjoy privileges in South Africa. They alone can vote and be elected to parliament and local government bodies. They have used this privilege to monopolise nearly all economic, educational, cultural and social opportunities. This gives the impression that the ruling class is composed of the entire White population. In fact, however, real power is in the hands of the monopolists who own and control the mines, the banks and finance houses, and most of the farms and major industries. The gold and diamond mines are owned by seven mining-financial corporations and controlled by a handful of powerful financiers. These seven corporations are closely linked with British and American imperialist interests. They control capital investment in mining alone of R490 million, and employ almost 500,000 workers. In addition, they dominate large sections of manufacturing industries. They are linked with the main banks, two of which control assets of over R2,000 million, mainly in the form of loans to industry, commerce and estate. They own vast tracts of arable land and mining rights in almost every part of the country. In agriculture too monopoly dominates. 4 per cent of the farms make up an area amounting to almost four-tenths of the total White-owned farmland. Thus, in mining, industry, commerce and farming, monopolists dominate the country's economy. They are also closely linked with state monopoly capital ventures, such as Iscor (Iron and Steel), Escom (Electricity) and Sasol (Petrol).

These monopolists are the real power in South Africa. The special type of colonialism in South Africa serves, in the first place, their interests. Low non-White wages; the reserves of poverty; the compound labour system and the importation of hundreds of thousands of contract labourers from beyond our borders; the pass laws and poll tax and rigid police control of labour and of movement – all are designed to keep their profits high. In 1961, these seven mining corporations and their subsidiaries made a working profit of nearly R212 million and paid out dividends of R101 million to shareholders.

The South African monopolists act as allies and agents of foreign imperialist interests. One quarter of the capital of the seven mining-financial groups is owned abroad, mainly by British and American investors. In 1958, dividends of R43 million were paid out abroad. The two biggest banks, Standard and Barclays, are largely controlled from Britain, and in recent years United States capital investment in South Africa has grown rapidly, exceeding all other American investments in the rest of Africa put together.

Effective economic domination in South Africa is thus exercised by an alliance of local White monopoly interests in mining, industry and agriculture, together with foreign imperialists and representatives of state monopoly capitalism. These interests have conflicts among themselves, which are reflected in the main White political parties and groupings. But they find common ground in the perpetuation of the colonial-type subjugation of the non-White population.

The system of colonial domination over and robbery of the non-White masses is not in the genuine, long-term interest of the workers, small farmers, middle-class and professional elements who make up the bulk of the White population. White domination means more and more police and military expenditure to burden the taxpayer and divert men and resources from useful production. It means that the poverty-stricken masses are unable to form an adequate market for South African industry and agriculture. It means more and more dictatorial police-state measures, the extinguishing of civil liberties for Whites as well as non-Whites. It means a South Africa despised and shunned by the whole world, subjected to economic, diplomatic, cultural and other forms of isolation, boycott and sanctions. It means a future of uncertainty and fear. The maintenance of White supremacy involves ever-increasing repression and violence by the government, resistance by the oppressed people and the steady drift to civil war. Only the complete emancipation of the non-White peoples can create conditions of equality and friendship among the nationalities of South Africa and eliminate the roots of race hatred and antagonism which are the greatest threat to the continued security and existence of the White population itself. The national liberation of the non-Whites which will break the power of monopoly capitalism is thus in the deepest long-term interest of the bulk of the Whites. Progressive and far-seeing Whites ally themselves unconditionally with the struggle of the masses of the people for freedom and equality.

On the whole, the White workers represent an 'aristocracy of labour'. The monopolists have extended numerous concessions to them. They receive relatively high wages. Non-white miners receive an average of R144 a year plus food and compound housing; White miners R2470. African male farm workers average R68 a year; Whites R1050. Whites have a monopoly of the best paid jobs, and of entry into skilled trades. They are invariably given positions of authority over non-Whites. The relatively high standards of life and wages enjoyed by White workers represent, in reality, a share in the super profits made by the capitalists out of the gross exploitation of the non-Whites. Systematically indoctrinated with the creed of White superiority, the White worker imagines himself to be a part of the ruling class and willingly acts as a tool and an accomplice in the maintenance of colonialism and capitalism. However, in reality, the White worker, like the non-White worker at his side, is subjected to exploitation by the same capitalist owners of the means of production. White workers' wages in general are high in comparison with those of non-Whites. But many categories of White workers are paid little more than non-Whites, and also struggle to support their families. The White worker is subject to the insecurity of the capitalist system, with its constant threats of depression, short-time and unemployment. The division of trade unions on racial lines weakens all sections of workers in their constant struggle with the bosses for better pay and conditions and shorter hours of work. The fundamental interests of all South African workers, like those of workers everywhere, lie in unity: unity in the struggle for the day-to-day interests of the working class, for the ending of race discrimination and division, for a free, democratic South Africa as the only possible basis for the winning of socialism, the overthrow of the capitalist class and the ending of human exploitation.

Non-White South Africa
More than two-thirds of the South Africans are people of indigenous African descent. Living and working in all parts of the country, they form the basic population and are at the same time the main victims of colonialism; the most oppressed and exploited of all. The former divisions of the African people along tribal lines, and their classification into chiefs and commoners, are breaking down with the collapse of the tribal system. This system was

suitable for the simple, self-contained economy of the past, based on subsistence farming and common ownership of land. There is no place for it in a modem exchange economy based on large-scale industry and mining, on the farming of products for sale on the market. The Nationalist Party government, following the maxim: 'Divide and Rule', is attempting to revive tribalism and tribal divisions. Their attempts cannot succeed. The African people of this country are moving inevitably and consciously towards the formation of a single, modern nation.

There are no acute or antagonistic class divisions at present among the African people. Most of them are wage-workers in industry or agriculture. There are no large-scale African employers of labour. The professional groups, mainly teachers, do not, as a rule, earn salaries or live differently from their fellow-Africans. Even the people of the Reserves, especially the menfolk, spend much of their lives as migrant wage labourers on the mines, in agriculture or industry

One-third of the African people live on the Reserves. The largest of these are the Transkei and Ciskei, in the Cape Province, but there are also other scattered areas widely separated in the other three provinces. The Nationalist government speaks of the Reserves as the 'homelands' of the African people, but so far from being able to sustain additional population, they are grossly overcrowded already and far too small to maintain their present population of 34 million. Most Africans on the reserves are not independent peasants and have no land or insufficient to make a living. To support their families and avert starvation, most of the men in the prime of life are usually away working for White employers, and leaving the farming to old people and womenfolk. The smallness and the overcrowding of the Reserves lead to soil exhaustion. There is no opportunity for intensive farming, crop rotation, and scientific cattle pasturing, because there is not enough land. The Reserves are the most backward and undeveloped areas in the country, typical of colonial Africa. They lack industries, communications and power resources. There is no capital for improvements or mechanisation.

The 'Bantustan' Fraud

Under its preposterous 'Bantustan' scheme the Nationalist government is proposing to partition South Africa. They pretend to be conferring 'independence' and 'self-government' on the Reserves, which they have rechristened 'Bantu Homelands', and thus to justify treating Africans in the remaining 87 per cent of South Africa as 'aliens' and 'temporary visitors'. They present this proposal as a concession to the African people and to world opinion. Africans and all freedom-loving people reject this proposal with contempt and indignation. There are no grounds, in history or in reality, for the Nationalists to claim any part of South Africa exclusively for Whites. Africans live in every part of our country; their labour has gone to develop its farmlands and its cities, its mines and industries, its railways and harbours; they claim every inch of South Africa as their homeland. The 'Bantustan' scheme is not only undemocratic and opposed to every principle of self-determination, it is also fraudulent. Though they pretend they are giving land to Africans they are not giving them any additional land at all – in many cases they are actually taking away land from them. The Nationalist Party promises independence and self-government to the Reserves, but the so-called 'Bantustan' schemes are both dishonest and impractical. The Nationalists have no intention of conferring any genuine independence on any group of non-White people. Even if they were compelled to make concessions in this direction, the land area of the Reserves is too small, the economy too backward, and completely lacking in capital to allow for the possibility of any real independence for these areas.

The government is attempting, through the 'Bantu Authorities' system, to enforce a return to tribalism, using chiefs who are prepared to collaborate, and deposing and deporting those who refuse. The effect is actually to hasten the breakdown of tribal institutions. Those chiefs who collaborate with the government have become the most hated group in the countryside, relying on dictatorship and terror, contrary to African traditions, to enforce the laws of the White authorities on the unwilling people. The people of the Reserves are boldly calling the government's 'Bantustan' bluff. They are fighting bitter struggles, including armed struggles, against the Bantu Authorities. The peasant in the countryside today is not the unsophisticated tribesman of the previous century. Millions have at some time or other come to work in the towns. They have come into contact with the challenging outlook and the advanced methods of organisation of the trade unions, the Congress movement and the Communist Party. These 'new peasants' have awakened the countryside, transforming the African peasantry from a reserve of conservatism into a powerful ally of the urban working class in the struggle against White colonialism, and for freedom, land, equality and democracy.

Millions of agricultural labourers and labour tenants are employed on White-owned farms throughout the country. These are the most exploited workers in South Africa. They work without any protection from labour laws, from dawn to sunset, at hard and exhausting labour, for wretchedly low wages. The food they are given is too little, it is always the same, and it is an unhealthy diet. On most farms the housing for them is worse than what is provided for the farm animals. The use of convict labour, and compound labour, and other forms of forced labour, is common on farms in many parts of South Africa. Farmers and their foremen frequently employ physical violence against African farm labourers, beating them with sjamboks, often to death. Wages for farm labour are the lowest in the country. Agricultural labourers are not really free workers. They are tied, often for life, to a particular farmer because of the operation of the labour tenancy system, the pass laws and in particular the so-called 'trek-pass', the Native Service Contract and the Masters and Servants Acts. Organisation of agricultural workers' unions and other bodies for farm workers is also made exceptionally difficult because of the close supervision maintained over them by the farmers.

The 400,000 African labourers working on the gold and coal mines have to do the most backbreaking, dangerous and unhealthy work, for wages which are a scandal and a disgrace in an industry which distributes millions of rands annually to its shareholders. They are separated, for long periods, from their wives and families. A large proportion of them are 'imported' from territories outside the Republic, the Protectorates, S.W. Africa, the Portuguese Colonies, Nyasaland, Tanganyika and elsewhere, although conferences of African states have decided to work towards ending this practice. The migratory labour system leads to a continual turnover of personnel, making the organisation of mine workers a difficult task and the mine owners go to great lengths to stamp out the development of trade unionism among them. Especially since the great strike led by the African Mineworkers' Union in 1946, they are subject to constant surveillance by police, spies and informers.

The special character of colonialism in South Africa, the seizing by Whites of all the opportunities which in other colonial countries have led to the growth of a national capitalist class, have strangled the development of a class of African capitalists. All positions of economic strength and influence are held as the jealously guarded monopoly of members of the White group alone. There are very few Africans who make profits by the exploitation of labour power. In some areas there are some independent African farmers, producing for the market along 'capitalist' lines. But, as a rule, the holdings are so small that they can be and are cultivated by the farmer himself and his family. There is quite a substantial number of African traders and shopkeepers. Because they have to contend with innumerable colour bars and special restrictions, and because their capital is usually too small, their businesses are rarely very big or very profitable. In a great many cases, in fact, the shop is in the hands of non-African bondholders or wholesalers, of whom the shopkeeper himself is little more than an employee. African businessmen are not allowed to own fixed property. They may not trade in the centres of the cities, the main areas of commercial activity, but are relegated to the African townships and the outskirts. They are subjected to the pass laws and all the restrictions and insecurities imposed on all Africans. An African businessman is not allowed to open a branch elsewhere or to trade anywhere outside his place of residence. The interests of the African commercial class lie wholly in joining the workers and rural people for the overthrow of White supremacy.

The intellectuals and professional groups among the Africans share with their people all the hardships and indignities of colonialism. The largest group, the teachers, receive salaries far below those of their white colleagues, and comparing unfavourably with those of many African industrial workers. They have to work in appalling conditions, in overcrowded classrooms, lacking modern equipment, teaching half-starved children. The Nationalist policy of 'Bantu Education' imposes upon them syllabuses designed to indoctrinate their pupils with servility and apartheid theories, and containing a minimum of genuine educational content. They are compelled to teach in the African languages although there are no adequate text books in these languages. Under the Nationalist regime there has been a catastrophic fall in the standard of African education. The few places once open to African students for professional training in some White universities, have been closed. The new 'tribal colleges' set up instead by the Nationalist government are a travesty of institutions of higher education. They have no facilities to train architects, engineers, scientists, dentists or technicians in most fields. Passports for those who wish to study abroad are usually refused. Opportunities for cultural development among Africans are restricted to a minimum. Nearly all public libraries, theatres, concert halls and other cultural facilities are reserved for Whites and the few for non-Whites are inferior. The exceptionally sharp contradictions of South Africa, and their own conditions of life, which are a challenge to their self-respect and human dignity, face the African intellectuals with a clear-cut choice. Either they align themselves with the struggles of the masses, or else they accept the role of assistants and agents in maintaining White colonialism. To their credit, many African professional men, teachers and even chiefs have sacrificed all hopes of privilege and advancement in order to join wholly with their people.

The workers of the towns, the Africans employed in factories and in transport, in steelworks and power stations, in shops and offices, comprise the most dynamic and revolutionary force in South Africa. The wages of urban African workers, in relation to their high living costs, are scandalously low. They are forced to live far from their places of work, involving exhausting and expensive journeys by bus or train. In shops and factories they are relegated to the most arduous and least rewarding work. Pass laws and urban areas legislation make the tenure of their jobs and their residences precarious, and they are subjected to never-ending raids and surveillance by the police. It is illegal for African workers to strike and their trade unions are unrecognised and vigorously discouraged by the State. Even when employers are prepared to enter into collective bargaining with African workers, the State intervenes to stop it. Despite these and many other disabilities, and the daily struggle for existence, this class, the most numerous and experienced working class on the African continent, has time and again shown that it is the vanguard of the African people. It has built up a number of stable and effective trade unions, devoted to the cause of African liberation and of workers' unity on our continent and throughout the world. African workers constitute the core of the African National Congress and the Communist Party. They have repeatedly come out on nationwide political general strikes and have been the leading force in every major struggle of the liberation movement. Disciplined and taught the lessons of organisation and unity in the harsh school of capitalist production, driven by their conditions of life into united struggle for survival, this class alone is capable, in alliance with the masses of rural people, of leading a victorious struggle to end White domination and exploitation.

The Coloured and Malay people, a population of 1½ million living mainly in the Western Cape Province, are a national group comprising workers, farm labourers, professional people and small businessmen. Like all non-Whites, the Coloured people are subjected to many forms of racial discrimination, reflected in low standards of living, education, housing, nutrition and health. Coloured workers, despite a tradition of craftsmanship which is the oldest in the country, find access to senior posts is withheld from them and given to Whites. Coloured farm labourers work and live under wretched conditions. Their pay is scandalously low, and on the wine farms is partly made up by a liquor ration – the 'tot' system, which undermines their health. Coloured teachers and other state employees are paid much less than their White counterparts for doing the same work. Nevertheless, for many years, this community occupied a privileged position in relation to the Africans. The White ruling group extended various concessions – such as a qualified franchise, trade union rights, property rights – in order to prevent the emergence of a Coloured national consciousness, and the formation of a united front of oppressed non-White peoples for equality and the ending of White colonialism. This policy was not without success.

But, with the deliberate removal by the Nationalist government, one after another, of all the privileges extended to the Coloured people in the past – the abolition of the common roll franchise, the introduction of apartheid and job reservation, White baasskap in the trade unions and separate university education – working class and democratic leaders have come to the fore. The Coloured people are rejecting apartheid and moving towards the path of struggle, side by side with African and other freedom fighters.

The Indian community, of half a million, are mainly the descendants of indentured labourers who came to work in the Natal sugar fields a century ago. From the earliest times all sorts of degrading and discriminatory restrictions have been placed on South African Indians, restrictions which they have resisted in many historic struggles. Today there is a substantial class of Indian industrial and agricultural workers, especially in Natal, but also, increasingly in the Transvaal. There is also a considerable class of Indian merchants, factory owners and small shopkeepers. The Indian workers face appalling problems of unemployment and overcrowding in slum conditions. Indians do not enjoy voting and other democratic rights. Indian businessmen, and all sections of the community, are subjected to innumerable disabilities, especially relating to land and property ownership and economic and educational opportunities. They are not allowed to move from one Province to another without special permits, and are completely debarred from the Orange Free State. The Nationalist government has applied the Group Areas Act with particular ferocity against the Indian communities in the cities and small towns, uprooting them from their homes and livelihood and threatening to 'resettle' them in isolated areas where they face complete ruination. The Indian people have turned their backs on the reformist bourgeois leadership which counselled paths of compromise with oppression and the seeking of sectional privileges regardless of democratic principle and the fate of the masses. They have unreservedly joined in the many united struggles of the African and other oppressed peoples over the past two decades.

5
The Forces of Change
The system of colonialism and racial oppression in our country is powerfully challenged and will be overthrown by the unified struggle of national liberation and working class movements that have grown, developed in experience and maturity and become steeled in many years of complex and difficult struggle.

The impact of capitalism destroyed the traditional economy and fabric of African tribal society. It scattered and disarmed the tribal armies. It turned the chiefs from people's leaders into instruments for implementing the laws devised by Whites. But the spirit of the African people was not broken. Patriotic African intellectuals, with the backing of many chiefs, began forming a new type of organisation, a national political organisation of the African people. A number of such bodies was formed, and in 1912 these united to form the African National Congress. The establishment of the A.N.C. is a profoundly important landmark not only for South Africa, but for our Continent as a whole. It was the forerunner of similar bodies in very many other countries of the Continent, movements which led the African revolution, and today take part in African governments.

As a national liberation organisation, the A.N.C. does not represent any single class, or any one ideology. It is representative of all the classes and strata which make up African society in this country. With the advance of members of the working class, together with revolutionary young intellectuals, to leading positions in the A.N.C., the organisation steadily developed and went forward in its policy and methods of struggle. Congress has steadfastly rejected narrow nationalism, Black chauvinism, anti-Communism and other outlooks which are harmful to the people's cause. It was precisely on these issues that the right-wing Pan-Africanist Congress broke away from the A.N.C. to form a rival organisation. The A.N.C. has formed a firm alliance between itself and patriotic organisations of the Indian and Coloured people, the democratic Europeans and the non-racial Trade Union movement – the Congress Alliance. Even though driven underground since 1960, the A.N.C. has carried on the struggle.

The representative organisation of the Indian people is the South African Indian Congress. For many years, under the leadership of representatives of the wealthy commercial classes, the Indian Congress contented itself with sectional struggles, aimed at maintaining and improving the status of its community alone as a minority group. But, in the middle forties, a dynamic new leadership, representing the mass of exploited Indian workers and peasants, as well as radical intellectuals who had absorbed the teachings of Marxism-Leninism and identified themselves with the working class, pointed out that the future of the Indian community in South Africa was dependent upon the establishment of conditions of true democracy for the country as a whole. The struggle of the Indian people was one with that of the African national movement for freedom and equality for all in this country. This new policy and leadership was accepted by the great majority of the members of the South African Indian Congress, and since that time this Congress has taken full part in the major struggles of the Congress Alliance.

The pioneer Coloured political movement, the African People's Organisation, conducted militant campaigns and pursued a radical united front policy, but this tradition was not maintained. For many years, leadership of the Coloured people's organisations and trade unions was dominated by middle class elements, who either collaborated openly in the maintenance of White supremacy, or – under the cover of wordy denunciations of 'Herrenvolkisrn' – preached a policy of abstention from political activity and hostility to the African national liberation movement. In recent years the Nationalist government's attacks on their longstanding rights have led to a revival of militancy among the Coloured people. The masses of Coloured working people and radical youth are turning increasingly towards the Coloured People's Congress, an ally of the African National Congress.

There has always been a minority of Whites in South Africa who fought against racial oppression and courageously came out for the rights of the oppressed. The African people will never forget the memory of such democrats, Christians, liberals and Communists as Van der Kemp, Pringle, Olive and W.P. Schreiner, Ivon Jones and S.P. Bunting, who swam against the stream of racialism. From its formation in 1953 until it was outlawed in 1962, the Congress of Democrats represented the most advanced and progressive section of the White population. In spite of unceasing persecution by the State which banned and restricted the greater part of its membership, the C.O.D. joined all the major campaigns of the people for freedom, and shared all the trials and tribulations of the other members of the Congress Alliance.

This alliance headed by the African National Congress, which has been joined by the non-racial Congress of Trade Unions, has adopted a revolutionary democratic programme, emanating from the masses, the Freedom Charter, which envisages profound democratic changes in every field of South Africa's political, social, economical and cultural life. During the grim years of the Nationalist regime, the Congresses have conducted one stirring campaign after another – the May Day and June 26 strikes of 1950 and many general strikes in the years that followed, the campaign of Defiance of Unjust Laws and the Congress of the People are examples. In its foreign relations, the Congress Alliance has done much to bring the outrages of apartheid to the attention of the outside world, and to evoke acts of international solidarity which have greatly inspired and encouraged the peoples of our country.

The labour movement of South Africa has reflected, in an especially acute way, the profound international cleavage of the working class between reformists and revolutionaries, social-democrats and Communists. It began almost exclusively as a movement of the White skilled workers. During the first quarter of the present century the White working class fought many a bitter and stirring struggle against the monopoly capitalists. The miners and other White workers of the Witwatersrand formed armed commandos to defend themselves against the attempts of the Smuts government in 1922, to smash their strike by force. But, led by Right-wing renegades from socialism, and bribed by concessions and privileges extended to them by the monopolists, the great majority of the White workers repudiated the principles of socialism and working class unity. So far from joining hands with their oppressed and exploited fellow-workers of a dark skin colour, they have turned their backs on them and joined in an alliance with the White capitalists and wealthy farmers to maintain White colonialism and to subjugate and exploit the non-White peoples. The years since 1922 have seen a steady decline in the militancy and class-consciousness of the White workers. The once powerful Labour Party is dead. The White trade unions – with a few honourable exceptions – collaborated in the implementation of apartheid in industry and job reservation. In fact, most of these unions have become little more than societies to preserve a White monopoly of skilled jobs. For the most part, the White workers of this country support their capitalist rulers and exploiters in the maintenance of White supremacy and colonialism.

The labour laws of South Africa, accepted in the main by the White trade unionists, have compelled the African workers to form their own trade unions. In spite of all the disabilities under which they have to function, these unions have played a notable part in raising the wages and improving the conditions of the workers. They have educated the workers in the spirit of class unity and international solidarity. Following the exclusion of African trade unions from the White-dominated Trade Union Council in 1956, these came together with workers of other races who remained loyal to the principles of trade unionism, to establish the South African Congress of Trade Unions. S.A.C.T.U. has consistently campaigned to organise the hundreds of thousands of unorganised workers, particularly the Africans. It has opposed every manifestation of racialism and White privilege in the economic life of the country and in the trade union movement. It has endorsed the Freedom Charter and played an important part in the Congress Alliance. The Congress of Trade Unions has consistently upheld the principle of working class internationalism as expressed by the World Federation of Trade Unions. It has opposed the efforts of the so-called International Confederation of Free Trade Unions to split the workers' movement in Africa and elsewhere. S.A.C.T.U. is a foundation member of the All-Africa Federation of Trade Unions.

The Communist Party

Established on July 29, 1921, the Communist Party of South Africa was the first Marxist-Leninist Party on the African Continent. It was itself based mainly on the International Socialist League, which in 1915, under the leadership of men like Bill Andrews, had broken from the S.A. Labour Party over the issue of opposition to the imperialist war. It spread socialist teachings among the people and strove unceasingly against racialism and for the unity of the working class. It demanded complete freedom and equality for the African and other subject nationalities and led the workers and oppressed people in struggles, many of them historic, against pass laws and unemployment, against fascism at home and abroad, and for a democratic South Africa. The Communist Party brought about profound changes in the thinking, political outlook, demands, forms of organisation and methods of struggle of the oppressed and exploited people of this country. Members of the Party worked hard to build up the trade union movement, the African National Congress and other organisations of the people. Hated, slandered and persecuted by the ruling classes, the Party grew to become the outstanding champion of the oppressed and working people in every struggle against exploitation and national oppression. Nevertheless, despite its great achievements and struggles, the Communist Party of South Africa proved incapable of surviving under illegal conditions. Legalistic illusions had penetrated into the ranks of the Party, including its leading personnel. The Party was unprepared and unable to work underground. These errors culminated in the dissolution of the Party upon the passing of the Suppression of Communism Act by the Nationalist Government in 1950. Under this law hundreds of 'listed' Communists were victimised, banned, banished and forced to resign from organisations which they had given their lives to build.

The Nationalists boasted that they had 'destroyed Communism in South Africa'. It was an idle boast. Defying the Nazi laws of the Nationalists, the most steeled and determined Communists of South Africa came together in 1953 to form the South African Communist Party, to carry forward and raise still higher the banner of the Communist movement under the new and testing conditions of illegality. Combining legal mass work with the illegal work of building the Marxist-Leninist Party as the disciplined vanguard of the fight for freedom, democracy, peace and socialism, the South African Communist Party is the heir to the tradition created by the

Communist Party of South Africa. It is a tradition of unflinching struggle against oppression and exploitation, for unity of the workers and freedom-loving people of our country, irrespective of race and colour.

The South African Communist Party is the party of the working class, the disciplined and advanced class which has no property stakes in present-day South Africa and has been the core and inspiration of other classes in every struggle of our time. The working class seeks a close alliance with the rural people, and with the urban middle classes and intellectuals in the national democratic revolution. Only under its leadership can the full aims of the revolution be achieved. It is to enable the working class to fulfil this historic mission that the workers have founded and built their own political party, the South African Communist Party.

The historic task of the Communist Party is the abolition of the capitalist system, and through socialist transformation of the economy of the country, to attain a classless Communist Society. However, at a time when the majority of the people are subject to the most vicious and degrading national oppression, when White colonialist reaction imposes a rule of terror on the whole population and sacrifices the people's living standards on the altar of White supremacy, the central and immediate task of the Communist Party is to lead the fight for the national liberation of the non-White people, and for the victory of the democratic revolution. The Party will strive continuously for the building and strengthening of a united front of national liberation, the unity of Communists and non-Communists, the unity of freedom-loving people of all nationalities and all anti-colonialist classes in the national democratic revolution.

The South African Communist Party is a part of the world Communist movement. It participates in meetings of fraternal Communist and Workers' Parties and abides loyally by their common decisions. True to the principles of working class internationalism, the Party works for unity of the workers of the whole world, and especially of the Marxist-Leninist parties. The Party works for the unity of all anti-imperialist and sane forces in the world in the life-and-death struggle against a devastating nuclear war, for peaceful co-existence of nations of whatever stage of social development, for universal and complete disarmament. This policy coincides with the fundamental interests of the people of our country. It is in harmony with the aims of the independence and integrity of our country and of all-African co-operation and unity.

The structure of the Party is based on the principles of democratic centralism. While demanding strict discipline, the subordination of a minority to the majority and of lower Party organs to higher organs, and the prohibition of all factions within the Party, it upholds the principle of democratic election of all leading organs of the Party, collective leadership and full debate of policy. The curtailment of some aspects of democratic procedure is inevitable under illegal conditions; this temporary situation must be compensated for by all members, regarding it as their duty to participate in the formulation of policy and by the leadership, encouraging and making it possible for them to do so.

6
The National Democratic Revolution

The Nationalist Party, which has governed South Africa since 1948, has brought this country to the verge of revolution. The Afrikaner nationalist movement, which was always corrupted by White chauvinism, has today lost all trace of the anti-imperialist element it once had, during the period of its struggle against British rule. Dominated by the Afrikaner capitalist class and large-scale farmers, the Nationalist Party is controlled by the fascist 'Broederbond' secret society. Deeply influenced by the Nazi movement in Germany, it adopted many of Hitler's ideas and worked for a fascist victory in the second world war. The Nationalist Party has become the instrument of the most racialistic and imperialistic sections of the capitalist class. The declaration of a Republic in May 1961 in no way lessened the dependence of the South African economy on British and American finance-capital. The Republic left the British Commonwealth not by choice of the Nationalist government but because the unpopularity of its racial policy among African and Asian member countries faced it with expulsion. In all major questions of international policy the Nationalist government identifies itself with the most aggressive elements of international imperialism in the United States, Britain, France, West Germany and Japan. It is dependent on financial and armaments aid from these countries to maintain its rule in South Africa.

The Nationalist Party relies on violence and terror to maintain itself in office. It has disfranchised the few non-Whites who once enjoyed the vote and otherwise altered the electoral system to ensure that it cannot be removed by Parliamentary means. It has outlawed workers' and liberation organisations, meetings, newspapers and other publications, and resorted to arbitrary bannings, deportations, arrests, confinements and house-arrests of freedom-fighters. It has closed the door to every possibility of peaceful advance of the non-White peoples to social, political and economic rights. It is mobilising and arming the White population for the express purpose of 'shooting down the black masses'. Already its police have committed massacres of unarmed Africans, such as those of Sharpeville and Langa, which have shocked the whole world. A powerful international movement has developed, supported by African, Asian and socialist governments, for the diplomatic, economic, cultural and sporting isolation of South Africa, and for boycotts and sanctions against the Republic. The policy of the Nationalist government has brought about a state of permanent and deepening crisis in the country.

The other White parliamentary parties can offer no way out of this crisis. The United Party, traditionally the instrument of the gold-mining interests and the English-speaking capitalists, laid the basis for all the excesses of the Nationalists during the many years in which it governed South Africa prior to 1948. As the main 'opposition' group in Parliament it has steadily retreated before Nationalist reaction. It is compromised by its own antidemocratic class character and afraid lest genuine opposition to the government might result in disturbances which would adversely affect business and the confidence of foreign investors. It vies with the Nationalists in appealing to the racial prejudices of the White voters. It has actively or passively assisted the Nationalist Party at every stage of its march to fascism.

Disgusted with the surrender of the United Party and alarmed at the dangers to the country's stability and future presented by Nationalist policy, a number of former U.P. M.P.s and members broke away in 1959 to form the Progressive Party. Backed by influential imperialist interests, such as the Oppenheimer mining group, and supported by a section of urban, middle-class Whites, the Progressive Party seeks to avert the coming democratic revolution in South Africa by offering a 'qualified' franchise to middle-class non-Whites and concessions to ease the intolerable burden of apartheid.

A more radical tendency among progressive middle-class and intellectual circles is represented by the Liberal Party. This Party proposes a universal franchise, but since it expressly confines itself to 'parliamentary and constitutional methods', it suggests no realistic or convincing method to obtain this. Its insistence on anti-Communist and anti-socialist policies and its failure to attack the roots of race-oppression in the economy of the country seriously lessen the Liberal Party's usefulness and effectiveness. Its adherence to the 'West' in the cold war continually conflicts with its opposition to the Nationalist government, and makes the liberation movement doubt its reliability as an ally in the struggle.

The deep-rooted crisis in South Africa cannot be resolved by the Nationalist government, using methods of force and violence or attempting to deceive home and world opinion with fraudulent schemes of 'Bantu self-government'. Nor can it be resolved by a mere change of government to another section of the White ruling class which would make superficial concessions while leaving the essence of the colonial system and monopoly control intact. The crisis springs from the fundamental contradictions of South African society: between the oppressed people and their rulers; between South African colonialism and the world-wide movement against colonialism and imperialism; between the working class and the rural masses, together with the middle classes, on the one side, and the handful of monopoly capitalists on the other.

This crisis can only be resolved by a revolutionary change in the social system which will overcome these conflicts by putting an end to the colonial oppression of the African and other non-White people. The immediate and imperative interests of all sections of the South African people demand the carrying out of such a change, a national democratic revolution which will overthrow the colonialist state of White supremacy and establish an independent state of National Democracy in South Africa.

The main content of this revolution is the national liberation of the African people. Its fulfilment is, at the same time, in the deepest interests of the other non-White groups, for in achieving their liberty the African people will at the same time put an end to all forms of racial discrimination. It is in the interests of the White workers, middle class and professional groups to whom the establishment of genuine democracy and the elimination of fascism and monopoly rule offers the only prospect of a decent and stable future.

The main aims and lines of the South African democratic revolution have been defined in the Freedom Charter, which has been endorsed by the African National Congress and the other partners in the national liberation alliance. The Freedom Charter is not a programme for socialism. It is a common programme for a free, democratic South Africa, agreed on by socialists and non-socialists. At the same time, in order to guarantee the abolition of racial oppression and White minority domination, the Freedom Charter necessarily and realistically calls for profound economic changes: drastic agrarian reform to restore the land to the people; widespread nationalisation of key industries to break the grip of White monopoly capital on the main centres of the country's economy; radical improvements in the conditions and standards of living for the working people. The Communist Party pledges its unqualified support for the Freedom Charter. It considers that the achievement of its aims will answer the pressing and immediate needs of the people and lay the indispensable basis for the advance of our country along non-capitalist lines to a communist and socialist future. To win these aims is the immediate task of all the oppressed and democratic people of South Africa, headed by the working class and its party, the Communist Party

Violence and Non-Violence
In their long and difficult struggles the national liberation organisations of South Africa, including the Communist Party, have always sought peaceful methods of struggle. In the past they have counselled non-violent methods not because they are cowardly or believers in pacifist illusions but because they wished to avoid the bitterness and bloodshed of civil war. But the ruling class has invariably replied to non-violence with violence; to peaceful protests with suppression and police massacres of unarmed men, women and children. The Nationalist government has closed, or is closing, every channel of legal protest and normal political activity. It is openly preparing for civil war.

In the face of these provocations, the liberation movement has had to reconsider its attitude towards 'non-violence' as a universal principle. The patience of the people is not endless. They are determined to win freedom in our lifetime. They would prefer to achieve their liberation by non-violent means. But today they are left with no alternative but to defend themselves and hit back; to meet violence with violence. The Nationalists are forcing a solution upon South Africa in which patriots and democrats will take up arms to defend themselves, organise guerrilla armies and undertake various acts of armed resistance, culminating in a mass insurrection against White domination. In such a conflict, however long and costly, the fighters for freedom must win, for they will enjoy the support of the overwhelming majority of the people of our country and the whole world.

The Communist Party considers that the slogan of 'non-violence' is harmful to the cause of the democratic national revolution in the new phase of the struggle, disarming the people in the face of the savage assaults of the oppressor, dampening their militancy, undermining their confidence in their leaders. At the same time, the Party opposes undisciplined acts of individual terror. It rejects theories that all non-violent methods of struggle are useless or impossible, and will continue to advocate and work for the use of all forms of struggle by the people, including non-collaboration, strikes, boycotts and demonstrations.

The Party does not dismiss all prospects of non-violent transition to the democratic revolution. This prospect will be enhanced by the development of revolutionary and militant people's forces. The illusion that the White minority can rule forever over a disarmed majority will crumble before the reality of an armed and determined people. The crisis in the country, and the contradictions in the ranks of the ruling class, will deepen. The possibility would be opened of a peaceful and negotiated transfer of power to the representatives of the oppressed majority of the people

Whether its end is brought about through such a peaceful transition or by insurrection, the vicious type of colonialism embodied in the present Republic of South Africa cannot long endure. Its downfall and the victory of the South African democratic revolution are certain in the near future.

The Communist Party unreservedly supports and participates in the struggle for national liberation headed by the African National Congress in alliance with the S.A. Indian Congress, the Congress of Trade Unions, the Coloured People's Congress and other patriotic groups of democrats, women, peasants and youth. With them, it demands the immediate summoning of a sovereign national convention to draw up and promulgate the constitution of a state of national democracy in South Africa. It considers that it is important and urgent for all the forces and movements for freedom to agree upon all their main goals and aims at this time.

It is in this situation that the Communist Party advances its immediate proposals before the workers and democratic people of South Africa. These are not proposals for a socialist state. They are proposals for the building of a national democratic state. These proposals are put forward within the framework of the Freedom Charter which the Party considers to be suitable as a general statement of the aims of a state of national democracy. Our proposals are not directed towards communists and socialists alone, but are submitted as a basis for discussion for all democratic and patriotic people, and in particular for members and supporters of the national liberation and trade union movements.

7
Immediate Proposals of the Communist Party

State Structure
The Party stands for a unitary South African state with a Republican form of government. All local and national representatives in legislative bodies should be subjected both to election and recall by universal, equal, direct, adult franchise, without regard to race, colour, sex or property, educational or other qualifications whatsoever. The Party declares that the revolutionary people of South Africa cannot merely take over existing State and government institutions designed to maintain colonialism, but must destroy them and create new people's institutions in their place. The Senate and all institutions based on property or other undemocratic qualifications must be abolished.

New territorial administrative regions should be established, enjoying full powers of local government corresponding to the progressive traditions and the wishes of the people of each area, but conforming to the overall character and laws of the people's democratic state.

Every vestige of apartheid and racial discrimination should scrupulously be removed from every field of state service and public life. Every rank of the Civil Service, of the army, navy and air force, of the judiciary, police, municipal services and other public institutions should be open to all South Africans. The aim of the state should be to replace all officials who are disloyal to democratic non-racial principles. Special measures should be taken rapidly to promote African and other non-White personnel, so as to ensure that all state institutions are fully representative of the nature of the population of South Africa.

Civil Rights and State Security
The state must guarantee the fullest liberty of speech and thought, of the press and of organisation, of conscience and religion, to all citizens. The people's freedom of movement must be guaranteed. Racialistic and counterrevolutionary propaganda must be forbidden. People must be free to discuss and debate all schools of democratic and progressive opinion.

In order to preserve and extend the gains of the revolution, particularly in the conditions of South Africa, the utmost vigilance must be exercised against those who would seek to organise counter-revolutionary plots, intrigues and sabotage, against all attempts to restore White colonialism and destroy democracy.

While extending the greatest measure of democracy to the people, and ensuring their fullest participation in the public life of the country, a vigorous and vigilant dictatorship must be maintained by the people against the former dominating arid exploiting classes. Towards this end, the Party will propose the disbandment of the police and military forces maintained by White colonialism. A new people's militia and people's liberation army, composed of and led by trusted representatives of the people, must be created.

The Party will work unceasingly to oppose the development of any form of cult of individual leadership, of illegal and arbitrary methods, or of misuse of power in any way. It will uphold proper legal and judicial procedures, and fight to protect the security of the citizen, the inviolability of his home, his privacy and his correspondence.

Economic Development
In order to ensure the rapid development of South Africa as a well balanced industrial-agricultural country, overcoming the lopsidedness caused by

colonialism, to abolish unemployment, and to ensure continuously rising material and cultural standards of the people, the Party advocates the large-scale, planned development of the economy of the country, controlled and directed by the state.

In order to ensure South Africa's independence, the Party will press for the strengthening of the state sector of the economy, particularly in the fields of heavy industry, machine tool building and fuel production. It will seek to place control of the vital sectors of the economy in the hands of the national democratic state and to correct historic injustice, by demanding the nationalisation of the mining industry, banking and monopoly industrial establishments, thus also laying the foundations for the advance to socialism.

At the same time, the state should protect the interests of private business where these are not incompatible with the public interest. It should offer assistance, by way of state loans, to non-monopolist producers, in return for a state share in their undertakings, thus paving the way for a gradual and peaceful transition to socialism.

The state should encourage and develop the initiative, talents and crafts of the people and provide opportunities and the fullest encouragement for those who show inventiveness, mechanical skill and other socially useful talents.

Agriculture
In order to rally the support of the great masses of rural people, to raise their living and cultural standards and to rectify the injustices committed by the colonialists in seizing most of the land of South Africa, the revolutionary state must take immediate and drastic measures to restore the land to the people. The Reserve system, and any laws restricting land ownership on a racial basis, must be abolished.

All land must immediately be confiscated which is in the hands of financial monopolies and land speculators, absentee-owners, farmers who use convict labour or indentured compound labour, and other idlers, exploiters and parasites who allow the land to lie idle while the masses starve. This confiscated land must be placed in the hands of those who live and work upon the land. At the same time, the state should guarantee security of tenure to peasant farmers and smallholders who fruitfully cultivate the land by their own labour. All agricultural land transactions should be regulated to avoid accumulation of land once again in the hands of the rich.

Radical reform must be undertaken in regard to all communally-held and tribally-held lands, with respect to land tenure and social relationships.

Backward tribal and other relationships should be replaced by democratic institutions. Special attention should be given to building industries in these areas, electric power stations, modern roads and railways, and all other things required to enable them soon to catch up with the economic and cultural development of the rest of the country. Advanced and efficient agricultural methods and techniques should be introduced.

The state should encourage the widespread development of democratically administered co-operative and collective farms rather than individual peasant smallholdings. Vigorous measures should be taken to mechanise and electrify farming operations, to conserve water supplies and create large-scale irrigation schemes, to encourage scientific livestock breeding and the diversification of crops. The state should aim at the development of a prosperous, cultured and progressive rural community, close in its standards of living and education, social outlook and interests, to the people of the towns and cities.

Labour and Social Welfare

As the party of the working class, the Communist Party demands the protection and substantial advancement of the workers' standards of living, housing, working conditions, wages, leisure and recreation. It proposes that all workers, including farm, mine and domestic workers, be entitled to full trade union rights and the protection of labour laws, including a national minimum wage, annual paid holidays, sick leave unemployment and workmen's compensation benefits for all, and adequate safety regulations in all mines, factories, farms and other places of work.

The Party demands that the state provide special protection for women workers, the removal of all restrictions against married women employees, and the provision of adequate maternity leave before and after birth. The Party will fight for full and equal rights for women in every aspect of state, social and private life. It will work for the elimination of polygamy. It will fight vigorously against all vestiges and manifestations of contempt for or unequal treatment of women, or their being regarded as mere cooks, domestic servants, nannies and housekeepers. It will fight for the admission of women on an equal basis to every sphere of state, industrial, commercial, agricultural, scientific, academic and professional life.

The Party proposes that a state medical service be instituted providing free preventive and curative medical and health services to all, including hospitals, medicines, spectacles, dentures and all other aspects of a comprehensive health service.

The Party proposes the provision of free meals at school to all children:

that all workers be guaranteed cheap transport to and from work; and that the state provide adequate pensions, without discrimination, to all old people. It demands adequate allowances for all who are unemployed, disabled, orphaned, or otherwise unable to earn a living.

The Party demands the abolition of all residential segregation and the provision of adequate housing for all, with special attention to the needs of those living in slums.

Education
There must be no segregation in education. All children must receive free primary and secondary education from the state. Standards of education must be the same for all children, irrespective of race, home language or economic status, and designed to develop citizens imbued with a love of their people, their country and humanity.

There must be equal opportunities for all to receive higher education and specialised technical training. However, in order to correct the legacy of colonialism, priority must be given to the training of African and other non-White specialists in every field.

The state must organise a campaign among the masses for the complete elimination of adult illiteracy.

All teachers must be guaranteed decent standards of living and the right to take part in public life. They must be enabled to attain the highest qualifications and their remuneration and promotion must be on the basis of qualifications and merit alone.

National Rights
In view of the ravages wrought by the White colonialists, the Party demands exceptional measures to uphold the rights, dignity, culture and self-respect of all national groups inhabiting our country.

All languages used by the people of South Africa should enjoy equal rights and status. In local administrative regions, organs of local government, laws, and courts, the language used should normally be that spoken by the majority of people in that region.

The state should encourage in particular the unity of the African people and foster the spirit of unity of all South Africans. At the same time it should encourage and stimulate the development of healthy, non-antagonistic national consciousness and legitimate pride among all sections of the people. It should encourage the development of national cultures, art and literature.

While standing for a united South African state, the Party recognises the rights of all national groups in the country to develop and to determine their own future. To enable these rights to be realised, the Party demands the abolition of the Reserve system and the even development of agriculture, industry and communications throughout South Africa.

Freedom of movement must be an inviolable right of all citizens and all citizens must enjoy equal rights and status in every part of the country.

Vigorous measures must be taken to train and promote non-Whites, especially Africans, as managers and directors of industrial, agricultural, mining and commercial enterprises; as professors, doctors, chemists, architects, scientists and engineers; as leading personnel of every sort.

While regarding as its main task in the sphere of national rights, as being to correct the injustice and crime perpetrated against the African majority, the state must also safeguard and guarantee the rights of minority groups, whether of European, Coloured, Indian, Chinese or any other descent. The state must protect the rights of all citizens equally, and vigorously oppose and suppress all senseless acts of revenge which have their roots in the past. All manifestations of racialism, including the use of derogatory terms to designate people of various national groups, must be prohibited by law.

Foreign Relations

The national democratic state of South Africa should be fully independent. It should base its policy on the peaceful coexistence of states with different social systems. South Africa should aim to strengthen the United Nations and make it more democratic and effective as an instrument of peace. It should work for universal disarmament and the abolition of war as a means of settling disputes between nations.

South Africa should not join any imperialist military alliance or power bloc, or allow imperialist bases to be set up on its territory.

A democratic South Africa should aim at the closest and most fraternal relationships between all African states, towards a united Africa.

Democratic South Africa must seek the closest and most brotherly relations upon a basis of complete equality between our country and its neighbouring territories of South West Africa, Basutoland, Bechuanaland, Swaziland, Mozambique and Rhodesia. It must proclaim and scrupulously observe the right of self-determination and independence of South West Africa, Basutoland, Bechuanaland and Swaziland.

A free South Africa will render every assistance to all other Africans in their struggles to liberate themselves from colonialism.

A democratic South African state should enter into diplomatic, cultural, commercial and economic arrangements with all countries, irrespective of their social system, seek to conclude equal and mutually beneficial agreements with them and to strengthen the ties of friendship and brotherhood amongst the peoples of the whole world.

Part Two

The Road to Power

Forward to Freedom: Strategy and Tactics of the ANC

(Adopted by a conference of the ANC, Morogoro, 25 April – 1 May 1969)

The struggle of the oppressed people of South Africa is taking place within an international context of transition to the Socialist system, of the breakdown of the colonial system as a result of national liberation and socialist revolutions, and the fight for social and economic progress by the people of the whole world.

We in South Africa are part of the zone in which national liberation is the chief content of the struggle. On our continent sweeping advances have been registered which have resulted in the emergence to independent statehood of forty-one states. Thus the first formal step of independence has been largely won in Africa and this fact exercises a big influence on the developments in our country.

The countries of Southern Africa have not as yet broken the chains of colonialism and racism which hold them in oppression. In Mozambique, Angola, South West Africa, Zimbabwe and South Africa white racialist and fascist regimes maintain systems which go against the current trend of the African revolution and world development. This has been made possible by the tremendous economic and military power at the disposal of these regimes built with the help of imperialism.

The main pillar of the unholy alliance of Portugal, Rhodesia and South Africa is the Republic of South Africa. The strategy and tactics of our revolution require for their formulation and understanding a full appreciation of the inter-locking and interweaving of International, African and Southern African developments which play on our situation.

Rule by Force

South Africa was conquered by force and is today ruled by force. At moments when white autocracy feels itself threatened, it does not hesitate to use the gun. When the gun is not in use, legal and administrative terror, fear, social and economic pressures, complacency and confusion generated by propaganda and 'education' are the devices brought into play in an attempt to harness the people's opposition. Behind these devices hovers force. Whether in reserve or in actual employment, force is ever present and this has been so since the white man came to Africa.

Unending Resistance to White Domination
From the time alien rule was imposed there has been – historically speaking – unbroken resistance to this domination. It has taken different forms at different times but it has never been abandoned. For the first 250 years there were regular armed clashes, battles and wars. The superior material resources of the enemy, the divided and often fragmented nature of the resistance, the unchallenged ascendancy of imperialism as a world system up to the beginning of the 20th century, the historically understandable absence of political cohesion and leadership in the people's camp; these and other factors combined to end the first phase of resistance against alien domination. But the protracted character of this resistance unequalled anywhere else in Africa is underlined by the fact that the armed subjugation of the indigenous people was only really accomplished at the beginning of this century. The defeat of the Bambatha Rebellion in 1906 marked the end of this first phase and set the stage of the handing over of the administration of the country to local whites in 1910. The fifty years which followed was not a period of resignation or of acceptance. It was a period of development and of regrouping under new conditions; a period in which newly created political formations of the people continued to struggle with the enemy and grew into maturity; a period in which, above all, national consciousness began to assert itself against tribal sectionalism. This period witnessed the emergence and development of the primary organisation of the liberation movement – The African National Congress. It also saw the evolvement of national organisations reflecting the aspirations of other oppressed non-white groups – the Coloureds and the Indians – and the creation of economic and political organisations – the South African Communist Party and Trade Unions which reflected the special aims and aspirations of the newly developed and doubly exploited working class. This was a period of organisational growth. It was punctuated by struggles involving techniques ranging from orthodox mass campaigning to general strikes, to mass acts of defiance. It culminated in the decision taken in 1961 to prepare for armed confrontation. December 1961 saw the opening stages of the campaign in the simultaneous acts of sabotage which occurred in most of the main urban centres on the 16th.

The Move to Armed Struggle

Why was the decision for armed struggle taken in 1961? Why not 1951 or 1941 or 1931? Is it that the character of the state had so altered fundamentally that only in 1961 did armed struggle become the only alternative? Not at all. There has never been a moment in the history of South Africa since 1952 in which the white ruling class would have given privileges without a physical battle. Why then did organisations like the African National Congress not call for armed struggle? Was it perhaps that they were not really revolutionary or that it was only in the early 1960s that they began to appreciate the correct strategy? Is there perhaps substance in accusations by some of our detractors that until the early sixties the liberation movement was lacking in military fervour and the desire for radical change? In other words was its policy not a revolutionary one? What is our measuring rod for revolutionary policy? A look at this concept will help towards a more profound understanding not only of the past but of the future. It is therefore not out of place to devote a word to it.

In essence, a revolutionary policy is one which holds out the quickest and most fundamental transformation and transfer of power from one class to another. In real life such radical changes are brought about not by imaginary forces but by those whose outlook and readiness to act is very much influenced by historically determined factors.

To ignore the real situation and to play about with imaginary forces, concepts and ideals is to invite failure. The art of revolutionary leadership consists in providing leadership to the masses and not just to its most advanced elements; it consists of setting a pace which accords with objective conditions and the real possibilities at hand. The revolutionary-sounding phrase does not always reflect revolutionary policy, and revolutionary-sounding policy is not always the spring-board for revolutionary advance. Indeed what appears to be 'militant' and 'revolutionary' can often be counter-revolutionary. It is surely a question of whether, in the given concrete situation, the course or policy advocated will aid or impede the prospects of the conquest of power. In this – the only test – the advocacy of armed struggle can, in some situations, be as counter-revolutionary as the advocacy of its opposite in other situations. Untimely, ill-planned or premature manifestations of violence impede and do not advance the prospect for revolutionary change and are clearly counter-revolutionary. It is obvious therefore that policy and organisational structures must grow out of the real situation if they are not to become meaningless clichés.

Future historians may well be able to pause at some moments during the evolution of our struggle and examine critically both its pace and emphasis. But, in general, without the so-called reformist activities of the previous half-century, the prospect of advancing into the new phase would have been extremely small. This is so because even in the typical colonial-type situation armed struggle becomes feasible only if:

- There is disillusionment with the prospect of achieving liberation by traditional peaceful processes because the objective conditions blatantly bar the way to change;
- There is readiness to respond to the strategy of armed struggle with all the enormous sacrifices which this involves;
- There is in existence a political leadership capable of gaining the organised allegiance of the people for armed struggle and which has both the experience and the ability to carry out the painstaking process of planning, preparation and overall conduct of the operations; and
- That there exist favourable objective conditions in the international and local plans.

In one sense conditions are connected and interdependent. They are not created by subjective and ideological activity only and many are the mistakes committed by heroic revolutionaries who give a monopoly to subjective factors and who confuse their own readiness with readiness of others.

These conditions are brought about not only be developing political, economic and social conditions but also by the long, hard grind of revolutionary work. They depend on such factors as the response of the enemy, the extent to which he unmasks himself and the experience gained by the people themselves not in academic seminars but in actual political struggle. We reject the approach which sees as the catalyst for revolutionary transformation only the short-cut of isolated confrontations and the creation of armed resistance centre. Does this mean that before an actual beginning can be made by the armed challenge we have to wait for the evolvement of some sort of deep crisis in the enemy camp which is serious enough to hold out the possibility of an immediate all-round insurrection? Certainly not! We believe that given certain basic factors, both international and local, the actual beginning of armed struggle or guerrilla warfare can be made and having begun can steadily develop conditions for the future all-out war which will eventually lead to the conquest of power. Under the modern highly sophisticated police state (which South Africa is) it is questionable whether a movement can succeed in a programme of mass political organisation beyond a certain point without starting a new type of action. Also, it is not easy to determine the point at which sufficient concrete political and organisational preparations have been carried out to give our armed detachments the maximum chances of survival and growth within any given area. There is no instrument for measuring this. But we must not overdo the importance of the subjective factors and before embarking upon a path which is in one sense tragic, although historically inevitable and necessary, certain of the basic minimum conditions already mentioned must be present and certain minimum preparations must have been made.

Tempered in Struggle
In the light of those considerations, it is clear that it was only after the victory of the anti-imperialist forces in the Second World War and the tide of independence in Africa, Asia, and Latin America, combined with the zig-zags of struggle inside South Africa in the last fifty years, which by the beginning of the sixties demanded a move in the direction of armed struggle. The fifties were among the most stirring and struggle-filled decades in the history of the liberation movement. Thousands upon thousands of militant cadres were tempered during this period and masses of our people both in town and countryside participated in a variety of forms of struggle. The moulding of mass political consciousness reached a new intensity. The response of the authorities was such that the overwhelming majority of the people learnt, through their own participation in the struggle and confrontation with the state, that in the long run the privileges of the minority will only be wrenched from it by a reversion to armed combat. Indeed, during this 'peaceful' stage in our struggle hardly a year passed without massacres of our people by the army and police.

Each phase in the unfolding of the struggle of the fifties played a part in setting the stage of our new approach. A rebirth of the spirit of deliberate defiance of the white man's law was stimulated by the great Defiance Campaign of 1952. The response of the state towards the Congress of the People Campaign and the adoption of the Freedom Charter demonstrated its intention to crush what had previously been accepted as legitimate expressions for equality. The numbers of highly successful national general strikes motivated in the main by political and not economic demands proved the growing maturity of the urban non-white working class. The magnificent resistance by the peasants in Pondoland, Sekhukhuneland and Natal in the late fifties pointed also to the new spirit of militancy and struggle in the countryside. The general strikes as a method of political mobilisation was suppressed with the utmost vigour and by the end of the fifties could no longer be effectively employed as an instrument of mass struggle. Other protests were increasingly broken by police brutality and the use of orthodox mass demonstration as an effective weapon was demonstrably not feasible. Legal opposition was rendered ineffective by bannings, exiles and the imprisonment of activists and leaders to long terms for the most trivial infringements. Finally, by such laws as the Terrorism and Sabotage Acts, all opposition by legal or peaceful means was rendered impossible.

Heightened Political Ferment

In the field of representation, any reformist illusion that may still have existed of a slow advance towards democracy was shattered by the removal of the historic remains of non-white representation including even undemocratic and powerless bodies such as the Native Representative Council. Thus the enemy unmasked himself completely not only to a group of advanced thinkers but to the mass of the people as a whole. The liberation surge towards independence of the African continent which marked the late fifties and early sixties had an important bearing on our own situation. Not only were friendly borders creeping closer but in a very real way these events stimulated and excited people in the unliberated territories in the direction of self-rule. The basic drive for this in our country had never been suppressed. But the events in South Africa in the previous decade and what was happening on the continent confirmed that conquest of power by the people was a realisable goal in our lifetime. The enormous material power of the enemy and by contrast the material weakness of the people was to them no more than a temporary impediment. Memory was fresh of Cuba and – on our own continent – Algeria, both of which had proved that in the long run material resources alone are not a determining factor.

The heightened political ferment both here and on our continent reflected itself in the growth and further maturing of all sections of the liberation front. These leaders who were unable to adjust to the new revolutionary mood (even before the policy of the preparations for organised armed resistance) fell by the wayside. The cohesion and unity of action between the various national and social groupings comprising the liberation front reached new heights. All this constituted not only moral justifications for a move towards armed struggle, but, what is more important, conditions had been created – they were not always there – making a departure in direction correct, necessary and, in the true sense, revolutionary.

Our Approach to Revolutionary Armed Struggle

In a way, the decision taken in 1961 was, historically speaking, in the tradition of the earlier armed resistance to the entrenchment of the foreigner. But it is now occurring in a new situation. Not only had this situation to be understood but the art and science – both political and military – of armed liberation struggles in the modern epoch had to be grasped and applied. The head-on mobile warfare of the traditional African armies of the past could not meet the challenge. The riot, the street fight, the outburst of unorganised violence, individual terrorism; these were symptoms of the militant spirit but not pointers to revolutionary technique. The winning of our freedom by armed struggle – the only method left open to us – demands more than passion. It demands an understanding and an implementation of revolutionary theory and techniques in the actual conditions facing us. It demands a sober assessment of the obstacles in our way and an appreciation that such a struggle is bitter and protracted. It demands, too, the dominance in our thinking of achievement over drama. We believe our movement acted in accordance with these guidelines when it embarked upon the detailed preparation for the launching of guerrilla struggle. We understood that the main physical environment of such a struggle in the period is outside the enemy strongholds in the cities, in the vast stretches of our countryside. The opening steps in 1961 – organised sabotage mainly in the urban areas – served a special purpose and was never advanced as a technique which would, on its own, either lead to the destruction of the state or even do it great material damage (although guerrilla activity in the urban areas of a special type is always important as an auxiliary). At the same time there was a threefold need to be met in order to lay the foundations for more developed and meaningful armed activity of the guerrilla type.

The first was the need to create a military apparatus and, more particularly to recruit large numbers of professional cadres who were to be trained and who would form the core of future guerrilla bands.

The second was the need to demonstrate effectively to all that we were making a sharp and open break with the processes of the previous period which had correctly given emphasis to militant struggle short of armed confrontation.

The third was the need to present an effective method for the overthrow of white supremacy through planned rather than spontaneous activity. The sabotage campaign was an earnest indication of our seriousness in the pursuit of this new strategy. All three needs were served by this convincing evidence that our liberation movement had correctly adjusted itself to the new situation and was creating an apparatus actually capable of clandestinely hitting the enemy and making preparations for a more advanced phase. The situation was such that without activity of this nature our whole political leadership may have been at stake both inside and outside the country and the steps which were simultaneously taken for the recruitment and preparation of military cadres would have met with less response.

The Relationship between the Political and Military

When we talk of revolutionary armed struggle, we are talking of political struggle by means which include the use of military force even though once force as a tactic is introduced it has the most far-reaching consequences on every aspect of our activities. It is important to emphasise this because our movement must reject all manifestations of militarism which separates armed people's struggle from its political context.

Reference has already been made to the danger of the thesis which regards the creation of military areas as the generator of mass resistance. But even more is involved in this concept. One of the vital problems connected with this bears on the important question of the relationship between the political and military. From the very beginning our Movement has brooked no ambiguity concerning this. The primacy of the political leadership is unchallenged and supreme and all revolutionary formations and levels (whether armed or not) are subordinate to this leadership. To say this is not just to invoke tradition. This approach is rooted in the very nature of this type of revolutionary struggle and is borne out by the experience of the overwhelming majority of revolutionary movements which have engaged in such struggle against a foe with formidable material strength does not achieve dramatic and swift success. The path is filled with obstacles and we harbour no illusions on this score in the case of South Africa. In the long run it can only succeed if it attracts the active support of the mass of the people. Without this lifeblood it is doomed. Even in our country with the historical background and traditions of armed resistance still, within the memory of many people and the special developments of the immediate past, the involvement of the masses is unlikely to be the result of a sudden natural and automatic consequence of military clashes. It has to be won in all-round political mobilisation which must accompany the military activities. This includes educational and agitational work throughout the country to cope with the sophisticated torrent of misleading propaganda and 'information' of the enemy which will become more intense as the struggle sharpens. When armed clashes begin they seldom involve more than a comparative handful of combatants whose very conditions of fighting-existence make them incapable of exercising the functions of all-round political leadership. The masses of the peasants, workers and youth, beleaguered for a long time by the enemy's military occupation, have to be activated in a multitude of ways not only to ensure a growing stream of recruits for the fighting units but to harass the enemy politically so that his forces are dispersed and therefore weakened. This calls for the exercise of all-round political leadership.

All-round Political Leadership

Guerrilla warfare, the special, and in our case the only form in which the armed liberation struggle can be launched, is neither static nor does it take place in a vacuum. The tempo, the overall strategy is to be employed, the opening of new fronts, the progression from lower to higher forms and thence to mobile warfare; these and other vital questions cannot be solved by the military leadership alone, they require overall political judgements intimately involved with the people both inside and outside the actual areas of armed combat. If more awareness of oppression combined with heroic examples by armed bands were enough, the struggle would indeed be simple. There would be no collaborators and it would be hard to find neutrals. But to believe this is to believe that the course of struggle is determined solely by what we do in the fighting units and further involves the fallacious assumption that the masses are rock-like and incorruptible. The enemy is as aware as we are that the side that wins the allegiance of the people wins the struggle. It is naive to believe that oppressed and beleaguered people cannot temporarily, even in large numbers, be won over by fear, terror, lies, indoctrination and provocation to treat liberators as enemies. In fact history proves that without the most intensive all-round political activity this is the more likely result. It is therefore all the more vital that the revolutionary leadership is nation-wide and has its roots both inside and outside the actual areas of combat. Above all, when victory comes, it must not be a hollow one. To ensure this we must also ensure that what is brought to power is not an army but the masses as a whole at the head of which stands its organised political leadership. This is the perspective which is rooted at all levels of our liberation movements whether within or outside the army. Our confidence in final victory rests not on the wish or the dream but on our understanding of our own conditions and the historical processes. This understanding must be deepened and must spread to every level of our Movement. We must have a clear grasp not only of ourselves and of our own forces but also of the enemy – of his power and vulnerability. Guerrilla struggle is certainly no exception to the rule that depth of understanding, and knowledge of realities, both favourable and unfavourable, make for more lasting commitment and more illuminating leadership. How then do we view the enemy we face – his strength and his weakness? What sort of structure do we face and how dogged will the enemy resistance be?

The Enemy: His Strength and Weakness

On the face of it the enemy is in stable command of a rich and varied economy which, even at this stage when it is not required to extend itself, can afford an enormous military budget. He has a relatively trained and efficient army and police force. He can draw on fairly large manpower resources. In addition the major imperialist powers such as Britain, West Germany, France and the United States and Japan who have an enormous stake in the economy of our country constitute a formidable support for the Apartheid regime. Already now before the crisis deepens the imperialist partners of South Africa have done much to develop the economy and armament programme of South Africa. In a situation of crisis they may pass over from support to active intervention to save the racist regime. If there is one lesson that the history of guerrilla struggle has taught it is that the material strength and resources of the enemy is by no means a decisive factor. Guerrilla warfare almost by definition presents a situation in which there is a vast imbalance of material and military resources between the opposing sides. It is designed to cope with the situation in which the enemy is infinitely superior in relation to every conventional factor of warfare. It is par excellence the weapon of the materially weak against the materially strong. Given its popular character and given a population which increasingly sides with and shields the guerrilla whilst at the same time opposing and exposing the enemy, the survival and growth of a people's army is assured by the skilful exercise of tactics. Surprise, mobility and tactical retreat should make it difficult for the enemy to bring into play its superior firepower in any decisive battles. No individual battle is fought in circumstances favourable to the enemy. Superior forces can thus be harassed, weakened and, in the end, destroyed. The absence of an orthodox front, of fighting lines; the need to protect the widely scattered installations on which his economy is dependent; these are among the factors which serve in the long run to compensate in favour of the guerrilla for the disparity in the starting strength of the adversaries. The words 'in the long run' must be stressed because it would be idle to dispute the considerable military advantages to the enemy of his high-level industrialisation, his ready-to-hand reserves of white manpower and his excellent roads, railways and air transportation which facilitate swift manoeuvres and speedy concentration of personnel. But we must not overlook the fact that over a period of time many of these unfavourable factors will begin to operate in favour of the liberation forces:

- The ready-to-hand resources, including food production, depend overwhelmingly on non-white labour which, with the growing intensity of the struggle, will not remain docile and co-operative.
- The white manpower resources may seem adequate initially but must become dangerously stretched as guerrilla warfare develops. Already extremely short of skilled labour – the monopoly of the whites – the mobilisation of a large force for protracted struggle will place a further burden on the workings of the economy.
- In contrast to many other major guerrilla struggles, manpower resources are all situated within the theatre of war and there is no secure external pool (other than direct intervention by a foreign state) safe from sabotage, mass action and guerrilla action on which the enemy can draw.
- The very sophistication of the economy with its well-developed system of communications makes it a much more vulnerable target. In an undeveloped country the interruption of supplies to any given region may be no more than a local setback.
- In a highly sensitive modern structure of the South African type, the successful harassment of transport to any major industrial complex inevitably inflicts immense damage to the economy as a whole and to the morale of the enemy.

One of the more popular misconceptions concerning guerrilla warfare is that a physical environment which conforms to a special pattern is indispensable – thick jungle, inaccessible mountain areas, swamps, a friendly border and so on. The availability of this sort of terrain is, of course, of tremendous advantage to the guerrillas, especially in the early non-operational phase when training and other preparatory steps are undertaken and no external bases are available for this purpose. When operations commence, the guerrilla cannot survive, let alone flourish, unless he moves to areas where people live and work and where the enemy can be engaged in combat. If he is fortunate enough to have behind him a friendly border or areas of difficult access which can provide a temporary refuge it is, of course, advantageous. But guerrilla warfare can be, and has been, waged in every conceived type of terrain, in deserts, swamps, in farm fields, in built-up areas, in plains, in the bush and in countries without friendly borders or islands surrounded by the sea. This whole question is one of adjusting survival tactics to the sort of terrain in which operations have to be carried out.

In any case, in the vast expanse that is South Africa, a people's force will find a multitude of variations in topography, deserts, mountains, forests, veld and swamps. There might not appear to be a single impregnable mountain or impenetrable jungle but the country abounds in terrain which in general is certainly no less favourable for guerrilla operations than some of the terrain in which other guerrilla movements operated successfully. Also the issue must be looked at in the context of guerrillas, who are armed and operate in the terrain. The combination makes an area impregnable for the guerrilla. South Africa's tremendous size will make it extremely difficult, if not impossible, for the white regime to keep the whole of it under armed surveillance in strength and in depth. Hence, an early development of a relatively safe (though shifting) rear is not beyond the realm of practicality.

The White Group
The above are only some of the important factors which have not always been studied and understood. It is necessary to stress these factors not only because they give balance to our efforts but because – properly assessed – they help destroy the myth of the enemy's invincibility.

But above all a scientific revolutionary strategy demands a correct appreciation of the political character of the forces which are ranged against one another in the South African Struggle for liberation. Is the enemy a monolith and will he remain so until his final defeat? What is the main content of the struggle for liberation and, flowing from this, which is the main revolutionary force and who are its potential allies and supporters? These are questions of capital importance. They play a vital part in determining the tactics of the revolutionary struggle, the broad organisational structures we create and many other fundamental approaches. They must be considered within the framework of the special feature of the objective situation which faces us. South Africa's social and economic structure and the relationships which it generates are perhaps unique. It is not a colony, yet it has, in regard to the overwhelming majority of its people, most of the features of the classical colonial structures. Conquest and domination by an alien people, a system of discrimination and exploitation based on race, technique of indirect rule; these and more are the traditional trappings of the classical colonial framework. Whilst at the one level it is an 'independent' national state, at another level it is a country subjugated by a minority race. What makes the structure unique and adds to its complexity is that the exploiting nation is not, as in the classical imperialist relationships, situated in a geographically distinct mother country, but is settled within the borders. What is more, the roots of the dominant nation have been embedded in our country by more than three centuries of presence. It is thus an alien body only in the historical sense.

The material well-being of the white group and its political, social and economic privileges are, we know, rooted in its racial domination of the indigenous majority. It has resisted and will resist doggedly and passionately any attempt to shift it from this position. Its theorists and leaders ceaselessly play upon the theme of 'We have nowhere else to go'. They dishonestly ignore and even twist the fact that the uncertainty about the future of the oppressor in our land is an uncertainty born not of our racialism but of his. The spectre is falsely raised of a threat to the white men's language and culture to 'justify' a policy of cultural discrimination and domination. By economic bribes and legal artifices which preserve for him the top layers of skills and wage income, the white worker is successfully mobilised as one of racialism's most reliable contingents. In every walk of life white autocracy creates privilege by operation of the law and, where necessary, the gun and with a primitive and twisted 'proof' of its own superiority.

Nevertheless, the defence of all-round economic, social and cultural privileges combined with centuries of indoctrination and deeply felt theoretical rationalisation which centre on survival, will make the enemy we face a ferocious and formidable foe. So long as the threat from the liberation movement was not powerful enough to endanger the very existence of white baasskap, there was room for division, sometimes quite sharp, in the white political camp.

Its motivation amongst the ruling class was competition for the lion's share of the spoils from the exploitation of the non-white people. It always centred round the problem of the most effective way of 'keeping the native in his place'. In such an atmosphere there were even moments when white workers adopted militant class postures against the small group which owns South Africa's wealth. But the changed world mood and international situation inhibited these confrontations. The laager-minded white group as a whole moves more and more in the direction of a common defence of what is considered a common fate.

These monolithic tendencies are reinforced by a Hitler-like feeling of confidence that the fortress is impregnable and unassailable for all time. This process of all white solidarity will only be arrested by the achievements of the liberation movement. For the moment the reality is that apart from a small group of revolutionary whites, who have an honoured place as comrades in the struggle, we face what is by and large a united and confident enemy which acts in alliance with, and is strengthened by, world imperialism. All significant sections of the white political movement are in broad agreement on the question of defeating our liberation struggle.

This confrontation on the lines of colour – at least in the early stages of the conflict – is not of our choosing; it is of the enemy's making. It will not be easy to eliminate some of its more tragic consequences. But it does not follow that this will be so for all time. It is not altogether impossible that in a different situation the white working class, or a substantial section of it, may come to see that their true long term interest coincides with that of the non-white workers. We must miss no opportunity either now or in the future to try and make them aware of this truth and to win over those who are ready to break with the policy of racial domination. Nor must we ever be slow to take advantage of differences and divisions which our successes will inevitably spark off to isolate the most vociferous, the most uncompromising and the most reactionary elements amongst the whites. Our policy must continually stress in the future (as it has in the past) that there is room in South Africa for all who live in it, but only on the basis of absolute democracy.

The African Masses: The Main Force for Liberation
So much for the enemy. What of the liberation forces? Here too we are called upon to examine the most fundamental features of our situation which serve to mould our revolutionary strategy and tactics. The main content of the present stage of the South African revolution is the national liberation of the largest and most oppressed group – the African people. This strategic aim must govern every aspect of the conduct of our struggle whether it be the formulation of policy or the creation of structures. Amongst other things, it demands in the first place the maximum mobilisation of the African people as a dispossessed and racially oppressed nation. This is the mainspring and it must not be weakened. It involves a stimulation and deepening of national confidence, national pride and national assertiveness. Properly channelled and properly led, these qualities do not stand in conflict with the principles of internationalism. Indeed, they become the basis for more and more meaningful co-operation; a co-operation which is self imposed, equal and one which is neither based on dependence nor gives the appearance of being so.

The national character of the struggle must therefore dominate our approach. But it is a national struggle which is taking place in a different era and in a different context from those which characterised the early struggles against colonialism. It is happening in a new kind of world – a world which is no longer monopolised by the imperialist world system; a world in which the existence of the powerful socialist system and a significant sector of newly liberated areas has altered the balance of forces; a world in which the horizons liberated from foreign oppression extend beyond mere formal political control and encompass the element which makes such control meaningful – economic emancipation. It is also happening in a new kind of South Africa; a South Africa in which there is a large and well-developed working class whose class consciousness and in which the independent expressions of the working people – their political organs and trade unions – are very much part of the liberation front. Thus, our nationalism must not be confused with chauvinism or narrow nationalism of a previous epoch. It must not be confused with the classical drive by an elitist group among the oppressed people to gain ascendancy so that they can replace the oppressor in the exploitation of the mass.

But none of this detracts from the basically national context of our liberation drive. In the last resort it is only the success of the national democratic revolution which – destroying the existing social and economic relationship – will bring with it a correction of the historical injustices perpetrated against the indigenous majority and thus lay the basis for a new – and deeper internationalist – approach. Until then, the national sense of grievance is the most potent revolutionary force which must be harnessed. To blunt it in the interests of abstract concepts of internationalism is, in the long run, doing neither a service to revolution nor to internationalism.

The Role of the Coloured and Indian People

The African, although subjected to the most intense racial oppression and exploitation, is not the only oppressed national group in South Africa. The two million strong Coloured Community and three-quarter-million Indians suffer varying forms of national humiliation, discrimination and oppression. They are part of the non-white base upon which rests white privilege. As such, they constitute an integral part of the social forces ranged against white supremacy. Despite deceptive, and, often, meaningless concessions, they share a common fate with their brothers and their own liberation is inextricably bound up with the liberation of the African people.

A unity in action between all the oppressed groups is fundamental to the advance of our liberation struggle. Without such a unity, the enemy easily multiplies and the attainment of a people's victory is delayed. Historically both communities have played a most important part in the stimulation and intensification of the struggle for freedom. It is a matter of proud record that amongst the first and most gallant martyrs in the armed combat against the enemy was a Coloured Comrade, Basil February. The jails in South Africa are a witness to the large scale participation by Indian and Coloured comrades at every level of our revolutionary struggle. From the very inception of Umkhonto they were more than well represented in the first contingents who took life in hand to help lay the basis for this new phase in our struggle.

This mood was not only reflected in the deeds of its more advanced representatives. As communities too, the Coloured and Indian people have often in the past, by their actions, shown that they form part of the broad sweep towards liberation. The first series of mass acts of deliberate defiance of the conqueror's law after the crushing of the Bambatha rebellion, was the campaign led by that outstanding son of the Indian people – Mahatma Gandhi. Thereafter the Indian community and its leaders – particularly those who came to the fore in the 1940s – played no small part in the injection of a more radical and more militant mood into the liberation movement as a whole. The stirring demonstrations of the fifties from the Defiance Campaign to the Congress of the People, to the general strike, and the peasant revolts and mass demonstrations, saw many examples of united action by all the oppressed people. Indian workers responded in large numbers to almost every call for a general strike. Indian shopkeepers, could always be relied upon to declare a day of Hartal in solidarity with any protest which was being organised. Memory is still fresh of the outstanding response by the Coloured workers of the Western Cape to the 1961 call by the ANC for a national general political strike.

The Alliance between the Congress organisations was a spur to the solidarity and reflected it. But events both before and after Rivonia put paid to the structures which had been created to express the Alliance.

How can we strengthen and make effective the co-operation between the communities, and how can we integrate committed revolutionaries irrespective of their racial background?

Our Fighting Alliance

Whatever instruments are created to give expression to the unity of the liberation drive, they must accommodate two fundamental propositions:

Firstly, they must not be ambiguous on the question of the primary role of the most oppressed African mass and,

Secondly, those belonging to the other oppressed groups and those few white revolutionaries who show themselves ready to make common cause with our aspirations, must be fully integrated on the basis of individual equality. Approached in the right spirit, these two propositions do not stand in conflict but reinforce one another. Equality of participation in our national front does not mean a mechanical parity between the various national groups. Not only would this practice amount to inequality (again at the expense of the majority), but it would lend flavour to the slander which our enemies are ever ready to spread of a multiracial alliance dominated by minority groups. This has never been so and will never be so. But the sluggish way in which the Movement inside the country responded to the new situation after 1960 in which co-operation between some organisations which were legal (e.g. SAIC, CPO, COD) and those that were illegal (e.g. ANC) sometimes led to the superficial impression that the legal organisations – because they could speak and operate more publicly and thus were more noticeable – may have had more than their deserved place in the leadership of the Alliance.

Therefore, not only the substance but the form of our structural creations must in a way which the people can see – give expression to the main emphasis of the present stage of our struggle. This approach is not a pandering chauvinism, to racialism or other such backward attitudes. We are revolutionaries, not narrow nationalists. Committed revolutionaries are our brothers to whatever group they belong. There can be no second-class participants in our Movement. It is for the enemy we reserve our assertiveness and our justified sense of grievance.

The important task of mobilising and gaining the support of other oppressed non-white groups has already been referred to. Like every other oppressed group (including Africans), we must not naïvely assume that mere awareness of oppression will, by itself push the Indian and Coloured people in the direction of opposing the enemy and alighting themselves with the liberation movement. The potential is of course there, because in a very real sense the future of the Indian and Coloured people and their liberation as oppressed groups is intimately bound up with the liberation of the Africans. But active support and participation has to be fought for and won. Otherwise the enemy will succeed in its never-ending attempt to create a gap between these groups and the Africans and even recruit substantial numbers of them to actively collaborate with it. The bottom of the barrel will be scraped in the attempt to create confusion about the objectives of the liberation movement. More particularly, the enemy will feed on the insecurity and dependency which is often part of the thinking of minority oppressed groups. They will try to raise a doubt in their minds about whether there is a place for them in a future liberated South Africa. They have already spread the slander that at best for the Coloureds and Indians, white domination will be replaced by black domination.

It is therefore all the more important, consistent with our first principle, that the Coloured and Indian people should see themselves as an integral part of the liberation movement and not as mere auxiliaries.

The Working Class

Is there a special role for the working class in our national struggle? We have already referred to the special character of the South African social and economic structure. In our country – more than in any other part of the oppressed world – it is inconceivable for liberation to have meaning without a return of the wealth of the land to the people as a whole. It is therefore a fundamental feature of our strategy that victory must embrace more than formal political democracy. To allow the existing economic forces to retain their interests intact is to feed the root of racial supremacy and does not represent even the shadow of liberation.

Our drive towards national emancipation is therefore in a very real way bound up with economic emancipation. We have suffered more than just national humiliation. Our people are deprived of their due in the country's wealth; their skills have been suppressed and poverty and starvation has been their life experience. The correction of these centuries-old economic injustices lies at the very core of our national aspirations. We do not understand the complexities which will face a people's government during the transformation period nor the enormity of the problems of meeting economic needs of the mass of the oppressed people. But one thing is certain – in our land this cannot be effectively tackled unless the basic wealth and the basic resources are at the disposal of the people as a whole and are not manipulated by sections or individuals be they white or black.

This perspective of a speedy progression from formal liberation to genuine and lasting emancipation is made more real by the existence in our country of a large and growing working class whose class consciousness complements national consciousness. Its political organisations – and the trade unions – have played a fundamental role in shaping and advancing our revolutionary cause. It is historically understandable that the double-oppressed and doubly exploited working class constitutes a distinct and reinforcing layer of our liberation. Its militancy and political consciousness as a revolutionary class will play no small part in our victory and in the construction of a real people's South Africa.

Beyond our borders in Zimbabwe, Angola, Mozambique and Namibia are our brothers and sisters who similarly are engaged in a fierce struggle against colonialist and fascist regimes. We fight an Unholy Alliance of Portugal, Rhodesia and South Africa, with the latter as the main economic and military support. The historic ZAPU–ANC Alliance is a unique form of co-operation between two liberation movements which unites the huge potential of the oppressed people in both South Africa and Zimbabwe. The extension of co-operation and coordination of all the people of Southern

Africa as led by FRELIMO, ZAPU, SWAPO, MPLA and the ANC is a vital part of our strategy.

What then is the broad purpose of our military struggle? Simply put, in the first phase, it is the complete political and economic emancipation of all our people and the constitution of a society which accords with the basic provisions of our programme – the Freedom Charter. This, together with our general understanding of our revolutionary theory, provides us with the strategic framework for the concrete elaboration and implementation of policy in a continuously changing situation. It must be combined with a more intensive programme of research, examination and analysis of the conditions of the different state of our people (in particular those on the land), their local grievances, hopes and aspirations, so that the flow from theory to application – when the situation makes application possible – will be unhampered.

Advance to People's Power!
75 Years of Struggle
(Adopted by the ANC, 1987)

South Africa is a land of extreme wealth for the privileged white colonial population, and extreme poverty and destitution for the oppressed black majority. Whites, 17 per cent of the population, receive more than 70 per cent of all income. The poverty that prevails in our country is the direct result of apartheid – the result of white greed and military strength.

When we talk of struggle against apartheid we talk of what operates, for the vast majority of South Africans, as a police state. Apartheid is not merely racial discrimination. Its central feature is not the segregation of public amenities. Apartheid means not only inequality, racism, national and racial oppression and exploitation of the black majority in our country, but also the means necessary to enforce it, to defend it and to guarantee its survival in the face of powerful forces of resistance fighting to defeat it. Apartheid is a form of violence that operates, every moment of every day, against our people and the other peoples of Southern Africa, to perpetuate a white monopoly of political and economic power. Apartheid is everything progressive humanity opposes, and as such we call on all peace-loving people to make common cause with us to ensure its total destruction.

Since the townships were invaded by Pretoria's soldiers in 1984, thousands of people have lost their lives, many more have been injured and maimed, tens of thousands have been detained, while many have simply 'disappeared'.

Lives have been lost ever since the colonialists came to our country. The formation of the African National Congress on January 8th, 1912 created a people's organisation which transcended tribal, religious and class barriers in the fight for freedom in the land of our birth, an organisation which continued, under the new conditions prevailing, the anti-colonial struggle of our people.

Our struggle is fundamentally a national liberation struggle to rid our nation of the colonial oppressor. South Africa, a country of some 30 million people, is being run as two countries, the one colonising the other, the white country of 4.5 million people colonising the 27 million black majority, and maintaining control through force and international support.

Mass meetings, deputations, demonstrations, protests, passive resistance and strikes were the hallmark of the half-century of peaceful struggle waged by the people of South Africa. Every avenue of non-violent protest was met with violent repression on the part of the regime, culminating in the banning of the ANC after the Sharpeville Massacre in 1960, and the declaration of a state of emergency. The regime turned South Africa into an armed camp. The ANC went underground, determined to find new methods of struggle. 1961 saw the formation of Umkhonto weSizwe, our people's army, our striking force for final liberation. The violence of the regime was now to be met by the revolutionary violence of the people. Since then, the ANC has combined political and armed struggle to defeat apartheid.

Our aim is a war fought by the entire people – in strikes, demonstrations, resistance to forced removals, as well as in the field of armed struggle. Our call, to make apartheid unworkable and South Africa ungovernable, has resulted in the severest crisis the Pretoria regime has yet had to face.

The African National Congress stands for a new South Africa, a South Africa in which racism shall be a thing of the past, where human dignity and equality shall prevail in the life of the country and its people, where the goals enshrined in the Freedom Charter shall be transformed into a living reality. Before that day dawns, many lives will be lost. Our people will suffer great hardship. But we are prepared to meet this challenge; to make whatever sacrifices are necessary for achieving freedom in South Africa.

Pre-1912: Organisational History of the ANC

On January 8th, 1987 the African National Congress commemorates the 75th anniversary of its foundation. It was the first African nationalist political organisation in South Africa, and indeed on the continent of Africa. Many political organisations of neighbouring countries, now independent, can trace their origins to the ANC. Since its modest beginnings in the form of the regional Native congresses during the first decade of this century, the ANC has grown from strength to strength, sparing no effort to fulfil its goal of a united South African nation free from the chains of imperialism and racism. It has succeeded in uniting African, Coloured, Indian and democratic whites of South Africa under one, forward-marching body in the struggle for freedom.

The formation of the ANC in 1912 signified the birth not only of the ANC, but also of the South African nation. The ANC was assigned the task of midwife in this process of national rebirth and regeneration. The formation of the ANC meant the creation of a loyalty of a new type, a non-tribal loyalty, a loyalty which was inherently anti-colonial. It was an act of national salvation, a continuation – under new historical conditions – of the anti-colonial struggle of our people which had begun with colonialism itself.

South Africa was conquered by force and is today ruled by force. Whether in reserve or in actual employment force is ever-present. This has been so ever since the colonialists came to our country. As time has progressed, force in the fascist mould has been implemented in greater and by more terrifying methods. Children, women, youth and the aged are subjected to brutal and systematic violence comparable only to that perpetrated under Nazi tyranny.

In order to fully appreciate the political and social significance that the ANC, as the liberation movement of oppressed South Africans, expresses, and the necessity for the type of organisation we have today, it is necessary to look at the past.

European settlement in South Africa dates back to April 6th, 1652. Because of the intrusive, predatory and aggressive policies of the invaders, disputes, which soon led to war, ensued. In the Cape alone, nine wars of resistance against colonial encroachment were waged. Our people fought courageously and heroically and, in fact, were at no time ever conquered by the Boers. It was the arrival of the British military forces in South Africa which marked a qualitative and quantitative change in the resistance struggle. Immensely strengthened, the forces of colonisation and oppression, with their overwhelming superiority in arms and numbers of well-trained men, were able, after grim and bitter battles, to eventually subdue all military opposition.

Effectively, the defeat of the Bambata Rebellion in 1906 brought to a close this first, 250-year phase of resistance and set the stage for the handing over of the administration of the country to local white settlers by British imperialism.

Defeated militarily and totally disarmed, robbed of their land by foreign invaders, denied any say in the governing of their country, our people realised that new ways had to be found to continue the struggle. Old forms of organisation and methods of struggle were proving inadequate to meet the new conditions. The people were looking for new forms of organisation, and learning new methods of struggle; they were learning the ways of mass meetings, demonstrations, deputations, protests, passive resistance and strikes.

The ANC was born out of the lessons learnt from the past. The need for African unity in the face of the common enemy and common problems, a need long recognised by far-sighted African leaders, was forcefully brought home with the promulgation of the Act of Union in 1910, when General Louis Botha moved to consolidate white hegemony within the system established by the South African Act of Union, passed in the British House of Commons in 1909, uniting the formerly embittered feuding sections of the white minority.

These underlying factors led to the formation of the ANC on January 8th, 1912. There was full recognition of the need for the strength achieved in unity – unity of purpose and unity in action. Furthermore, the far-sighted founders of the ANC recognised the urgency for united action to oppose the imminent Land Act, due to be implemented in 1913, which was to further rob the African people of their land, reducing their territorial rights to a mere 13 per cent of South Africa.

The formation of the ANC was not an accident of history. It was a logical development of history, a continuation of the anti-colonial struggle of our people which began with colonialism itself. There were many factors that led to the formation of the ANC. The introduction of Christianity in South Africa led to the emergence of black Christians who later rejected the white Christian values, formed their own independent churches with new concepts and values. The first of these black converts to form an independent church was Nehemiah Tile, who played a significant religious and political role. He formed the Tembu Church in 1883 in the Transkei. The founding of the Ethiopian Church by the Rev. MM Mokone on the Witwatersrand in 1892 was tantamount to widening the battlefront started by Tile.

This period saw the emergence of young African intellectuals who came from mission schools established throughout the country. They helped in establishing the early beginnings of what later became an African press. They wrote articles in English and African languages, and therefore helped to develop the African languages. The first political organisation, Imbumba yama Afrika (Union of Africans), was formed in the Cape in 1882. It advocated African unity as opposed to denominational diversity and planned representations to white authorities. In 1884 two additional organisations were formed, again in the Cape, namely the Native Education Association and the Native Electoral Association, which were concerned mainly with electoral politics – in those days, Africans in the Cape could vote.

But it was during the Anglo-Boer War and immediately after the Treaty of Vereeniging in May 1902 that concrete steps were taken by Africans to form a movement which would devise some method of presenting grievances and complaints of Africans to the government.

This growing awareness and consciousness of a need for a political organisation of Africans on a broader basis led Martin Lutuli, Saul Msane and Josiah Gumede to meet Harriet Colenso to discuss the formation of an African political organisation. In July 1900, the Natal Native Congress was formed, its first secretary being HC Matiwane. Its chairman was Martin Lutuli – an uncle of the late former President-General of the ANC, Chief Albert Lutuli. Martin Lutuli was chairman for three years, being replaced by Skweleti Nyongwana, while he became vice-chairman. Local committees managed local affairs and the object and intention of Congress was to represent the whole African community in Natal.

In 1902 in the Eastern Cape, Africans close to the East London newspaper *Izwi Labantu*, and therefore opposed to Jabavu's *Imvo Zabantsundu*, and his preoccupation with European politics, founded the South African Native Congress. The tasks of this organisation were to co-ordinate African activities in the Cape Colony, particularly in connection with electoral politics. The political orientation of the South African Native Congress is contained in a 1903 statement of its Executive, 'Questions affecting the Natives and Coloured People resident in British South Africa'. The Native Vigilance Association of the Orange River Colony presented testimony before the South African Native Affairs Commission on September 23, 1904. What was striking, but not surprising if one takes into account the ethnic composition of the province, was the 'non-tribal' composition of the leadership of this organisation, judging by the delegation which saw the Native Affairs Commission.

These testimonies and petitions to King Edward VII, for example from the Native United Political Associations of the Transvaal Colony (April 25, 1905), or the Orange River Colony Native Congress (June 1906), or the Natal Native Congress (October 1908), or from the 'Aboriginal Natives of South Africa resident in the Transvaal' (October 22, 1908), and resolutions of the South African Native Congress (April 10, 1908), give an insight into the problems and grievances of the Africans who showed an acute awareness of the magnitude of their disabilities and a sharp antagonism to any continuation of the political system of the Boer Republics.

These petitions (the Transvaal Native Union collected 3,764 signatures) asked for a common roll franchise throughout South Africa, plus separate representation for the mass of the African people unable to qualify for this. Within four months these organisations held congresses. The draft South Africa Act was discussed at these meetings. Resolutions deprecating the colour bar and the failure to extend the African franchise from the Cape to the North were passed. It was from these regional conferences that 60 elected delegates came to Bloemfontein to attend the South African Native Convention on March 24–26, 1909.

The South African Native Convention consisted of delegates from the Cape Colony, Natal, Transvaal, Orange Free State and Bechuanaland (now Botswana). The Rev. Walter Rubusana, leader of the Cape delegation of the South African Native Congress, chaired the convention and was elected president of the Convention. They discussed those clauses of the draft Union Act which related to African and Coloured people.

These resolutions, which attacked the racism inherent in the Draft Act, were delivered to the Governors and Prime Ministers of the four colonies (Cape, Natal, OFS and Transvaal) and to the British High Commissioner for transfer to the Secretary of State for Colonies. If the Draft Act was not amended, a deputation was to be sent to England. The delegation was to comprise the Rev. Rubusana, president of the Native Convention, TM Mapikela of the Orange River Colony and D Dwanya of the Cape Congress. The Transvaal Native Congress appointed Alfred Mangena, who was already in London, and instructed him to work in co-operation with the other delegates. WP Schreiner was invited to join them and Tengo Jabavu represented his tiny Cape Convention. The Coloured community was represented by Dr Abdurahman, leader of the African People's Organisation, while Advocate Gandhi represented the Indian community. This defiant deputation was later to be disappointed by the attitude of the British government, which once more deliberately ignored the express wishes of the black population of South Africa.

Faced with these problems and the fact that their interests had been totally disregarded in the absence of a political organisation of their own which could voice their grievances and aspirations, the Africans started to work towards unity for a common action and to educate themselves towards promotion of mutual help, a feeling of brotherhood and a spirit of togetherness. Pixley ka Isaka Seme, who became the convenor of the January 8 meeting, was in fact impatient about the formation of the ANC. In October 1911 he wrote: 'It is conclusively urgent that this meeting should meet this year because a matter which is so vitally important to our progress and welfare should not unnecessarily be postponed by reason of personal differences and selfishness of our leaders.' In what seemed to be a statement of policy or an item on the agenda of the coming meeting – the central theme of his contribution – he said: 'The demon of racialism, the aberrations of the Xhosa-Fingo feud, the animosity that exists between the Zulus and the

Tongas, between the Basotho and every other Native, must be buried and forgotten ... We are one people! These divisions, these jealousies, are the cause of our woes and all the backwardness and ignorance that exists today.'

Thus on January 8, 1912, when the ANC was formed, Seme gave the keynote speech. After the opening speeches were made, the gathering sang Tiyo Soga's 'Lizalis 'idinga lakho, Thixo, Nkosi yenyaniso' (Fulfil Thy Promise, Thou True Lord). Seme, seconded by Alfred Mangena, moved that the assembly should establish the South African Native National Congress. He was unanimously supported. A committee was appointed to draw up a constitution. George Montsioa suggested that seven paramount chiefs be appointed as Honorary Presidents of the South African Native National Congress (the ANC). Thus the conference resolved that two houses, the Upper and Lower House, should be established. The Upper House consisted of Dalindyebo of the Thembus; Montsioa of the Barolong; Lewanika of Barotseland (part of Zambia); Letsie II of Basotholand (now Lesotho), who was elected President of the Upper House; Khama of Bechuanaland (now Botswana); Mareclane of Pondoland; and Moepi of the Bakgatla. Dinuzulu, the Zulu chief who was deposed and exiled to the Transvaal by the British, was also included.

The Executive of the Lower House, the executive proper, consisted of the Rev. John L Dube, President; Solomon T Plaatje, Secretary; Pixley ka Isaka Seme was elected Treasurer; Thomas Mapikela of the Orange Free State became Speaker; and Montsioa Recording Secretary. The Rev. Mqoboli of the Wesleyan Church became Chaplain-in-chief with the Rev. HR Ngcayiya, President of the Ethiopian Church, as his Assistant. The Rev. Walter Rubusana, Meshack Pelem, Sam Makgatho and Alfred Mangena were elected vice-presidents.

The first National Executive Committee consisted of ministers of religion, lawyers, an editor (Plaatje), a building contractor (Mapikela), a teacher and estate agent (Makgatho) and an interpreter, teacher and Native labour agent (Pelem). These are people who went through mission schools; five of them studied abroad (Britain and USA) and others had attended conferences overseas. These men were prominent both in local political organisations and nationally. They were relatively young – in their thirties, and early fifties. The four provinces were represented on the Executive. The chiefs were honoured in accordance with African tradition. They represented the rural masses who were then the majority of the people.

At the inaugural conference of the ANC eleven papers were read, the topics ranging from discussions about schools, the burning current issues of 'Native' labour, segregation, the land question and the 'Squatters' law. To conclude the proceedings John Knox Bokwe's Give a Thought to Africa' was sung and the delegates returned to report back to their local organisations on the practical means of implementing their vision of African unity and the fight against white domination. These resolutions could only be implemented in the course of struggle.

The Road from the 1912 Bloemfontein Conference

The closing notes of John Knox Bokwe's 'Give a Thought to Africa' were still ringing in the ears of those who participated in the ANC foundation conference at Mangaung (Bloemfontein) when the first battles confronted the newly formed ANC. The years following 1912 were a period of development and regrouping under new conditions; a period in which newly created political formations of the people continued to struggle and grew to maturity; a period in which, above all, national consciousness began to assert itself against tribal sectionalism. This period witnessed the emergence of the primary organisation of the liberation movement – the African National Congress.

This was a time of organisational growth punctuated by struggles ranging from mass campaigning and general strikes to mass acts of defiance. The aims of the ANC campaigns at this time were:

- To highlight the grievances and demands of the African people who had been driven off the land; of those on white-owned farms where they were treated like serfs, working from dawn to dusk for a mere pittance; those in the overcrowded and arid reserves where poverty and hunger were the lot of the inhabitants; and in urban areas where they were harassed by pass laws and chased from pillar to post.
- To educate the African masses politically and to create national and political consciousness among them;
- To express the aspirations of the African people and to build mass pressure which could compel the regime to change its repressive policy towards the African people;
- To awaken the conscience of 'White South Africa' with regard to its inhumanity to fellow human beings.

The first major struggle the African National Congress launched was against the 1913 Land Act, which reduced our people in the countryside to landlessness, ruin and destitution. This fight was also carried to England. The African National Congress sent two deputations – in 1913–1914 and in 1919 – financed by both the chiefs and the people. Though it had its own parliament, South Africa was still under the British Crown, and our leaders and people correctly went to London to present our case and ask the British Government to intervene in the dispute. The deputations were, however, unsuccessful.

There was also an attempt by the authorities in the Orange Free State in 1913 to extend the pass system to African women. This, too, became a campaign issue, resulting in temporary victory.

It was these immediate campaigns, along with a number of smaller struggles, which steeled the ANC as a people's organisation. The ANC developed its identity as the true expression of African nationhood, the symbol of African unity, the mouthpiece of the oppressed people of South Africa and their instrument for national emancipation. It emerged as a new type of organisation, created to meet the complex and difficult situation and conditions arising from foreign domination and exploitation.

Through the anti-1913 Land Act campaign and the African women's anti-pass campaign, it was clearly demonstrated that the ANC embodied the aspirations of the people of South Africa, spearheading the fight to destroy foreign domination and injustice in the political, economic and social spheres. The ANC set out to win back for the African people their rightful position as controllers of the destiny of their country.

The Nats come to Power

1948 saw the Nationalist Party coming to power, entrenching white minority fascist domination of our country. In an attempt to stem the tide of reaction unleashed by the Nationalist Party, and in order to advance the cause of liberation and freedom, the Annual National Conference of the African National Congress in 1949 adopted a militant Programme of Action: the document commonly and popularly referred to as 'The 1949 Programme of Action'. Among other things the Programme laid down the forms and methods of struggle which the African National Congress would employ in its struggle for emancipation.

These were: strikes, boycotts, 'civil disobedience' and 'non-cooperation'. Civil disobedience means defiance of laws and Government orders. Non-cooperation means 'to cease to recognise a foreign authority on your soil; to cease to obey it; to ignore its law-courts; to refuse to pay taxes; and to decline to serve it as soldiers and policemen'.

For a variety of reasons the African National Congress decided that the programme laid down in its 1949 Programme of Action should be carried out in a non-violent way, under a policy of non-violence. Among the reasons advanced for this were:

- The poor state of organisation among the people;
- The tendency among our people to disregard or minimise the importance of organisation and organised way of fighting;
- That the people were unarmed and psychologically unprepared for a violent struggle, while the forces of the enemy were armed to the teeth;
- That limited non-violent forms of struggle were still open to us;
- Because of the urgent need for creating a powerful mass political pressure force; and
- The great need and necessity for educating the people politically, creating among them a feeling and spirit of national consciousness, determination, discipline, selflessness and readiness to make sacrifices.

The African National Congress at the time based its policy partly on two strategic and tactical propositions, namely:

- That while the right to meet, to speak, to organise and to move about still existed, we should use these opportunities to organise mass political pressure against the government; and
- That in a country with traditions of representative governing institutions, the possibility of the inner conscience being pricked always existed, and therefore our mass pressure and world opinion might be heeded even in South Africa!

Another important consideration was the avoidance of the massacre of our unarmed people. As the leader of the African people, the African National Congress had to see to it that, if possible, mass slaughter had to be avoided. It is a notorious fact that the Boers are always ready and happy to shoot down Africans. Where the lives of thousands of people are involved, a leader cannot afford the luxury of experiment, gambling or recklessness.

The 1952 Defiance Campaign
The ANC resolved to embark upon a massive campaign of defiance of apartheid laws. On June 26, 1952, together with the South African Indian Congress, the ANC launched the Campaign for the Defiance of Unjust Laws. The Defiance Campaign carried on through 1953, covering all major cities and centres in South Africa. Over 8,000 volunteers belonging to the ANC and its allies defied apartheid and were jailed. In 1954 the ANC launched a struggle against the imposition of the inferior Bantu Education system, calculated to reduce African youth to hewers of wood and drawers of water for the white people. Massive agitation took place among parents and

teachers and a boycott of Bantu Education was organised. This period is defined by some as the passive resistance period of the ANC, often because such people, who do not recognise the full viciousness of the regime, would have it that the ANC should have remained a 'pacifist', civil-rights type of movement. The ANC in the 1950s was never pacifist nor a movement for civil rights. To say this would be a distortion of history. Rather, our policy was one of non-violence.

The 1952 non-violent campaign was certainly not a passive affair. To avoid creating an impression of passivity, the campaign was advisedly called 'Campaign for Defiance of Unjust Laws'. The spirit of defiance engendered by this campaign produced, though indirectly, the riots of 1953 at Port Elizabeth, East London, Kimberley, Denver and elsewhere. It also produced the militant struggles in Winburg, Zeerust, Maloka (Rooijantjiesfontein), Sekhukhuniland, Pondoland, Zululand, Transkei, Peddie, the African women's fight against dipping and passes in Natal, as well as the struggle of the people of Mabieskraal and other areas. Nor can we overlook the numerous successful militant boycott campaigns already referred to earlier.

Last but not least, the activities carried out under the policy of non-violence forced the government of Verwoerd to abandon all pretences of legality, to throw overboard all its laws and to rely entirely on martial law and brute force. They caused the Verwoerd government to declare a state of emergency four times in the years 1960 to 1962!

Unity of Democratic Forces and Pretoria's Response
In the 1950s the question of unity among all genuine democratic forces, which had always had the serious attention of the ANC, was beginning to take more concrete shape. A firm base of solidarity and joint action in the struggle among Africans, Indians and Coloureds was firmly established. Later, during the Defiance Campaign of 1952, some progressive Whites joined the struggle on the side of the oppressed people, and the Congress of Democrats was formed.

This alliance was further strengthened with the South African Congress of Trade Unions, formed in March 1955. As the only non-racial trade union federation in South Africa, it brought the weight of thousands of organised workers into the struggle.

Having succeeded substantially in mobilising the various African ethnic groupings into a single fighting nation, the ANC, in keeping with its overall strategy to lead a united front of all anti-racist and democratic forces, hammered out a common programme with the representatives of the various racial groups and the democratic trade union movement.

This programme was further crystallised when early in 1955 the ANC called for 50,000 volunteers from all sections of the South African people to go among the people and collect freedom demands to be incorporated into a common programme for South Africa. Thus began one of the greatest campaigns in the history of the South African liberation movement. Demands flowed into the offices of the ANC from every corner of South Africa; from Africans, Indians, Coloureds and Whites; from workers and peasants; from shopkeepers and intellectuals.

On June 26 that year at the historic Congress of the People, the fighting demands of all South Africans were enshrined in the Freedom Charter.

The success of this campaign and the widespread support the Charter received from the people did not go unnoticed by the racist regime in South Africa. In 1956, the political police swooped and arrested 156 leaders of the ANC and its allies and charged them with High Treason, using the Freedom Charter as the basis of its charge.

After a trial lasting over four years all the accused were found not guilty and discharged. However, many were served with banning and restriction orders.

The progressive developments of the 1950s were not without effect within the African National Congress. The transformation of the ANC into a greater mass movement, the formation of the Congress Alliance and the adoption of the Freedom Charter provoked a backlash from a minority group of 'Africanists'. Some now familiar phrases were bandied about. According to this faction, the ANC leadership under Chief Albert Lutuli had 'abandoned' the genuine African nationalism of the 1949 Programme of Action and had become the tools of the 'white communists' of the Congress of Democrats. These 'Africanists' opposed joining with the democratic organisations of national groups other than African in the Congress Alliance, and violently rejected the Freedom Charter, particularly its provision that South Africa belongs to all who live in it. They also opposed what they called the 'leftist' economic clauses of the Freedom Charter and the general 'leftist' influence in the ANC. They left the ANC in 1958, and in 1959, led by Robert Sobukwe and PK Leballo, they formed the Pan Africanist Congress (PAC), which today is little more than an organisation in name only.

In 1957, the ANC, together with local residents' associations, organised the Alexandra and Pretoria bus boycotts. In April 1958, the ANC organised another one-day national strike. In 1959 at its national conference in Durban, the ANC resolved to conduct a massive nationwide struggle against the pass laws over the following year. This campaign was already under way when the PAC sought to wreck it by launching its passive resistance campaign only ten days before the National Anti-Pass Campaign was to begin on March 31st, 1960. When the police massacred the people at Sharpeville, the PAC was in disarray. The ANC called a national one-day strike on March 29, 1960 and ordered massive burning of passes. The South African regime, alarmed by the powerful wave of mass action by our people, declared the African National Congress illegal. The ANC refused to accept the order and decided to continue the struggle as an underground and illegal organisation. The ANC was not the only organisation to suffer this silencing. Ten years previously, the Communist Party of South Africa was banned following the passing of the 1950 Suppression of Communism Act. But in 1960 it announced its functioning as the South African Communist Party, which had been reconstituted, operating underground since 1953. On March 30, 1960, the regime declared a State of Emergency and arrested over 2,000 people. The following March saw the convening of the All-in African Conference, attended by 1,400 delegates, under the leadership of Nelson Mandela. It called for a national convention to decide a new constitution.

By May 31, 1961 the country was placed on a war footing to smash the nationwide strikes called to protest against the establishment of the so-called Republic of South Africa. On June 26, 1961 Mandela declared the next stage of the struggle was to be one of non-collaboration and stated that he would remain underground to lead it. He would continue to act as the spokesman for the National Action Council.

The regime unleashed a reign of terror and turned South Africa into an armed camp. New methods of struggle had to be found.

Armed Struggle and Morogoro: Forward into the 1970s and 1980s

In 1960, under conditions of a state of emergency and a harsh crackdown on the ANC, a number of our leaders were sent abroad to establish an external mission under the then Deputy President-General of the ANC, Oliver Tambo. Faced with the regime's reign of terror and the closing of all avenues of legal protest and organisation, the ANC decided to form an army of liberation. In 1961 the ANC, together with the South African Communist Party, formed Umkhonto weSizwe (MK), a people's army, with Nelson Mandela as the first Commander-in-Chief. Large numbers of cadres left the country for military training.

On December 16th, 1961 organised acts of sabotage took place throughout the country, marking the emergence of MK - the Spear of the Nation, the armed wing of the ANC. A leaflet issued by the High Command of Umkhonto stated in part that: 'Umkhonto weSizwe will be at the front line of the people's defence. It will be the fighting arm of the people against the government and its policies of race oppression. It will be the striking force of the people for liberty, for rights and for their final liberation …

In these actions, we are working in the best interests of all the people of this country – black, brown and white – whose future happiness and well-being cannot be attained without the overthrow of the Nationalist Government, the abolition of white supremacy and the winning of liberty, democracy and full national rights and equality for all the people of this country.'

The violence of the regime was now to be met by the revolutionary violence of the people. To prepare effectively for this new stage of our struggle, Nelson Mandela illegally left the country and travelled extensively in Africa and Europe. He returned to South Africa in July 1962, and worked underground until his arrest in August of the same year. He was sentenced, at that time, to five years' imprisonment.

The early actions of MK were based mainly on sabotage attacks against state installations, and were initially very successful. However, on July 11, 1963, our underground movement suffered a serious setback with the capture of some of our leaders at Rivonia. The Rivonia trialists – Mandela, Mbeki, Sisulu, Goldberg, Kathrada, Mhlaba, Mlangeni and Motsoaledi – were sentenced to life imprisonment. The state had demanded the death penalty, and it was only the massive international campaign on their behalf, inspired by their courageous and uncompromising stand, which saved their lives.

Despite such setbacks, the struggle continued. 1967 saw the Lutuli Combat Detachment comprising ZAPU and ANC guerrillas cross the Zambezi into Rhodesia at the start of the Wankie and Sipolilo battles, which lasted until late 1968.

In May 1969 a seven-day ANC Consultative Conference took place in Morogoro, Tanzania. The main aim was to bring about a qualitative change in the organisational content of our movement in keeping with the new situation – namely a Revolutionary People's War. The pace for the 1970s was set by the historic Morogoro Conference, where the strategy and tactics that would guide our movement in the pursuit of our cherished goal – total liberation – were adopted. Thus by the early 1970s the strength of the people was manifested in the extensive strike waves, the militancy of the youth and students, and the oppressed people's clear identification with the armed struggle being waged – and won – in neighbouring Angola and Mozambique. The whole world reverberated with the barbarity of racist aggression in the 1976 nationwide uprisings which left more than a thousand of our youth dead, but marked a new stage in our struggle, raising mass resistance on all fronts to unprecedented heights.

The Seventies also saw the situation in the whole of Southern Africa change dramatically. The political and military defeat of Portuguese colonialism in Africa significantly altered the balance of power in favour of the revolutionary forces. There emerged people's power in Mozambique and Angola. These countries evolved new kinds of state power, new types of social and property relations, and therefore sharpened the confrontation between the forces of progress and those of colonial and racist reaction in Southern Africa. Similarly, the liberation of Zimbabwe was to be of great significance to our struggle.

Of crucial importance, too, will be the victory of the people of Namibia under the leadership of SWAPO.

South Africa remains the last bastion of colonialism and racism on the African continent. The apartheid regime now faces an all-round offensive in the spirit of the ANC's rallying call for united action.

Armed Struggle Complements People's Struggle
The struggle of the people of South Africa consists of four inter-linked elements – the vanguard role of the underground structures of the ANC; the united mass political action of the people; the international campaign to isolate the Pretoria regime; and the armed struggle, spearheaded by our people's army, Umkhonto weSizwe.

Our struggle embraces a variety of methods and tactics, the different forms of struggle complementing and strengthening each other. We are freedom fighters set out on the road to build a new society. We are waging a political struggle with arms in hand. We have always defined the enemy in terms of a system of domination, and not as a people or race. Our war efforts are directed at the state machinery, not at civilian targets.

The liberation war we are engaged in is often referred to as people's war, a war which actively involves all the people of South Africa, a war where all the oppressed people are involved in battle against the oppressor, a war in which men and women, young and old, are active fighters.

We hold the firm view that there can be no separation between the military and political leaderships. The army is, and must remain, the instrument of the political movement. Revolutionary armed struggle is political struggle by means which include the use of military force, and the victory we strive for has as its aim the seizure of power by the people led by their political vanguard, the ANC.

MK has to fulfil two main elements in our strategy. It must raise the level of mass action inside the country. This means that the army should reinforce the people's struggles. Such struggles are taking place along a very wide front. Our army has to step up its operations in order to imbue the masses with confidence in their ability to fight back. Building a people's army to fight a people's war means that our movement and our army must create and consolidate the conditions for the existence, survival, growth and expansion of our army among the people. These conditions should be so created that no matter how hard the enemy tries to uproot us, our existence and our capacity to attack over a large area increase.

Today, the people of South Africa are on the march. Our demand is for people's power. Apartheid cannot be reformed. It must be destroyed, root and branch. In his January 8th, 1985 address to the nation, President Tambo said: 'Through struggle and sacrifice we have planted the seeds of people's war in our country, that is, a war waged by the people against the white minority regime. One of our central tasks in the coming period is to transform the potential we have created into the reality of people's war. Guided by that perspective, we must build up the mass combat forces that are training themselves in mass political action for sharper battles and for the forcible overthrow of the racist regime. The mass combat forces that are and have been engaged in the popular offensive, these death-defying patriots, must now become part of Umkhonto weSizwe, the vital cutting edge of our onslaught. It is in this way that we will ensure that the people's army deepens its roots and grows inextricably among the popular masses. It is in this way that we will ensure that it grows in size, in the spread and quality of its operations and in the weight of every blow it delivers.'

Pretoria's response to the mass upsurge of our people has been to impose martial law, blanket press and media censorship, and the granting of unlimited licence to kill to the racist soldiers, police and death squads. Thousands of our people are paying the supreme sacrifice for liberty – laying down their lives in the bitter war that is raging. Pretoria is able to arm, deploy and finance its massive military machine because of the economic, political and diplomatic support granted by Western governments, in particular the United Kingdom and the USA.

Forward to People's Power!
In the decade of the Eighties what does an all-round offensive within South Africa mean? The ANC has decided to engage the enemy on all fronts – political struggle, trade union activity, mass women's campaigns, school boycotts, struggle on the religious front, peasant revolts and military actions. Umkhonto weSizwe always attempts to apply military theory to our concrete conditions.

We are aware that there is no victory possible without mass participation, that is to say active and conscious involvement of the oppressed black masses. No group of revolutionaries acting on their own, however gallant, disciplined and self-sacrificing they may be, can succeed in overthrowing the fascist regime.

The main content of the present stage of the South African revolution is the national liberation of the largest and most oppressed group – the African people. This strategic aim must govern every aspect of the conduct of our struggle, whether it be the formulation of policy or the creation of structures. Among other things, it demands in the first place the maximum mobilisation of the African people as a dispossessed and racially oppressed national majority. This is the mainspring and it must not be weakened. There can be no ambiguity on the question of the primary role of the most oppressed African masses. But the African, although subject to the most intense social oppression and exploitation, is not the only oppressed national group in South Africa.

The Coloured and Indian communities suffer from varying forms of humiliation, discrimination and oppression. They are part of the oppressed black base upon which is built white privilege, constituting an integral part of the forces ranged against white supremacy.

The ANC fights not only against the oppression of the black people by the white, but also for the establishment of a united South African nation, not based on race, tribe or creed. The struggle of the ANC for one nation embodies the aspirations of those democratic and peace-seeking white people who are prepared to throw their lives into the struggle with the oppressed majority in the cause of a non-racial, national identity.

Unity in action among all the oppressed groups is fundamental to the advance of our liberation struggle. Historically, all these communities have played a most important part in the intensification of our struggle for freedom. The jails in South Africa are witness to the large-scale participation by Indian, Coloured and White comrades at every level of our revolutionary struggle.

The Second National Consultative Conference, June 1985
The ANC held its Second National Consultative Conference at Kabwe, Zambia, on June 16 to 23, 1985. It was a representative Conference of 250 democratically elected delegates representing all sections of our movement: the workers, the women, youth, media workers, soldiers – everybody.

For seven days our people discussed issues connected with our struggle, our strategy and tactics, our strengths and weaknesses. The mood and spirit of Conference was that of comradeship and frankness. This Conference, which took place on the Ninth Anniversary of the Commemoration of the Soweto Uprising, also endorsed the principles enshrined in the Freedom Charter, whose 30th anniversary we commemorated on June 26, 1985. It reaffirmed the decisions of the 1969 Morogoro Conference and re-endorsed the anti-imperialist positions of the ANC.

Indeed, this Conference has been described as a Council of War precisely because it charted the way forward to the intensification of the armed struggle. It decided that the distinction between 'hard' and 'soft' targets should disappear. This was not a new idea. It had been discussed (like all other issues) in the numerous, continual regional pre-Conference discussions which involved everybody, including all those who were not elected as delegates to the Conference.

The question of intensifying armed struggle poses new challenges for, and responsibilities on, the ANC and on the international community which – by the look of things and the nature of the violence of the enemy – is going to be more involved in that struggle for liberation.

One of these questions is the question of sanctions, comprehensive sanctions. In 1977 the UN called for sanctions. We are far from suggesting that sanctions will bring apartheid to its knees. All we are saying is that sanctions will weaken apartheid and that will enable us to fight against a weakened enemy. This will minimise the loss of lives, shorten the duration of our struggle and lessen bloodshed. This will be a contribution to our struggle and an act of solidarity with our people.

Another important decision, taken at the Conference, was the question of opening ranks at all levels inside and outside the country, to all South Africans who have come to join the ANC. Conference felt that the ANC composition at all levels should reflect the South African society – people who are sacrificing and fighting for the national liberation of the blacks, especially the Africans, and social emancipation of both the blacks and whites.

Conference also adopted a new Constitution and a Code of Conduct. A new National Executive Committee was elected, and it was charged with the task of implementing Conference resolutions and leading the ANC in the coming battles.

As the ANC observes the 75th anniversary of its formation, it is conscious of the bitter struggle that lies ahead for our people. It is also conscious of the ever-growing solidarity, support and strength of the international democratic community, which has set itself against colonialism, apartheid, racism and fascism. The ANC has, for these 75 years, remained faithful to the cause of freedom. It leads the struggle for the emancipation of all oppressed and exploited black people. It stands for a new order in South Africa where racism shall be a thing of the past and human dignity and equality shall prevail in the life of the country. But before that new order is born many lives will be lost. We are prepared to meet the challenge.

Advance to People's Power!

The Path to Power: Programme of the South African Communist Party

(Adopted by a conference of the South African Communist Party, 1990)

Colonialism of a Special Type

South Africa has a developed capitalist economy. In our country, and wherever it exists, the capitalist mode of production has the same basic characteristics. It is an exploitative system based on the extraction of surplus value from wage labour. But the universal features of capitalism occur within concrete societies, each with its own specific balance of class forces and particular economic, political and ideological features. In different capitalist countries the bourgeoisie exerts its class rule through different kinds of domination, ranging from bourgeois democracy to fascism.

Like many earlier oppressor classes, the bourgeoisie also exerts its class rule across frontiers. In the imperialist epoch, capitalism has extensively developed its own variants of colonial, semi-colonial and neo-colonial rule, underpinning the brutal super-exploitation of working people in the dominated societies.

Within South Africa, bourgeois domination and capitalist relations of production, which emerged within the context of colonialism, have been developed and maintained since 1910 through a specific variant of bourgeois rule – colonialism of a special type. It is a variant of capitalist rule in which the essential features of colonial domination in the imperialist epoch are maintained and even intensified. But there is one specific peculiarity: in South Africa the colonial ruling class with its white support base on the one hand, and the oppressed colonial majority on the other, are located within a single country.

On the one hand, white South Africans enjoy political power, racial privileges and the lion's share of the country's wealth. On the other hand, the overwhelming black majority of our country are subjected to extreme national oppression, poverty, super-exploitation, complete denial of basic human rights, and political domination.

There are significant class differences within both the white colonial bloc and the oppressed black majority. However, the effect of colonialism of a special type is that all white classes benefit, albeit unequally and in different ways, from the internal colonial structure. Conversely, all black classes suffer national oppression, in varying degrees and in different ways. The social and economic features of our country are directly related to its colonial history.

The Origins of Colonialism of a Special Type
From the time of the first white settlement, established by the Dutch East India Company over 300 years ago, the pattern was set for the ruthless exploitation of the black people of our country, the seizure of their lands and the enforced harnessing of their labour power. The Dutch made war on the Khoi people of the Cape, whom they contemptuously called 'Hottentots', and rejected their appeals for peace and friendship. The San people, the so-called 'Bushmen', were all but exterminated. Slaves were imported from Malaya and elsewhere. White settlers gradually penetrated into the interior. They drove the indigenous people from the best farm lands and seized their cattle. They subdued them by armed conquest and forced them into their service – at first through direct slavery, later through a harsh system of pass laws and taxation.

Colonialist propaganda has emphasised the negative features of traditional African society: the relatively low development of productive techniques, the illiteracy, inter-tribal conflicts and wars, superstitions and poverty. It is true that such features existed in traditional African society just as they did among all peoples at the period of early communal economies. But hostile propaganda has presented a distorted image. Prior to colonial conquest, the indigenous peoples had developed their own independent culture and civilisation. They mined and smelted iron, copper and other metals and fashioned them into useful implements. They had developed a number of handicrafts. Their system of extensive agriculture and livestock breeding was well-suited to the type of country and the tools at their disposal. Their system of government, though simple, was essentially democratic and popular in character. Private property in land was unknown, and food and shelter were freely shared, even with strangers.

But when the colonists began their ceaseless acts of armed aggression, the African people resisted bravely to defend their cattle and their land from robbery and their people from enslavement. They took up the spear against the bullets of the invader with his horses and wagons. But, tribal society and a rural economy could not provide the material basis for successful warfare against an enemy with a more advanced economy and more destructive weapons. Disunity among the various African peoples prevented the development of a common front of resistance. Time and again in their wars of conquest against African peoples, the colonisers were able to play off one community against another and to enrol African auxiliaries.

In the last quarter of the 19th century, the development of capitalist industrial mining on the Kimberley diamond fields and on the goldfields of the Witwatersrand had profound and far-reaching consequences. British and European finance houses exported vast sums of investment capital to South Africa. To seize complete control over the goldfields, British imperialism waged a successful war against the Boers. The gold mining companies were now the real rulers of the country. They had only one interest in the Africans – to force them into labour on the mines at minimum rates of pay. The mine bosses found the harsh colonial policy of the Boer Republics admirably suited to this purpose. The poll tax and pass systems were intensified. Dispossession of Africans from the land was speeded up. Not a single move was made to introduce into the northern colonies even the minimum citizenship rights which had been conceded to some blacks in the Cape. In the oppression, dispossession and exploitation of blacks, British imperialism and Afrikaner nationalism found common ground. This was the basis for the establishment of the Union of South Africa in 1910.

In that year South Africa was established as a political entity with a centralised state power. This established the political conditions for the construction and development of a national capitalist economy and the national institutions of bourgeois political domination. The economic power and political influence of British imperialism were not abolished with the establishment of the Union of South Africa in 1910. They were now exercised indirectly through the political structures of the new state monopolised by the descendants of European settlers. These new national structures were based on the effects of centuries of colonial conquest and land dispossession. They reproduced, in changed forms, the essential features of colonial domination that had existed before the Union of South Africa.

The new Union of South Africa perpetuated the inferior colonial status of Africans who were recognised only as the objects of administration, without any citizenship rights. In elected bodies, as well as in public administration, whites occupied all positions of authority, skill and competence. Africans occupied only subordinate, unskilled positions without any authority over whites.

The form of domination developed by the Union of South Africa also perpetuated the racialised economic structures of the pre-Union period. There was a white monopoly of capitalist means of mining, industrial and agricultural production and of distribution. There was also a virtual white monopoly of skilled and supervisory jobs in the division of labour. Whites had privileged access to trading and petty commodity production. The 1913 Land Act, confining land ownership for the African majority to a tiny arid proportion of the country, legally entrenched and intensified the results of centuries of colonial land dispossession.

The South African capitalist state did not emerge as a result of an internal popular anti-feudal revolution. It was imposed from above and from without. From its birth through to the present, South African capitalism has depended heavily on the imperialist centres. Capital from Europe financed the opening of the mines. It was the colonial state that provided the resources to build the basic infrastructure – railways, roads, harbours, posts and telegraphs. It was an imperial army of occupation that created the conditions for political unification. And it was within a colonial setting that the emerging South African capitalist class entrenched and extended the racially exclusive system to increase its opportunities for profit. The racial division of labour, the battery of racist laws and political exclusiveness guaranteed this. From these origins a pattern of domination, which arose in the period of external colonialism, was carried over into the newly-formed Union of South Africa. From its origins to the present, this form of domination has been maintained under changing conditions and by varying mechanisms. In all essential respects, however, the colonial status of the black majority has remained in place. Therefore we characterise our society as colonialism of a special type.

The Class and Social Structure of Colonialism of a Special Type
Since 1910 South African capitalism has developed enormously. From a typical extractive, colonial economy, whose core was gold mining based on cheap migrant labour and agriculture based on cheap forced labour, South Africa is now a relatively advanced capitalist society with the most developed infrastructure on the African continent. Today monopoly capital dominates every single sector of the South African economy. The development of capitalist forces of production has led to the extensive growth of a modern proletariat. Numerically, the working class, of which the core is a large industrial proletariat, is by far the largest class in our society. Even in the South African countryside, the agrarian working class, and migrant workers and their families, constitute the great majority of

the population. Bourgeois class domination is, however, still based on the colonial oppression of the black and, in particular, African majority.

The special colonial domination is based on an alliance of white classes and strata. The maintenance of this system, producing as it does increasing instability, violence and a growing isolation from the international community, is not in the overall long-term interests of the majority of South Africans, black or white. However, in the short term, all white classes and strata benefit from the oppression of the black majority.

Within the white colonial bloc, it is the bourgeoisie and in particular monopoly capital that is the leading class force. In every sector of the economy – mining, manufacturing, finance, and increasingly even in agriculture and services – monopoly capital is now overwhelmingly dominant. Enormous power is wielded by a handful of companies controlling vast economic empires. By the mid-1980s, 2.7 per cent of enterprises controlled over 50 per cent of our country's total turnover; 6.3 per cent of all enterprises employed over half of the national workforce; and a mere 6 per cent had 85 per cent of all fixed assets. Monopoly concentration of capital is a universal trend within capitalism – but the level of concentration in South Africa is virtually unprecedented. And the trend to ever greater concentration is increasing each year. By 1987, four companies (Anglo American, Sanlam, SA Mutual and Rembrandt) alone controlled 80 per cent of all shares on the Johannesburg Stock Exchange. Of these companies, Anglo American alone controlled 55 per cent.

Over the last decades Afrikaner-controlled monopoly conglomerates have developed, and their interests have interlocked and merged with those of the older monopolies traditionally controlled by English-speaking whites. A decisive role in the capitalist economy is also played by the state. State corporations in some of the key sectors – armaments, energy and transport – play a central role in propping up the entire capitalist economy. With all of these developments, the level of collusion between the state and private monopoly capital, and between English and Afrikaans big business, has increased substantially on the economic and political fronts.

Faced with a deepening crisis and the prospect of a national democratic revolution, these monopoly interests are now calling for some restructuring of race domination. At the heart of the various political arrangements they are advocating is an attempt to keep South Africa safe for monopoly capitalism. Under the guise of protecting 'group rights', they seek to perpetuate their monopoly control over the wealth of our country. In fact, their stranglehold over the great bulk of our country's productive land, machinery and capital is the accumulated result of more than a century of colonial dispossession, oppression and exploitation of the majority. There can be no true liberation from colonial oppression in our country without transforming this fundamental economic legacy.

Although monopoly capitalism has now become dominant in every sector, there are also non-monopoly capitalists. In particular, there is still a large number of non-monopoly white farms. This is the most backward sector of the capitalist economy. The national farming debt in 1986 exceeded the gross agricultural income, and it was ten times the sum of annual profits to farming capitalists. A large number of white-owned capitalist farms are only able to survive as a result of the most barbaric oppression and exploitation of their black labourers, and extensive government loans and other forms of protection.

Among the white middle strata, particularly from the Afrikaans-speaking community, large numbers are now integrated into the state bureaucracy. They are highly dependent for their positions on having in power a political organisation committed to a strong, racially privileged state bureaucracy. Other sectors of the white middle strata, professionals and particularly the intelligentsia, often feel least threatened among the white community by the prospect of a non-racial future. It is necessary to detach significant numbers of these sectors from an unquestioning support for white minority rule, and win them over to the struggle for national democracy.

The two million economically active whites mostly hold clerical, supervisory, administrative and technical positions. In many ways white wage-earners constitute a classical 'labour aristocracy'. Although their long-term interests lie in making common cause with their black working class brothers and sisters, decades of racial privilege have brought them real material gains. These have instilled an extremely reactionary outlook within a significant proportion of white workers. It is from this stratum that the ultra-rightwing, neo-fascist parties receive their major support. With the deepening crisis of South African capitalism, and with the growing collusion between the state and the monopolies, the economic situation of white workers has deteriorated. Their trade unions, which have for a long time been in deep collusion with management, are now proving less and less effective in defending the interests of their members. While organising white workers into progressive trade unions, and winning them away from racism is not an easy task in the present situation, every endeavour must be made in this direction.

The alliance of white classes and strata is not without contradictions and counter-tendencies. Although historically all white classes and strata have united around the system of white minority rule, the different interests that draw them together in this alliance are not static. Monopoly capitalism now tends to secure its labour from a more stable, better qualified and higher consuming workforce. From the perspective of monopoly capital these economic changes require a political and economic restructuring of colonialism of a special type. This restructuring is resisted by sections of the white working class and petty bourgeoisie, and by some of the non-monopoly capitalists in agriculture and manufacture.

Above all, the growing revolutionary challenge, and increased international isolation are now dramatically weakening the cement uniting the white bloc. Today, the white community is more confused, more divided and more demoralised than in many decades. While certain sectors are in favour of reform to ward off revolution, others are increasingly swept into the ranks of the ultra-right and various neo-fascist groupings that propagate the most rabid race hatred. Generally speaking, these differences and conflicts within the white bloc are not centred around the abolition of colonial domination of the majority, but around how best to maintain stability and privilege.

However, with the deepening political and economic crisis, increasing numbers of whites are beginning to doubt whether apartheid is in their own long-term interests, and whether it can ever bring them peace and security. White domination means more and more police and military expenditure to burden the taxpayer, diverting resources from useful production. It means enforced conscription of white males into the apartheid armies, to serve and even die for an unjust cause. It means more and more dictatorial police-state measures, and the extinguishing of civil liberties for whites themselves. It means a South Africa despised and shunned by the whole world, subjected to economic, sports and cultural isolation. It means a future of uncertainty and fear.

There are now many possibilities for detaching significant sectors of whites from at least an unquestioned faith in white minority rule. Indeed, increasing numbers of whites are now espousing an anti-apartheid position, joining the broad front of forces aligned against the Pretoria regime. There is also a long tradition within South Africa, pioneered in the 1920s by our Party, of whites renouncing colonial privileges and standing shoulder to shoulder with their black brothers and sisters in the revolutionary struggle for a united, non-racial and democratic South Africa. One of the features of the struggles of the 1980s has been the still small but growing number of whites actively making this fuller, revolutionary commitment.

Within the colonially oppressed black majority, the six-million-strong working class is by far the largest and most significant class force. Neither the profound economic changes that have occurred in South Africa, nor the restructuring that monopoly advocates, amount to an abolition of the special colonial oppression of the black working class. Despite the changes, black workers still occupy the less skilled and lower paid jobs. Inferior education, the unequal provision of resources and the denial of political rights all continue to reproduce a racially divided, colonial-type workforce. The system of national oppression has guaranteed a low paid black labour force, while allowing for changes in size and technical understanding. Until the 1960s there were relatively few black clerical workers and still fewer black employees who were formally described as skilled, semi-skilled, or supervisors, foremen and workers in service capacities.

By the beginning of the 1970s the present shape of the working class had been established. A more literate black workforce entered occupations previously dominated by whites, although the apartheid educational system still limits the vast majority of black people to low levels of education. Colonial oppression of the black proletariat has been retained through the changes. Whites work alongside blacks who, at a lower wage and with a lower status, increase their capacity to run a modern industry. Job descriptions are redefined, as blacks move into them at wages only a fraction of those paid to whites.

Oppressed by the special colonial form of bourgeois domination in South Africa and super-exploited, black workers stand to gain the most from the immediate abolition of national oppression. It is also black workers whose longer-term interests are for the complete and final eradication of all forms of oppression and exploitation in our country. The South African industrial proletariat, concentrated in the large urban complexes, has emerged as the most organised and powerful mass revolutionary contingent in our country. Its proletariat class consciousness has been developed and deepened by decades of militant trade unionism. This tradition is today embodied in the South African Congress of Trade Unions (SACTU) and in the giant federation, the Congress of South African Trade Union (COSATU). It is a working class that has responded in its millions to calls for national stayaways, shutting down the mines, factories, shops, and bringing the capitalist economy to a grinding halt for days at a time. It is a working class from among whom increasingly large numbers are actively rallying to the Marxist-Leninist positions of the SACP, openly espousing the perspectives of socialism. Within our own country this proletariat is gathering its forces to fulfil the historical role predicted over one hundred years ago by Marx and Engels for the working class movement on a world scale. Assembled in millions within the very heartland of an advanced capitalist economy, and leading the struggle against national oppression, the South African working class is poised to be the gravedigger of capitalist exploitation itself.

Large-scale and chronic unemployment has now become a central feature of South Africa's capitalist economy. Some 300 000 new job-seekers enter the labour market each year, while a stagnating economy is only able to absorb an extremely small proportion. Official figures deliberately underestimate the number of unemployed Africans by many millions. The most reliable estimates in the late 1980s were between six and eight million unemployed Africans. Other groups, in particular the Coloured people, have been seriously affected by unemployment. This enormous wastage of the human wealth and potential of our country is characteristic both of colonial oppression and of capitalism, a system based on private profits and not on social needs.

Closely allied to the South African industrial proletariat are the oppressed rural masses. There are some 1.3 million black workers on white-owned farms. Conditions for black workers on these farms are invariably bad. They are often treated with brutality, wages are extremely low, and they are not covered by labour laws in effect in other sectors of the economy. Malnutrition is common among black children on white farms, and many children are themselves also forced to work to supplement their family income.

The vast majority of about thirteen and a half million people in the bantustans are landless and without livestock or agricultural implements. While landlessness is acute, the land that is available to African peasants tends to be both overgrazed and barren. Among households with some land it is virtually only those that receive remittances from family members at regular intervals, in the form of wages or pensions, who are able to engage in any agricultural production beyond a garden plot.

The apartheid regime has tried to develop a stratum of middle peasants, so called '*bona fide* farmers', in the bantustans. This strategy has generally failed because patronage and corruption have led to resources for development and the little effective farming land available falling into the hands of bantustan civil servants, and bantustan government ministers in particular. These collaborative strata do not engage in small-scale farming, but set themselves up in commercial agricultural enterprises, often in joint ventures as junior partners to white farmers and commercial interests.

Within the economy of apartheid colonialism the bantustans serve as suppliers of cheap labour and as dumping grounds for the unemployed, the aged and the sick. Apart from migrant labourers and 'commuters', who are forced to travel many hours from dormitory townships, the vast majority of people in the bantustans are workers, families, unemployed workers and poor peasants. They are linked in many ways, direct and indirect, to the South African working class in their outlook and in their objective interests. Their demands are for land, for the right to settle where they choose, for secure and rewarding work, and for an end to the corruption and repressive actions of the bantustan authorities. In their struggle to achieve these demands, the rural masses are the major social ally of the working class in the broad struggle for national liberation, and the longer-term struggle for the socialist transformation of our country.

Among the oppressed black majority of our country there is a fairly small but growing and relatively significant range of middle strata, made up of a commercial petty bourgeoisie, and various professional categories. These middle strata suffer, with their fellow black, under the brutal and humiliating system of colonialism. The majority of these middle strata, in terms of their living conditions, their social origin and their political aspirations are closely linked to the oppressed black proletariat. Despite the regime's attempts to woo these black middle strata, hoping to transform them into a buffer between the masses and the white colonial bloc, the overwhelming majority have rejected these ploys. Indeed, the active participation of black middle strata within the national democratic movement has been an important feature of our revolutionary struggle. This is not to say that there are no other, contradictory tendencies among sections of the black middle strata. The apartheid regime has not abandoned its attempts to win them over, and their continued allegiance to the people's cause requires active and on-going work.

There is also a very small but emerging black bourgeoisie in South Africa. At present it controls means of production that are responsible for less than two per cent of our country's Gross National Product. One fraction of this emergent black bourgeoisie is closely associated with the various apartheid collaborative structures – like bantustan administrations, community councils, management committees, and the tricameral parliament. Using its control of subordinate bureaucratic apparatuses and by patronage and corruption it accumulates some capital resources. Because of its dependency on these apartheid structures, this fraction tends to be extremely reactionary, aligning itself to the colonial ruling bloc. However, its subordinate status and its very dependence upon the ruling bloc are sometimes the source of resentments and secondary contradictions which can be exploited by the liberation movement.

Other emergent fractions of the black bourgeoisie are developing out of petty bourgeois commercial activities, and also through the professional and managerial routes. Though growing in numbers, their hopes of entrepreneurial operations remain blocked by the economic stranglehold of the monopolies and by racial oppression. These strata can be won over into the broad national liberation movement.

The black majority includes two sizeable groups, the Coloured and Indian peoples. They share with the African majority the bitter suffering and humiliation of racial oppression. There have been considerable social changes over the last 30 years within these communities, with a growing process of class differentiation. The apartheid regime has used these changes, in particular the growing affluence of some of their upper strata, to intensify its attempts to win active collaboration from these communities. These attempts by the regime have failed dismally, and the Coloured and Indian people in their majority have soundly rejected and isolated the few collaborators drawn from their midst.

The Coloured community, numbering some three million, is predominantly working class in character. This community is subjected to many forms of racial discrimination, reflected in low standards of living, education, housing, nutrition and health. The changes in the national economy, with increased capital investment in the manufacturing sector in the 1970s, led to a significant growth in the number of Coloured workers in white-collar and skilled jobs, and a declining relative share of Coloured employment in the lower manual and skilled occupations.

Despite these advances the average Coloured monthly wage was still only 35 per cent of the average white earnings in 1986. Another significant change in the last decades has been the movement of Coloured women out of domestic service and agriculture into semi-skilled manufacturing, sales and clerical work. Coloured farm labourers still work and live under wretched conditions. The increased mechanisation of agriculture has resulted in over 100 000 Coloured farm workers losing their jobs since 1960. They and their families have swelled the ranks of the unemployed in the urban areas.

Although the Coloured community has always suffered racial oppression, in the first half of this century it occupied a privileged position in relation to Africans. The white ruling group extended various concessions – such as a qualified franchise, trade union rights and property rights – in order to prevent the emergence of a united front of oppressed blacks against white colonialism. This policy was not without success. However, with the accession of the National Party to power in 1948, many of these relative privileges were removed. In the late 1950s and 1960s the Coloured community was subjected to brutal, mass forced removals under the Group Areas Act.

In the 1980s the regime's attempts to incorporate Coloured people within the tricameral parliament have failed miserably. Increasing numbers of Coloured people have now come to align themselves unambivalently with the broader struggle of the African majority. One of the most significant developments in the 1980s has been the militant, mass participation of the Coloured community in the national democratic struggle.

The Indian community, nearly one million strong, originates mainly from the indentured labourers who came to work in the Natal sugar fields a century and a half ago. From the earliest times all sorts of degrading and discriminatory restrictions have been placed on South African Indians, restrictions which they have resisted in many historic struggles. Today there is a substantial number of Indian industrial workers. Like their fellow African workers they face appalling problems of unemployment and overcrowding in slum conditions. There is also a significant stratum of Indian merchants, factory owners and small shopkeepers. Indian business people, and all sections of the community, are subjected to numerous disabilities, especially relating to land and property ownership and economic opportunities. Until recently they were not allowed to move from one province to another without special permits. The apartheid regime has applied the Group Areas Act with particular ferocity against the Indian communities, uprooting them from their homes and livelihoods.

On the other hand, the Indian community in general has advanced economically and socially much more rapidly than other oppressed communities. There has been a significant increase in the number of Indian people in professional, managerial and supervisory positions in the last twenty years. In addition, the rigid application of the Group Areas Act for over 25 years, which has seen the enforced separation of Indian and African communities, has also had a political and cultural impact. Any negative tendencies resulting from these developments present special challenges to the national liberation struggle in the task of forging the broadest unity of action of the oppressed, while recognising real cultural and other differences. In accomplishing this task it is necessary to build upon the long traditions within the Indian community of united struggle with the African peoples. In the 1970s and 1980s these traditions have been actively reasserted through the Natal and Transvaal Indian Congresses.

Work amongst the Indian people has to take into account the class differentiation within this community. While there has been some economic advance within this community, it has not been evenly spread. The majority of the economically active Indian people in our country are exploited wage labourers, toiling shoulder to shoulder with African workers. In particular there is a large concentration of Indian workers in the garment industry, many of them working in appalling sweat-shop conditions. Deepening the class consciousness of Indian workers, and strengthening their class unity with the majority of workers, is a priority task.

The Crisis of Colonialism of a Special Type

Today, colonialism of a special type is in deep crisis. The crisis is the result of a combination of factors – the economic impasse of South African capitalism, international isolation, divisions in the ruling bloc, and, above all, the broad revolutionary struggle. The present crisis is more generalised, deep-rooted and enduring than those of the 1940s and the early 1960s.

The present crisis is intimately linked to the economic changes of the previous period, and to their interaction with the central features of colonialism of a special type. The development of an advanced capital economy, with its needs for a relatively settled and skilled workforce and an expanding market, has been distorted by apartheid colonialism.

On the economic front the crisis has many features: a severe shortage of skills as a result of the cultural and educational oppression of the majority, the large-scale under-utilisation of productive capacity, an increasing reluctance of capitalists to invest in fixed capital, and massive organic unemployment.

The capitalist economy is now stagnating, while the apartheid state itself sinks deeper into financial crisis. The state, with its large-scale investment in strategic industries and basic infrastructure, has in the past been a moving force for capitalist development. But it is now contributing directly to the overall crisis of the economy. Relying increasingly for its survival on naked repression and upon regional military adventures, the apartheid regime is squandering vast sums on its repressive machinery. In addition, the racial institutions of political control have spawned a huge state bureaucracy. There are numerous racially separate administration departments, bantustan apparatuses, and the tricameral parliament. These are a heavy drain on the regime's finances. The resulting fiscal crisis has, in turn, fuelled inflation and provoked severe difficulties in the repayment of foreign loans.

The ruling bloc's strategic objective of securing a manufacturing-led economic boom, to pull the economy out of its stagnation, has not materialised. The oppression of the black majority, with low wages and massive unemployment, has resulted in a very restricted home market. On the other hand, attempts to compete on international markets with South African manufactures have also failed to live up to the regime's expectations. South Africa's manufactured goods are, generally, not competitive on world markets. The attempts to compete have resulted simply in a greater dependence on foreign markets for imported machinery and high technology. The southern African market is more accessible to South African manufacturers, but the military and economic destabilisation of our neighbouring countries impoverishes the whole region, thus restricting its market potential.

But, above all, the crisis of apartheid colonialism is a political crisis. The ruling class and its political representatives realise that it is impossible to continue ruling in the old way. Amongst their major strategies is the attempt to secure black participation and collaboration in a subordinate form of civil government. At the political level the essence of the regime's crisis is precisely the failure of this strategy. As long as significant black participation is withheld, the regime's crisis will continue to fester and, in one form or another, upsurge and revolt will continue with increasing intensity and frequency.

Every racist constitutional and 'reform' initiative, designed to divert the revolutionary pressures, has landed on the rocks. Such initiatives have usually led to an increased tempo of struggle. The forced retreat from the concept that the bantustans would provide the 'final solution', and the self-evident ineffectiveness of the tricameral parliament, are amongst the most significant of these failures. The attempt to win black participation in the setting up of local ghetto councils – as a step towards the so-called 'Great Indaba' – has failed ignominiously.

The reform failures, the absence of any viable alternative political strategy, growing international isolation, the changing relation between racism and profit in important sectors, a bleeding economy and, above all, the unrelenting people's resistance, have led to significant splits and divisions at the top. Within the dominant race group the centuries-old confidence and belief in the eternal survival of white hegemony has begun to evaporate, leading to a significant shift in the traditional context of white politics.

The ideological cement which had for so long bonded the mainstream white politics together, has crumbled considerably and there is no substitute to fill the gaps. Afrikaner nationalism – the tribal pillar of white political power in the post-war period – is developing significant cracks. Its middle strata leaders had successfully exploited Afrikaner nationalism to win political office and with it access to the upper echelons of the economy. The embrace between English and Afrikaner capital is leading to a noticeable shift away from the purely ethnic divide within the white bloc.

The regime is less and less able to meet the expectations either of the capitalist class it represents or the mass of white workers who have, for over half a century, acted as its historic political support base. Mounting international pressures are having a serious effect on the economy and could reach a point which can no longer be tolerated by the capitalist class as a whole. The search for a way out of the crisis is also leading to increased vacillation and divisions within the power bloc.

The deep-rooted crisis and conflict in South Africa cannot be resolved within the confines of the apartheid colonial system. Nor can they be resolved by the National Party regime or any other section of the ruling class. The basic aims of all sections of the ruling class revolve around maintaining the essence of the system of oppression, and monopoly control over the wealth of South Africa. Our struggle is not, and cannot be, merely for civil rights within the framework of the existing system. This system is rooted in the special colonial subjugation of the majority of the South African people and the denial of their basic rights.

Part Three

Preparing to Govern

The Reconstruction & Development Programme: Introduction
(Published by the ANC, 1994)

1.1 What Is the Reconstruction and Development Programme (RDP)?

1.1.1 The RDP is an integrated, coherent socio-economic policy framework. It seeks to mobilise all our people and our country's resources toward the final eradication of apartheid and the building of a democratic, non-racial and non-sexist future.

1.1.2 Within the framework for policy represented by the RDP, the ANC will develop detailed positions and a legislative programme of government.

1.1.3 The RDP has been drawn up by the ANC-led alliance in consultation with other key mass organisations. A wide range of non-governmental organisations (NGOs) and research organisations assisted in the process.

1.1.4 This process of consultation and joint policy formulation must continue as the RDP is developed into an effective programme of government. Other key sectors of our society such as the business community must be consulted and encouraged to participate as fully as they may choose.

1.1.5 Those organisations within civil society that participated in the development of the RDP will be encouraged by an ANC government to be active in and responsible for the effective implementation of the RDP.

1.1.6 This inclusive approach to developing and implementing policy is unique in South Africa's political history. The special nature of the ANC as a liberation movement and the traditions of the Freedom Charter make it the only political organisation capable of unifying a wide range of social movements, community-based organisations and numerous other sectors and formations. Widespread and broad-based extra-parliamentary support will allow the ANC within a Government of National Unity to implement the programme.

1.2 Why Do We Need an RDP?

1.2.1 Our history has been a bitter one dominated by colonialism, racism, apartheid, sexism and repressive labour policies. The result is that poverty and degradation exist side by side with modern cities and a developed mining, industrial and commercial infrastructure. Our income distribution is racially distorted and ranks as one of the most unequal in the world – lavish wealth and abject poverty characterise our society.

1.2.2 The economy was built on systematically enforced racial division in every sphere of our society. Rural areas have been divided into underdeveloped bantustans and well-developed, white-owned commercial farming areas. Towns and cities have been divided into townships without basic infrastructure for blacks and well-resourced suburbs for whites.

1.2.3 Segregation in education, health, welfare, transport and employment left deep scars of inequality and economic inefficiency. In commerce and industry, very large conglomerates dominated by whites control large parts of the economy. Cheap labour policies and employment segregation concentrated skills in white hands. Our workers are poorly equipped for the rapid changes taking place in the world economy. Small and medium-sized enterprises are underdeveloped, while highly protected industries underinvested in research, development and training.

1.2.4 The result is that in every sphere of our society – economic, social, political, moral, cultural, environmental – South Africans are confronted by serious problems. There is not a single sector of South African society, nor a person living in South Africa, untouched by the ravages of apartheid. Whole regions of our country are now suffering as a direct result of the apartheid policies and their collapse.

1.2.5 In its dying years, apartheid unleashed a vicious wave of violence. Thousands and thousands of people have been brutally killed, maimed, and forced from their homes. Security forces have all too often failed to act to protect people, and have frequently been accused of being implicated in, and even fomenting, this violence. We are close to creating a culture of violence in which no person can feel any sense of security in their person and property. The spectre of poverty and/or violence haunts millions of our people.

1.2.6 Millions of ordinary South Africans struggled against this system over decades, to improve their lives, to restore peace, and to bring about a more just society. In their homes, in their places of work, in townships, in classrooms, in clinics and hospitals, on the land, in cultural expression, the people of our country, black, white, women, men, old and young devoted their lives to the cause of a more humane South Africa. This struggle against apartheid was fought by individuals, by political organisations and by a mass democratic movement.

1.2.7 It is this collective heritage of struggle, these common yearnings, which are our greatest strength, and the RDP builds on it. At the same time the challenges facing South Africa are enormous. Only a comprehensive approach to harnessing the resources of our country can reverse the crisis created by apartheid. Only an all-round effort to harness the life experience, skills, energies and aspirations of the people can lay the basis for a new South Africa.

1.2.8 The first decisive step in this direction will be the forthcoming one-person, one-vote elections. A victory for democratic forces in these elections will lay the basis for effective reconstruction and development, and the restoration of peace.

1.2.9 But an election victory is only a first step. No political democracy can survive and flourish if the mass of our people remain in poverty, without land, without tangible prospects for a better life. Attacking poverty and deprivation must therefore be the first priority of a democratic government.

1.2.10 How can we do this successfully? It is no use merely making a long list of promises that pretend to answer every need expressed. Making promises is easy – especially during election campaigns – but carrying them out as a government is very much more difficult. A programme is required that is achievable, sustainable, and meets the objectives of freedom and an improved standard of living and quality of life for all South Africans within a peaceful and stable society.

1.2.11 The RDP is designed to be such a programme. To reach the RDP's objectives we face many obstacles and we are setting ourselves a great challenge. Each and every expectation will not be realised and each and every need will not be met immediately. Hard choices will have to be made. The RDP provides the framework within which those choices can be made. Even more importantly, it will involve both government and the people in further identifying needs and the obstacles to satisfying those needs, and will involve both in jointly implementing realistic strategies to overcome these obstacles. The RDP is an expression of confidence in the wisdom, organisational abilities and determination of our people.

1.3 The Six Basic Principles of the RDP

1.3.1 Six basic principles, linked together, make up the political and economic philosophy that underlies the whole RDP. This is an innovative and bold philosophy based on a few simple but powerful ideas. They are:

1.3.2 *An integrated and sustainable programme.* The legacy of apartheid cannot be overcome with piecemeal and uncoordinated policies. The RDP brings together strategies to harness all our resources in a coherent and purposeful effort that can be sustained into the future. These strategies will be implemented at national, provincial and local levels by government, parastatals and organisations within civil society working within the framework of the RDP.

This programme is essentially centred on:

1.3.3 *A people-driven process.* Our people, with their aspirations and collective determination, are our most important resource. The RDP is focused on our people's most immediate needs, and it relies, in turn, on their energies to drive the process of meeting these needs. Regardless of race or sex, or whether they are rural or urban, rich or poor, the people of South Africa must together shape their own future. Development is not about the delivery of goods to a passive citizenry. It is about active involvement and growing empowerment. In taking this approach we are building on the many forums, peace structures and negotiations that our people are involved in throughout the land.

This programme and this people-driven process are closely bound up with:

1.3.4 *Peace and security for all.* Promoting peace and security must involve all people and must build on and expand the National Peace Initiative. Apartheid placed the security forces, police and judicial system at the service of its racist ideology. The security forces have been unable to stem the tide of violence that has engulfed our people. To begin the process of reconstruction and development we must now establish security forces that reflect the national and gender character of our country. Such forces must be non-partisan, professional, and uphold the Constitution and respect human rights. The judicial system must reflect society's racial and gender composition, and provide fairness and equality for all before the law. As peace and security are established, we will be able to embark upon:

1.3.5 *Nation-building.* Central to the crisis in our country are the massive divisions and inequalities left behind by apartheid. We must not perpetuate the separation of our society into a 'first world' and a 'third world' – another disguised way of preserving apartheid. We must not confine growth strategies to the former, while doing patchwork and piecemeal development in the latter, waiting for trickle-down development. Nation-building is the basis on which to build a South Africa that can support the development of our Southern African region. Nation-building is also the basis on which to ensure that our country takes up an effective role within the world community. Only a programme that develops economic, political and social viability can ensure our national sovereignty.

Nation-building requires us to:

1.3.6 *Link reconstruction and development.* The RDP is based on reconstruction and development being parts of an integrated process. This is in contrast to a commonly held view that growth and development, or growth and redistribution are processes that contradict each other. Growth – the measurable increase in the output of the modern industrial economy – is commonly seen as the priority that must precede development. Development is portrayed as a marginal effort of redistribution to areas of urban and rural poverty. In this view, development is a deduction from growth. The RDP breaks decisively with this approach. If growth is defined as an increase in output, then it is of course a basic goal. However, where that growth occurs, how sustainable it is, how it is distributed, the degree to which it contributes to building long-term productive capacity and human resource development, and what impact it has on the environment, are the crucial questions when considering reconstruction and development. The RDP integrates growth, development, reconstruction and redistribution into a unified programme. The key to this link is an infrastructural programme that will provide access to modern and effective services like electricity, water, telecommunications, transport, health, education and training for all our people. This programme will both meet basic needs and open up previously suppressed economic and human potential in urban and rural areas. In turn this will lead to an increased output in all sectors of the economy, and by modernising our infrastructure and human resource development, we will also enhance export capacity. Success in linking reconstruction and development is essential if we are to achieve peace and security for all.

Finally, these first five principles all depend on a thoroughgoing

1.3.7 *Democratisation of South Africa.* Minority control and privilege in every aspect of our society are the main obstruction to developing an integrated programme that unleashes all the resources of our country. Thoroughgoing democratisation of our society is, in other words, absolutely integral to the whole RDP. The RDP requires fundamental changes in the way that policy is made and programmes are implemented. Above all, the people affected must participate in decision-making. Democratisation must begin to transform both the state and civil society. Democracy is not confined to periodic elections. It is, rather, an active process enabling everyone to contribute to reconstruction and development.

1.3.8 An *integrated programme*, based on the *people*, that *provides peace and security for all* and *builds the nation, links reconstruction and development* and deepens *democracy* – these are the six basic principles of the RDP.

1.4 The Key Programmes of the RDP

1.4.1 There are many proposals, strategies and policy programmes contained in the RDP. These can be grouped into five major policy programmes that are linked one to the other. The five key programmes are:

- meeting basic needs;
- developing our human resources;
- building the economy;
- democratising the state and society, and
- implementing the RDP.

1.4.2 *Meeting basic needs.* The first priority is to begin to meet the basic needs of people – jobs, land, housing, water, electricity, telecommunications, transport, a clean and healthy environment, nutrition, health care and social welfare. In this way we can begin to reconstruct family and community life in our society. In this chapter, achievable programmes are set out for the next five years. These include programmes to redistribute a substantial amount of land to landless people, build over one million houses, provide clean water and sanitation to all, electrify 2,5 million new homes and provide access for all to affordable health care and telecommunications. The success of these programmes is essential if we are to achieve peace and security for all.

1.4.3 Our people should be involved in these programmes by being made part of the decision-making on where infrastructure is located, by being employed in its construction and by being empowered to manage and administer these large-scale programmes. These major infrastructural programmes should stimulate the economy through increased demand for materials such as bricks and steel, appliances such as television sets and washing machines, and many other products. In addition, the industrial sector must develop new, more efficient and cheaper products to meet our basic infrastructural needs.

1.4.4 *Developing our human resources.* The RDP is a people-centred programme – our people must be involved in the decision-making process, in implementation, in new job opportunities requiring new skills, and in managing and governing our society. This will empower our people but an education and training programme is crucial. This chapter of the RDP deals with education from primary to tertiary level, from child care to advanced scientific and technological training. It focuses on young children, students and adults. It deals with training in formal institutions and at the workplace.

1.4.5 The underlying approach of these programmes is that education and training should be available to all from cradle to grave. The RDP takes a broad view of education and training, seeing it not only as something that happens in schools or colleges, but in all areas of our society – homes, workplaces, public works programmes, youth programmes and in rural areas.

1.4.6 A key focus throughout the RDP is on ensuring a full and equal role for women in every aspect of our economy and society. With this emphasis and with the emphasis on affirmative action throughout the RDP, we must unlock boundless energies and creativity suppressed by racism and discrimination.

1.4.7 In training, particular attention is paid to the challenges posed by the restructuring of our industries as we fully re-enter the world economy. These challenges can only be met through the extensive development of our human resources.

1.4.8 An arts and culture programme is set out as a crucial component of developing our human resources. This will assist us in unlocking the creativity of our people, allowing for cultural diversity within the project of developing a unifying national culture, rediscovering our historical heritage and assuring that adequate resources are allocated.

1.4.9 Because of apartheid, sport and recreation have been denied to the majority of our people. Yet there can be no real socio-economic development without there being adequate facilities for sport and recreation in all communities. The RDP wants to ensure that all people have access to such facilities. Only in this way can all our peoples have a chance to represent their villages, towns, cities, provinces or country in the arena of sport and to enjoy a rich diversity of recreational activities.

1.4.10 The problems facing the youth are well known. If we are to develop our human resource potential, then special attention must be paid to the youth. Our human resource policy should be aimed at reversing youth marginalisation, empowering youth, and allowing them to reach their full potential. Programmes for training, education and job creation will enable our youth to play a full role in the reconstruction and development of our society.

1.4.11 This programme for the development of our human resources underpins the capacity to democratise our society, thus allowing people to participate on the basis of knowledge, skill and creativity.

1.4.12 *Building the economy.* The economy has strengths and weaknesses. Mining, manufacturing, agriculture, commerce, financial services and infrastructure are well developed. At present we have a large surplus of electricity. These are strengths we can build on. But so far they have not benefitted all our people. A process of reconstruction is proposed to ensure that these strengths now benefit all our people.

1.4.13 But we must also address serious weaknesses in our economy. There are still very clear racial and gender inequalities in ownership, employment and skills. Past industrial policies assisted in creating employment and were an important factor in developing industry but they were also accompanied by repressive labour practices, neglect of training, isolation from the world economy and excessive concentration of economic power. The result is a low level of investment in research and development, low and inappropriate skill levels, high costs, low productivity and declining employment.

1.4.14 Central to building the economy is the question of worker rights. Past policies of labour exploitation and repression must be redressed and the imbalances of power between employers and workers corrected. The basic rights to organise and to strike must be entrenched. And negotiations and participative structures at national, industry and workplace level must be created to ensure that labour plays an effective role in the reconstruction and development of our country.

1.4.15 In the world economy, the demand for raw materials including minerals has not grown rapidly and there is intense competition in the production of manufactured goods. The General Agreement on Trade and Tariffs (GATT) was recently updated to achieve substantial reductions in tariff levels. Our economy must adjust to these pressures if we are to sustain economic growth and continue to develop a large domestic manufacturing sector that makes greater use of our own raw materials and minerals.

1.4.16 A central proposal in this chapter is that we cannot build the South African economy in isolation from its Southern African neighbours. Such a path would benefit nobody in the long run. If South Africa attempts to dominate its neighbours it will restrict their growth, reducing their potential as markets, worsening their unemployment, and causing increased migration to South Africa. If we seek mutual cooperation, we can develop a large stable market offering stable employment and common labour standards in all areas.

1.4.17 The pressures of the world economy and the operations of international organisations such as the International Monetary Fund (IMF), World Bank and GATT, affect our neighbours and South Africa in different ways. In the case of our neighbours, they were pressured into implementing programmes with adverse effects on employment and standards of living. It is essential that we combine to develop effective strategies for all Southern African countrie1.4.18 In building the economy, programmes dealing with the following areas are dealt with: linking reconstruction and development;

industry, trade and commerce; resource-based industries; upgrading infrastructure; labour and worker rights, and Southern Africa.

1.4.19 *Democratising the state and society.* Democratisation is integral to the RDP. Without thoroughgoing democratisation the resources and potential of our country and people will not be available for a coherent programme of reconstruction and development.

1.4.20 In linking democracy, development and a people-centred approach, we are paving the way for a new democratic order. This chapter sets out the role of the Constitution and Bill of Rights, of national, provincial and local government, the administration of justice, the public sector, parastatals, the police and security forces, social movements and NGOs, and a democratic information system in facilitating socio-economic development.

1.4.21 *Implementing the RDP.* The RDP raises many challenges in its implementation because it involves processes and forms of participation by organisations outside government that are very different to the old apartheid order. To implement and coordinate the RDP will require the establishment of effective RDP structures in government at a national, provincial and local level.

1.4.22 This chapter deals with the proposals for coordinating and planning the implementation of the RDP. This requires substantial restructuring of present planning processes and a rationalisation of the complex, racist and fragmented structures that exist. The RDP can only be people-centred if the planning and coordinating processes allow the active involvement of democratic structures.

1.4.23 Understandably, the first questions asked are: What will the RDP cost? Who will pay for it? These are important questions and in developing a programme to finance the RDP, certain key points are taken into account:

* most of the expenditure on the RDP is not in fact new – rather it is the better organisation and rationalisation of existing systems that will unlock resources;
* we must improve the capacity of the financial sector to mobilise more resources and to direct these to activities set out in the RDP, from housing to small and medium-sized enterprises;
* we must ensure that electrification and telecommunications will be self-financing;
* existing funds must be reallocated and rationalisation must be effected in many areas;
* improved and reformed tax systems will collect more tax without

having to raise tax levels (as the RDP succeeds, more taxpayers will be able to pay and revenue will rise); and
* new funds will be raised in a number of areas.

1.5 Conclusion

1.5.1 All over South Africa, including in People's Forums, the same questions are posed over and over:

- how will the ANC create jobs?
- when will you build houses?
- how can we get water and electricity?
- what about education?
- when will we have a fair and effective police force?
- will you give us health care?
- what about pensions?

1.5.2 The RDP attempts to provide achievable, realistic and clear programmes to answer these questions. But it goes further than this and encourages people and their organisations to participate in the process. In the conclusion we outline proposed concrete steps to make such participation possible.

The Reconstruction & Development Programme: Building the Economy
(Published by the ANC, 1994)

4.1 Problem Statement

4.1.1 The South African economy is in a deep-seated structural crisis and as such requires fundamental reconstruction. For decades forces within the white minority have used their exclusive access to political and economic power to promote their own sectional interests at the expense of black people. Black people have been systematically exploited and oppressed economically and South Africa now has one of the world's most unequal patterns of distribution of income and wealth. A disproportionate share of the burden of poverty and inequality has fallen on black women who have been subject to systematic gender oppression. Economic deprivation has created a fertile base for the violence and instability now engulfing our country. The ever-changing and destabilising global economy has also adversely affected the local economy.

4.1.2 Marked regional disparities exist within the economy as a result of policies designed to ensure a migratory labour supply to the mines and of the ethnic division of South Africa under the apartheid system. Enforced segregation and industrial decentralisation have located whole communities in areas where their economic viability is threatened. A few metropolitan regions account for the bulk of national production, while some provinces are affected by a crisis of unemployment, and can barely afford to provide basic services. Almost half the black population was compelled to live in so-called 'homelands' where per capita incomes are less than a quarter of the national average.

4.1.3 Successive minority governments and business have tried to promote growth by encouraging local production of manufactured goods which were previously imported. This policy led to the emergence of a significant manufacturing sector in our country. However, the disparity between the low income levels of the majority of consumers and factors leading to rising price levels ensured that the manufacturing sector served the wealthy and excluded the poor. The sector is in general characterised by poor productivity and an undue dependence upon low wages. It makes little contribution to foreign exchange earnings, but depends to a very great extent on imported machinery and equipment paid for out of foreign exchange earned by mineral exports.

4.1.4 Over the past decade and more, growth stagnated, investment dropped precipitously and average real incomes declined. The economy remains dependent on mineral exports, and the manufacturing sector cannot create jobs, meet the basic needs of the majority or compete on world markets. The decline in investment within the public and private sectors, and capital flight, have contributed to an ageing capital stock and contraction in the manufacturing sector. Capacity utilisation of manufacturing plant and equipment remains at very low levels. Speculative investment has replaced productive investment, with a consequent decline in job creation and overall employment levels.

4.1.5 The South African economy is also characterised by excessive concentration of economic power in the hands of a tiny minority of the population. Through the pyramid system and the resultant control over a vast network of subsidiary companies, a small number of very large conglomerates now dominate the production, distribution and financial sectors. In addition there is a high degree of monopolisation and blatant anti-competitive tendencies such as predatory pricing and interlocking directorships in certain industries. With regard to land, white ownership and often corporate ownership are overwhelming. Not only does this create racial and social tension, but it is to be seriously doubted that such high levels of concentration can be economically beneficial.

4.1.6 A particular weakness of the economy, aggravated by racist and sexist policies, is the inability to maintain a dynamic small-scale and micro enterprise sector. Smaller firms, especially if owned by black people, can rarely develop productive linkages with the large-scale sector. Most people in the informal sector lack productive and managerial skills plus access to business sites, capital and markets. They face an array of repressive regulations originally designed to undermine black business and farming.

4.1.7 A critical cause of inefficiency and inequality lies in the position of labour. Economic growth depended on the centrality of the cheap labour system. Rigid hierarchies and oppressive labour relations ignored the skills latent in our experienced industrial workforce. Apartheid laws denied workers their basic rights. High levels of unemployment and oppressive legislation made it difficult even for organised workers to maintain a living wage. The lack of skills forms a major obstacle to the development of a modern economy able to support a decent living standard for all our people. The apartheid state also systematically excluded workers from collective bargaining and policy-making at national and shop-floor levels. While the struggles of organised workers have reversed this to some extent, the right to strike continues to be limited, farm and domestic workers do not have basic rights, the majority of workers earn low wages, and there are enormous wage differentials.

4.1.8 Only a quarter as many women as men hold jobs in the formal sector. High unemployment, the migrant labour system and the difficulties facing the informal sector hit women particularly hard. Within formal employment, women are discriminated against in many areas such as wages, job security, specific needs of women workers, and employment opportunities. The migrant labour system continues to disempower both workers and their families.

4.1.9 The agricultural sector and rural economy are also in crisis. Many white-owned farms are deeply indebted and vast tracts of land designated for occupation by whites are inefficiently cultivated. Many thousands of black rural households are, meanwhile, crammed into tiny plots unable to produce or buy affordable food. Government decentralisation policies have failed to channel resources to the rural areas, which remain the most deprived parts of the country.

4.1.10 The apartheid state's economic agencies have been contradictory and secretive, and were subordinate to apartheid's logic and the siege-economy mentality. Parastatals such as the Industrial Development Corporation (IDC), Development Bank of Southern Africa (DBSA) and the Small Business Development Corporation (SBDC) could be immensely important in driving industrial, socio-economic and infrastructural development. But in recent years, under the cloak of secrecy, the apartheid state privatised or commercialised many agencies in the public sector (such as Transnet, Eskom, Telkom, Iscor, Foskor, SAA, the Post Office, Forestry and others). Often this policy, unilaterally imposed for ideological reasons, harmed basic services to the poor or reduced the ability of the state to mobilise resources for development.

4.1.11 The consequences of such undemocratic state policies in a structurally unbalanced economy include a serious fiscal crisis, with high personal tax rates accompanying a large budget deficit. In addition, the country's balance of payments problems, exacerbated by capital flight, have made it difficult to service the foreign debt incurred during the apartheid era. The need to maintain tight controls over economic policy as a result has had a devastating effect on economic growth and employment.

4.1.12 In past years, South Africa's relations with its Southern African neighbours were hostile, and apartheid destabilisation destroyed much of their economic base. Within the South African Customs Union (SACU) there has been no consideration of the differing needs of the participating countries and no common developmental policies.

4.2 Vision and Objectives

4.2.1 The fundamental principles of our economic policy are democracy, participation and development. We are convinced that neither a commandist central planning system nor an unfettered free market system can provide adequate solutions to the problems confronting us. Reconstruction and development will be achieved through the leading and enabling role of the state, a thriving private sector, and active involvement by all sectors of civil society, which in combination will lead to sustainable growth.

4.2.2 Our central goal for reconstruction and development is to create a strong, dynamic and balanced economy which will:

4.2.2.1 eliminate the poverty, low wages and extreme inequalities in wages and wealth generated by the apartheid system, meet basic needs, and thus ensure that every South African has a decent living standard and economic security;

4.2.2.2 address economic imbalances and structural problems in industry, trade, commerce, mining, agriculture, finance and labour markets;

4.2.2.3 address economic imbalances and uneven development within and between South Africa's regions;

4.2.2.4 ensure that no one suffers discrimination in hiring, promotion or training on the basis of race or gender;

4.2.2.5 develop the human resource capacity of all South Africans so the economy achieves high skills and wages;

4.2.2.6 democratise the economy and empower the historically oppressed, particularly the workers and women and their organisations, by encouraging broader participation in decisions about the economy in both the private and public sectors;

4.2.2.7 create productive employment opportunities at a living wage for all South Africans;

4.2.2.8 develop a prosperous and balanced regional economy in Southern Africa based on the principles of equity and mutual benefit; and

4.2.2.9 integrate into the world economy in a manner that sustains a viable and efficient domestic manufacturing capacity and increases our potential to export manufactured products.

It is only by addressing the above that our economy will be capable of sustained growth.

4.2.3 To carry out programmes to meet these objectives, as well as those outlined in previous chapters, the democratic government must play a leading and enabling role in guiding the economy and the market toward reconstruction and development. Legislative and institutional reform will be effected to enable the implementation of the RDP. We aim to achieve a dynamic balance between government intervention, the private sector and the participation of civil society.

4.2.4 There must be a significant role for public sector investment to complement the role of the private sector and community participation in stimulating reconstruction and development. The primary question in this regard is not the legal form that government involvement in economic activity might take at any point, but whether such actions must strengthen the ability of the economy to respond to the massive inequalities in the country, relieve the material hardship of the majority of the people, and stimulate economic growth and competitiveness.

4.2.5 In restructuring the public sector to carry out national goals, the balance of evidence will guide the decision for or against various economic policy measures. The democratic government must therefore consider:

4.2.5.1 increasing the public sector in strategic areas through, for example, nationalisation, purchasing a shareholding in companies, establishing new public corporations or joint ventures with the private sector, and

4.2.5.2 reducing the public sector in certain areas in ways that enhance efficiency, advance affirmative action and empower the historically disadvantaged, while ensuring the protection of both consumers and the rights and employment of workers.

4.2.6 The RDP will foster a new and constructive relationship between the people, their organisations in civil society, key constituencies such as the trade unions and organised business, the democratic government, and the workings of the market.

4.2.7 We can only achieve our economic objectives if we establish transparent, participatory and accountable policy-making procedures in both the public and private sectors. The democratic government, the trade union movement, business associations and the relevant organisations of civil society must cooperate in formulating economic policy. The democratic government must review the inherited economic departments and agencies to streamline policy-making and implementation and to define appropriate relationships with forums and the various tiers of government.

4.2.8 Economic growth is critical for sustainable improvements in services and incomes. We must shape the expansion of the social and economic infrastructure to stimulate industry and agriculture. These policies must be coordinated with the development, on a cooperative basis, of the Southern African region as a whole. On this foundation, we must establish a dynamic, integrated economy able to provide higher incomes, reduce excessive dependence on imports and compete on foreign markets.

4.2.9 All of our policies must aim to alleviate inequalities in incomes and wealth and expand productive opportunities. Critical programmes in this area include urban and rural development, industrial strategy, support for small and micro enterprise (including small-scale farming), job creation, land reform and other programmes discussed in earlier chapters. The democratic government must also create laws and institutions to end discrimination in hiring, promotion and training.

4.2.10 Our economic policies require human resource development on a massive scale. Improved training and education are fundamental to higher employment, the introduction of more advanced technologies, and reduced inequalities. Higher labour productivity will be the result of new attitudes towards work in the context of overall economic reconstruction and development.

4.2.11 Basic to the consultative and interactive approach to economic policy is the protection of worker rights, labour standards and proactive labour market policies. The RDP makes a decisive break with the exploitative cheap-labour policies of apartheid and moves toward education, training, skills, a living wage, and collective bargaining as the basis for enhanced productivity in the economy.

4.3 Integrating Reconstruction and Development

4.3.1 One of the basic principles outlined in Chapter One was that of linking reconstruction and development. This is in contrast to the argument that growth is needed before development is possible, an approach which would leave intact the severe regional, racial and gender, and structural imbalances that characterise the present economy. To prevent this from happening, reconstruction and development must be an integrated process. Such integration must be basic to all economic policy. This is where the public sector must play a major enabling role, since it cannot be expected that the market will make such a structural transformation on its own. Yet without such a transformation democracy will not survive, because socio-economic stability will not be achieved.

4.3.2 The RDP's principles recognise the mutually reinforcing nature of urban and rural development strategies through, for example, the benefits of improved agriculture to the urban economy. Strategies for urban and rural development must be integrated within the RDP to ensure that the needs of all our people are met in a balanced and equitable manner. An integrated strategy is essential for the process of unifying our economy and linking reconstruction and development.

4.3.3 In general, the RDP recognises the need to break down apartheid geography through land reform, more compact cities, decent public transport, and the development of industries and services that use local resources and/or meet local needs. In this context, the RDP must seek to help people generate economic wealth in their chosen communities.

4.3.4 Macroeconomic policies must take into consideration their effect upon the geographic distribution of economic activity. Additional strategies must address the excessive growth of the largest urban centres, the skewed distribution of population within rural areas, the role of small and medium-sized towns, and the future of declining towns and regions, and the apartheid dumping grounds.

4.3.5 In order to foster the growth of local economies, broadly representative institutions must be established to address local economic development needs. Their purpose would be to formulate strategies to address job creation and community development (for example, leveraging private sector funds for community development, investment strategies, training, small business and agricultural development, etc.). If necessary, the democratic government must provide some subsidies as a catalyst for job creation programmes controlled by communities and/or workers, and target appropriate job creation and development programmes in the most neglected and impoverished areas of our country. Ultimately, all such projects should sustain themselves.

4.3.6 The incentives for decentralisation introduced under apartheid frequently proved excessively discretionary and open to misuse. Still, in many areas simply eliminating them would cause severe job losses. For this reason, the democratic government must establish clear-cut guidelines and procedures for reviewing decentralisation incentives. Where communities and workers can certify that the subsidies are being utilised in a sustainable, non-exploitative manner, the democratic government must maintain the incentives. Otherwise, it must redirect subsidies to ventures that promote linkages within the local economy.

4.3.7 The Interim Constitution will have a significant impact on economic growth. Setting up new provinces will affect investment flows, regional assets and fiscal transfers as well as the institutions that make and implement policies. Every province must develop a programme for regional reconstruction and development in the context of the national RDP.

4.3.8 **Rural development.** The RDP aims to improve the quality of rural life. This must entail a dramatic land reform programme to transfer land from the inefficient, debt-ridden, ecologically-damaging and white-dominated large farm sector to all those who wish to produce incomes through farming in a more sustainable agricultural system. It also entails access to affordable services, and the promotion of non-agricultural activities. In the 'homelands', where most rural people live, social services and infrastructure remain poorly developed, and this must be remedied.

4.3.9 Development efforts must address the special position of women, as they make up the majority of small-scale farmers, and bear the brunt of poverty, overcrowding and hunger in rural areas. They take responsibility for all aspects of their families' lives, including the need to obtain food, fuel and water, often over long distances, but are excluded from decision-making structures. They are the bulk of the seasonal labour force in agriculture, but receive the lowest wages. Their priorities include accessible water, sewage disposal, infrastructure, land rights, housing, training, local development committees, a disaster relief fund, markets for their production, and good representation in local government.

4.3.10 To correct the history of underfunding, misuse of resources and corruption, substantial transfers of funds from the central government to the rural areas will be required, targeted to meet the needs of the rural poor. The democratic government must institute a land reform process that allows people in the rural areas access to land for production and residence. It must support part-time activities, including small-scale farming, which can increase productivity, incomes and household food security. It must end the inequitable and inefficient subsidisation of the large farm sector.

4.3.11 Rural communities need practical access to health, education, support for entrepreneurship (including agriculture), financial services, welfare, and police and the courts. The objective of rural development policy must be to coordinate the activities of the relevant democratic government agents, and to pass much of the control of democratic government-funded services to the rural people for whom they are intended, within the framework of national and provincial policy in each sector. This will require fundamental changes to institutions and processes4.3.12 We must establish democratic structures to control the finances for local development activities. Elected councillors must replace the non-representative Regional Services Councils and Joint Services Boards at the district and local level.

4.3.13 Generally, the democratic government must support capacity-building in the District Councils, Local Councils, and voluntary community structures such as local development forums. To advise communities of their options, it must train a cadre of Community Development Officers. Their training must include sensitivity to gender issues. The Community Development Officers must work for the District Councils. Wherever possible, they must come from the areas they serve.

4.3.14 Educational opportunities in the rural areas lag far behind those in the cities. Human resource development forms a key component in building the rural economy. It must include the opening up and reorganisation of agricultural schools to meet the needs of the majority. Training and retraining of new and existing extension workers, community development officers and officials dealing with land reform are critical to the success of our rural development and land reform programme. These training and retraining programmes must be designed within the first 18 months of the RDP.

4.3.15 The democratic government must include a central Ministry of Rural Development and Land Reform. The Ministry must include a unit for rural data collection and an early warning system for food and water security.

4.3.16 **Urban development.** The importance of urban development strategies within the RDP is based on a recognition that the urban areas account for over 80 per cent of the country's gross domestic product (GDP), and accommodate approximately 60 per cent of South Africa's population. Continuing demographic shifts may increase urbanisation to over 70 per cent of the population by 2000. The three major metropolitan areas (the PWV, Greater Cape Town and Durban) account for 37.7 per cent of the total population and 67.7 per cent of the country's total manufacturing output. The PWV region alone accounts for 40 per cent of the country's total economic output.

4.3.17 Even with a strong rural development effort, economic activities will remain concentrated in the cities. Ensuring the quality of life, sustainability and efficiency in the urban areas will thus prove critical for renewing growth and promoting equity. The design of a comprehensive national urban strategy will help serve the cities' rapidly growing populations and address the inequities and structural imbalances caused by the apartheid system. The urban development strategy must also be aimed at fostering the long-term development and sustainability of urban areas while alleviating poverty and encouraging economic expansion.

4.3.18 The urban programme must therefore have several dimensions.

It must create a functionally integrated, efficient and equitable urban economy, as well as effective and democratic structures of urban governance and management; enhance the position of women in the cities; and initiate a social environment which contributes to a better quality of life.

4.3.19 Sustainable economic expansion must redress the imbalances in infrastructure, transportation and basic services in our cities. Housing, transport, electrification, and other infrastructure and service programmes should promote access to employment opportunities and urban resources, and the consequent densification and unification of the urban fabric. In particular, sites for industries and services that will not harm the environment should be located near existing townships. New low-income housing should be situated near employment opportunities wherever possible.

4.3.20 The environmental impact of urban reconstruction and development must form an integral part of an urban development strategy. This includes the encroachment of urban development on viable agricultural land, air pollution, water pollution and waste management.

4.4 Industry, Trade and Commerce

4.4.1 Our economy requires coordinated and effective policies that combine private sector initiatives and government support to address its structural weaknesses. Coherent strategies are required in industry, trade and commerce to meet the challenges of a changing world economy, while at the same time meeting the needs of the majority. We also require broadly accepted, well-designed programmes which minimise the costs of restructuring and change. A 5 per cent growth rate and the creation of 300,000 to 500,000 non-agricultural jobs per annum can be achieved within five years.

4.4.2 **Objectives of industry, trade and commerce policy**

4.4.2.1 The key goals of our industrial strategy are a substantial increase in net national investment, especially in manufacturing, job creation and the meeting of basic needs. Through the prudent implementation of macroeconomic policies such as monetary policies, and in particular such instruments as interest rates and an increase in public sector investment, gross investment in industry will increase. In general, our objective is to enhance our technological capacity to ensure that as part of the restructuring of industry, South Africa emerges as a significant exporter of manufactured goods. The industrialisation strategy aims at the promotion of a more balanced pattern of industrial development, capable of overcoming the acute over-concentration of industrial activities in certain metropolitan centres of the country.

4.4.2.2 Trade and industrial policy must respond to the demands of reconstruction and development. In particular, industrial expansion should follow from the extension of infrastructure to urban, peri-urban and rural constituencies. Some of this new demand will be met by utilising the considerable excess capacity that exists within industry. That should lower unit costs, raise productivity and foster innovation, providing a new impetus for international competitiveness.

4.4.2.3 While trade policy must introduce instruments to promote exports of manufactured goods in general, industrial policy must support and strengthen those internationally competitive industries that emerge on the basis of stronger internal linkages, meeting the needs of reconstruction and raising capacity utilisation.

4.4.2.4 Specific policies aim to expand the competitive advantage already enjoyed by the mining and capital- and energy-intensive mineral processing and chemical industries that lie at the core of the economy and provide the bulk of the country's foreign exchange as outlined in the section on mining and minerals below.

4.4.2.5 Policy must address the constraints on those segments of manufacturing that fall outside bulk steel, metals and chemical production. The recent GATT agreement has necessitated painful adjustment in certain quarters, and policy should aim to reduce and share out the impact of that adjustment while at the same time promoting efficiency. Substantial institutional development on a national and sectoral level is necessary for this process, as discussed in the 'Institutional Reform' section below.

4.4.2.6 The RDP must strengthen and broaden upstream and downstream linkages between the burgeoning mineral-based industries and other sub-sectors of industry. A broad range of instruments will be deployed, including closer scrutiny of pricing policies for intermediate inputs. Where conglomerate control impedes the objectives, anti-trust policies will be invoked.

4.4.2.7 Policies must aim to reduce the gap between conglomerate control of a wide range of activities within the financial, mining and manufacturing sectors and sub-sectors, on the one hand, and the difficulties faced by small and micro enterprises in entering those sectors, on the other. As outlined in the section on small and micro enterprise, instruments may include regulatory reform, supportive measures in terms of markets, credit and training, plus measures to prevent the abuse of market power.

4.4.3 Trade policy

4.4.3.1 Given the foreign-exchange constraints on growth in

South Africa, trade policies assume enormous importance. The agreements that a democratic South Africa enters into with her major trading partners will play a crucial role in future development.

4.4.3.2 A democratic South Africa must rapidly restructure the relationships with neighbouring African countries, who import about 20 per cent of our exports. More balanced and less exploitative trade patterns will result in more mutually beneficial outcomes. That will strengthen the Southern African region in its relations with emerging global trading blocs, as discussed in the section on Southern African regional policy below.

4.4.3.3 Tariff reductions on imports, which are a GATT requirement, also represent a strategic instrument for trade policy. Presently, they are subject to negotiation within the National Economic Forum. The government must develop democratic and consistent procedures for revising tariffs and export incentives. It must simplify the tariff structure and begin a process of reducing protection in ways that minimise disruption to employment and to sensitive socio-economic areas. National agencies concerned with international trade and tariffs must be sensitive to the interests of the Southern African region as a whole.

4.4.3.4 We must develop more cost-effective incentives schemes, designed to improve performance and not just the volume of exports. Trade policy strategies to promote exports must consider ways to reduce the bias against small and medium-sized exporters. They should facilitate the provision of short-term export finance to small business. Any duplication between the trade-promotion arms of the Department of Trade and Industry and the private-sector South African Foreign Trade Organisation should be eliminated.

4.4.4 Institutional reform

4.4.4.1 There should be a review of the functions of government departments, particularly those of importance to the RDP, and of the mandates of the various parastatals and development institutions. As they are key structures for the successful implementation of the RDP, such a review must be given priority. The evaluation should identify whether the body is appropriate and should continue more or less in its present form, or whether it should be significantly altered or merged or closed down. For instance, it should be considered whether there is an advantage in maintaining the science councils or whether some or all of them should be merged.

4.4.4.2 In order to promote greater accountability in parastatals, lines of funding and reporting must be restructured to ensure that each parastatal is directly accountable to a particular ministry. This means that funding and reporting lines must be the same.

4.4.4.3 The processes of commercialisation and privatisation of parastatals must be reviewed, to the extent that such processes are not in the public interest. This will require the elaboration of more appropriate business plans, and publication of those plans for open debate. The democratic government will reverse privatisation programmes that are contrary to the public interest.

4.4.5 Negotiating forums

4.4.5.1 The RDP must work with existing forums, such as the NEF, the National Electricity Forum and the National Housing Forum, and must develop a more coherent and representative system on a regional and sectoral basis. These forums must continue to build consensus around industrial and trade policy. In particular, they must address the needs of industrial sectors forced to adjust and the question of how to share the costs of adjustment; identify new economic sites of competitive advantage; develop aspects of industrial and trade policy; and deal with problems of extending infrastructure and meeting basic needs.

4.4.5.2 The democratic government must work together with organised labour and business in the NEF to ensure coordination between macroeconomic policies and trade, industrial and technology strategy. If necessary, it must restructure the NEF to ensure appropriate participation and powers.

4.4.5.3 Coordination of issues around energy may be facilitated by a National Energy Policy Council, as an advisory body, to oversee financing in the energy sector and to set out national policies on all aspects of energy, including liquid fuels, coal, gas, electricity, nuclear power, and other forms of energy for rural and urban consumers.

4.4.6 The corporate sector

4.4.6.1 Business can profit hugely from the new opportunities offered by economic and social changes, especially the increased engagement with regional and international trade and the development of social and economic infrastructure. To help bring about a more dynamic business environment, the democratic state must develop measures to encourage increased productive investment, greater investment in research and development, cooperation with small and micro enterprise, workplace democratisation, and more open and flexible management styles.

4.4.6.2 The RDP will introduce strict anti-trust legislation to create a more competitive and dynamic business environment. The central objectives of such legislation are to systematically discourage the system of pyramids where they lead to over-concentration of economic power and interlocking directorships, to abolish numerous anti-competitive practices such as market domination and abuse, and to prevent the exploitation of consumers. Existing state institutions and regulations concerned with competition policy must be reviewed in accordance with the new anti-trust policy. The democratic government should establish a commission to review the structure of control and competition in the economy and develop efficient and democratic solutions. It must review existing policy and institutions with the aim of creating more widely spread control and more effective competition. To that end, it must consider changes in regulation or management in addition to anti-trust measures.

4.4.6.3 The domination of business activities by white business and the exclusion of black people and women from the mainstream of economic activity are causes for great concern for the reconstruction and development process. A central objective of the RDP is to deracialise business ownership and control completely, through focused policies of black economic empowerment. These policies must aim to make it easier for black people to gain access to capital for business development. The democratic government must ensure that no discrimination occurs in financial institutions. State and parastatal institutions will also provide capital for the attainment of black economic empowerment objectives. The democratic government must also introduce tendering-out procedures which facilitate black economic empowerment. Special emphasis must also be placed on training, upgrading and real participation in ownership.

4.4.6.4 Stable, consistent and predictable policies as well as a dynamic economy should create a climate conducive to foreign investment. The democratic government must ensure treatment of foreign investors equivalent to treatment of national investors. They should abide by our laws and standards (especially with respect to labour), and obtain the advantages available to all investors. The democratic government must develop policies to ensure that foreign investment creates as much employment, technological capacity and real knowledge transfer as possible, allowing greater participation by workers in decision-making.

4.4.7 Micro, small and medium-sized enterprises

4.4.7.1 Small businesses, particularly those owned and operated by black entrepreneurs, must form an integral part of the national economy and economic policy. Micro producers should develop from a set of marginalised survival strategies into dynamic small enterprises that can provide a decent living for both employees and entrepreneurs. Policies to that end must focus on women, who are represented disproportionately in this sector, especially in the rural areas.

4.4.7.2 Government agencies must provide infrastructure and skills to raise incomes and create healthier working conditions in small businesses. They must protect the rights of workers, both family members and others, and provide training in productive and managerial skills.

4.4.7.3 Experience shows that four major constraints face small and micro enterprises: the lack of access to credit, markets, skills and supportive institutional arrangements. In collaboration with small-scale entrepreneurs themselves, the democratic state must develop an integrated approach to all four problems.

4.4.7.4 In the context of a supportive industrial strategy, all levels of the democratic government – central, regional and local – must where possible foster new, dynamic relationships between large, small and micro enterprises in ways that do not harm the interests of labour. As discussed in the chapter 'Implementing the RDP', the government must require financial institutions to lend a rising share of their assets to black-owned enterprise. All levels of the state should also, as far as possible, support joint marketing strategies and technological development within the small-scale sector.

4.4.7.5 The democratic government must rationalise and restructure existing parastatals to support small enterprise as far as their underlying purposes allow. It should reorganise the SBDC and reform the lending criteria of other agencies such as the IDC and the development corporations so that they incorporate small and micro enterprise in their plans as far as this is feasible, and end corruption and nepotism in their lending programmes.

4.4.7.6 Local governments must review zoning and licensing regulations to end discrimination against micro and small enterprise.

4.4.7.7 All levels of the democratic government must review their procurement policies to ensure that, where costs permit, they support small-scale enterprise. In particular, we must explore new policies on the procurement of furniture and school uniforms, which micro producers might supply. Procurement regulations must, however, require appropriate labour standards for suppliers.

4.4.7.8 A specific programme must be established to ensure government support for women entrepreneurs. It must be easily accessible and include skills training and access to credit.

4.4.7.9 In addition to policies to support small-scale producers in general, the micro enterprise sector requires special attention. It will benefit from measures ranging from welfare support to activities that enhance competitiveness. Since the majority of sector workers are women, all agencies set up to support the informal sector should address their needs.

4.4.7.10 The development of social and economic infrastructure, including pre-schools, water supplies, roads and electrification, will go a long way to improving productivity. Infrastructural programmes must therefore take the implications for micro enterprise into account.

4.4.7.11 To better serve micro enterprise, the democratic government must double the existing number of local service centres and satellites. These satellites must enable the democratic government to provide for rural women involved in small, micro and medium-sized enterprises. All training programmes for micro enterprise must provide appropriate child care.

4.4.7.12 A variety of other measures should lower the barriers to micro enterprise. Laws should be improved to allow people in this sector to collect debts. Market sites must be established and access to existing sites facilitated. Land reform initiatives must reduce the land hunger which drives more and more people into the informal sector. Finally, as a basis for sound policy-making in future, the statistical system must incorporate micro enterprises.

4.4.8 Science and technology policy

4.4.8.1 Technology policy is a key component in both industrial strategy and high-quality social and economic infrastructure. It is critical for raising productivity in both small- and large-scale enterprise.

4.4.8.2 Science and technology policy should pursue the broad objectives of developing a supportive environment for innovation; reversing the decline in resources for formal science and technology efforts in both the private and public sectors; enabling appropriate sectors of the economy to compete internationally; ensuring that scientific advances translate more effectively into technological applications, including in the small and micro sector and in rural development; and humanising technology to minimise the effect on working conditions and employment.

4.4.8.3 Technology policy must support inter-firm linkages that facilitate innovation. In research and development, the democratic government should support pre-competitive collaboration between local firms and public-domain efforts, combining enterprises and scientific institutes.

4.4.8.4 Incentives should support expansion in technological capacity in both existing firms and new start-ups. A greater share of government initiatives which facilitate technological development, knowledge acquisition and training must directly benefit small and micro enterprise.

4.4.8.5 Girls and women should be encouraged to obtain

technical and scientific skills. The Ministry of Education must establish targets in the study of science and technology in the educational institutions it subsidises. Research in the science and technology arena by the democratic government, parastatals and educational institutions must cater equally to the needs of women in this area.

4.4.8.6 New legislation must ensure that agreements to import foreign technology include a commitment to educate and train local labour to use, maintain and extend technology. Appropriate technology for small and medium-sized enterprises must be purchased where necessary and applicable from other developing countries. The democratic government must limit excessive payment of royalties and licence fees.

4.4.8.7 The democratic government must develop programmes to make university-based science more responsive to the needs of the majority of our people for basic infrastructure, goods and service. Scientific research should link up with technological advance in industry, commerce and services and in small and micro production. In particular, there must be research into appropriate and sustainable technologies for the rural areas.

4.4.8.8 The democratic government must redirect military/strategic production to civilian production. Policies should encourage former employees to develop spin-offs.

4.4.8.9 The democratic government must develop extensive institutional support and enhance government capacities to ensure successful research foresight. Because science and technology play a crucial role in the RDP, a strong coordinating agency in government must maintain on-going consultation with key stakeholders.

4.4.9 Commerce and distribution

4.4.9.1 Distribution patterns have been severely distorted by apartheid and, in the last two decades, by particular investment patterns. Problems have emerged, including the biased location of distribution outlets, a distorted relationship between property investment and shopping malls, and excessive concentration of ownership, particularly in the link with the large conglomerates and in racial composition.

4.4.9.2 These issues must be addressed in order to achieve more geographically balanced and accessible distribution, lowered costs of distribution, modernised linkages between production and distribution, and greater participation by black people in the distribution chain.

4.5 Resource-based Industries

4.5.1 Mining and minerals

4.5.1.1 South Africa is one of the world's richest countries in terms of minerals. Up to now, however, this enormous wealth has only been used for the benefit of the tiny white minority.

4.5.1.2 The minerals in the ground belong to all South Africans, including future generations. Moreover, the current system of mineral rights prevents the optimal development of mining and the appropriate use of urban land. We must seek the return of private mineral rights to the democratic government, in line with the rest of the world. This must be done in full consultation with all stakeholders.

4.5.1.3 Our principal objective is to transform mining and mineral-processing industries to serve all of our people. We can achieve this goal through a variety of government interventions, incentives and disincentives. Estimates suggest that the establishment of a government minerals marketing auditors' office and the national marketing of certain minerals would enable South Africa to realise greater foreign-exchange earnings. The management and marketing of our mineral exports must be examined together with employers, unions and the government to ensure maximum benefits for our country.

4.5.1.4 Minerals and mineral products are our most important source of foreign exchange and the success of our RDP will in part depend on the ability of this sector to expand exports to avoid balance of payments constraints in the short to medium term.

4.5.1.5 Mining and mineral products contribute three-quarters of our exports and the industry employs three-quarters of a million workers, but this could be much higher if our raw materials were processed into intermediate and finished products before export. Our RDP must attempt to increase the level of mineral beneficiation through appropriate incentives and disincentives in order to increase employment and add more value to our natural resources before export. Moreover, this policy should provide more appropriate inputs for manufacturing in South Africa.

4.5.1.6 Minerals are a vital input for numerous mineral-based industries. These industries, however, have difficulty in becoming internationally competitive due to the fact that the refining companies usually set higher prices for the domestic market than their export prices, a practice known as import parity pricing. A democratic government must consider mechanisms to encourage companies to sell to local industries at prices that will enhance their international competitiveness.

4.5.1.7 Existing tripartite structures such as the Mining Summit must be strengthened in order to facilitate national development strategies for the mining and mineral-processing industry.

4.5.1.8 Democratisation of the mining sector must involve new laws to build workplace democracy for miners by requiring employers to negotiate the organisation of work with their employees and their unions. Programmes must be established to allow financial participation by workers in mining companies in a meaningful way (including measures to influence the policies of financial institutions, especially insurance companies and pension funds, which hold significant stakes in the mining sector and in which our people have substantial investments). And anti-trust legislation and other measures must be implemented to permit the monitoring and appropriate control of mining, mineral processing and marketing.

4.5.1.9 International demand and supply patterns for metals and minerals have undergone fundamental changes in recent years which necessitate the restructuring of this major industry. In the medium term, this probably means a continued decline in the number of people employed in the mines. Up to now, the heaviest burdens associated with down-scaling have been borne by miners, one-third of whom have been retrenched. The RDP must put into place mechanisms to ensure orderly down-scaling of our mines so as to minimise the suffering of workers and their families. Measures should include the re-skilling and training of workers for other forms of employment.

4.5.1.10 Mining is a hard and dangerous job, and mineworkers labour under stressful conditions, often deep under the earth. The RDP envisages a new set of minimum standards for the mining industry that ensure fair wages and employment conditions for all workers and a health and safety system that recognises the special hazards related to mining.

4.5.1.11 Most mineworkers are forced to live in single-sex hostels and remit part of their salaries. In future all workers must have the right to live at or near their place of work in decent accommodation and shall have full control over their after-tax salaries. In addition, the mining companies must take some responsibility for the education, training and social needs of miners and their families as an integral part of labour policy on the mines.

4.5.1.12 Mining can be extremely destructive of our natural environment. Our policy is to make the companies that reap the profits from mining responsible for all environmental damage. Existing legislation must be strengthened to ensure that our environment is protected. Before a new mine can be established, there must be a comprehensive environmental impact study.

4.5.1.13 The Southern African region also has enormous mineral resources that have not been mined, due in part to the destabilisation policies pursued by the apartheid state in the last twenty years. In the spirit of mutual cooperation, the RDP should extend across our borders by using our considerable expertise in mineral exploration and exploitation to rehabilitate and develop the mineral potential of our neighbours. In this regard a special facility should be created to promote investment in the sub-continent.

4.5.1.14 The government must consider ways and means to encourage small-scale mining and enhance opportunities for participation by our people through support, including financial and technical aid and access to mineral rights. However, standards in respect of the environment, health and safety, and other working conditions must be maintained.

4.5.2 Agriculture

4.5.2.1 A vibrant and expanded agricultural sector is a critical component of a rural development and land reform programme. Agriculture contributes 5 per cent of GDP and over 10 per cent of employment. Sixty-six per cent of its output is in the form of intermediates, and its forward and backward linkages are high. The industry is characterised by a high degree of concentration in the hands of 60,000 white farmers, who own over 87 per cent of the land and produce more than 90 per cent of its product. Agriculture in the bantustans is starved of resources.

4.5.2.2 For every additional unit of capital invested, agriculture ultimately yields a larger number of job opportunities than all other sectors, with the exception of construction. The RDP aims to create a restructured agricultural sector that spreads the ownership base, encourages small-scale agriculture, further develops the commercial sector, and increases production and employment. Agriculture should be oriented towards the provision of affordable food to meet the basic needs of the population and towards household food security. The pursuit of national food self-sufficiency proves too expensive and will not meet these aims. Moreover, it could undermine trade with neighbouring countries better able to produce foodstuffs.

4.5.2.3 The present commercial agricultural sector will remain an important provider of food and fibre, jobs and foreign exchange. The RDP must provide a framework for improving its performance by removing unnecessary controls and levies as well as unsustainable subsidies.

4.5.2.4 Support services provided by the democratic government, including marketing, finance and access to cooperatives, must concentrate on small and resource-poor farmers, especially women. This requires a shift from the current pattern of expensive and inefficient support for commercial farmers, as well as reform of the marketing boards and agricultural cooperatives.

4.5.2.5 Comprehensive measures should be introduced to

improve the living and working conditions of farm workers. All labour legislation must be extended to farm workers, with specific provisions relating to their circumstances.

4.5.2.6 Efficient, labour-intensive and sustainable methods of farming must be researched and promoted. To this end, extension workers should be trained and retrained, and the agricultural education and research institutions restructured. The RDP must support effective drought management by providing agro-meteorological advice to farmers rather than subsidising losses, which in the past encouraged environmentally destructive farming methods.

4.5.2.7 Increased attention must be paid to additional processing and value-adding activities derived from agriculture. This is linked to modernising marketing and exporting activities, and to the considerable potential for supplying a growing tourist industry.

4.5.3 **Fisheries and forestry**

4.5.3.1 The marine resources along the South African coastline form the basis of a fishing industry which employs some 26,000 persons. The industry, however, is concentrated in the hands of a few major companies which own not only the harvesting rights, but also the processing and marketing concerns. In general wages are low, work is very often seasonal and provides little security, and it is dangerous. In addition, some fish stocks have been overexploited.

4.5.3.2 The primary objective of fisheries policy is the upliftment of impoverished coastal communities through improved access to marine resources and the sustainable management of those resources through appropriate strategies.

4.5.3.3 The administration of fisheries should be transferred from the Department of Environmental Affairs to a Department of Agriculture, Forestry and Fisheries. The Sea Fisheries Advisory Committee and the Quota Board should be retained, but their membership and functions should be revised. For inshore fisheries and monitoring of catches, there should be greater community involvement in enforcement. For offshore resources, consideration must be given to establishing a regional 'Coastguard' involving the Southern African Development Community countries.

4.5.3.4 Policies must also enhance the potential for inland fisheries to improve the livelihood of rural communities through fish farming.

4.5.3.5 The RDP recognises the vast potential of the wood-based industries in South Africa. Given that the state owns almost a third of South Africa's commercial forests, the democratic government has a special responsibility to manage the development of this sector. Forests use important tracts of land, they limit the water supply in some areas, and there are potential environmental hazards in single-crop plantations such as commercial forests. The current usage of timber resources is wasteful, and we are opposed to the massive and growing export of raw wood-chips.

4.5.3.6 For these reasons the RDP promotes the tightening of regulations governing land use in sensitive areas. There is enormous scope to add value to our raw timber materials prior to export. The local pulp and paper industry can meet the growing need for paper, especially as education expands. But the price of paper products must be lowered to the benefit of local consumers as well as to enable more effective competition in international markets for value-added paper products. To achieve this, we must improve efficiency and make substantial investments. The trade unions have a significant contribution to make in restructuring this industry and enhancing its performance.

4.5.4 Tourism

4.5.4.1 Tourism in South Africa has been geared essentially to the local white and overseas markets, and has been adversely affected by apartheid and the resultant sanctions. All aspects of tourism were provided on a racial basis, including infrastructure, lodgings, and even national parks, game reserves and recreational areas. Natural resources are part of our national patrimony and we must develop a culture of appreciation.

4.5.4.2 A process of reconstruction and development must take place within tourism in view of the distortions created by apartheid. In the process of restructuring, a vast potential could be realised, both in terms of the local mass market, and in terms of increased foreign exchange. This would also result in the creation of large numbers of sustainable jobs in tourism and allied industries, and would take advantage of South Africa's extraordinary human and natural resources.

4.5.4.3 To achieve the desirable results, sound planning is needed, which should be predicated on thorough research and consultation. With respect to the local mass market, education, access to facilities and the support of black entrepreneurship are critical. In addition, promotion of ecotourism and enhancement of South Africa's unique cultural and political heritage must be prioritised. These afford opportunities for integrating traditional knowledge into tourism.

4.5.4.4 Community involvement in tourism projects must be encouraged, stressing partnerships with other agencies and initiation and ownership of enterprises. Communities must be given access to finance, management skills, upgrading of tourist service skills, language proficiency and connections with marketing infrastructure. Training institutions should be located in areas accessible to local communities to prevent leakage of skills from the area. This could be combined with other extension services and development training programmes at regional and local level.

4.5.4.5 The Southern African dimension offers enormous tourist potential. A coordinated, mutually beneficial policy within the region could offer some of the world's greatest natural and recreational tourist attractions.

4.5.4.6 Tourism is potentially a major source of employment and foreign exchange, and could ease balance of payments constraints in a short period of time, provided that resources required for the tourism industry are locally sourced. This requires tourism to be carefully integrated into provincial and local-level development programmes.

4.5.4.7 Without effective support from the democratic government, communities and hospitality industry workers, however, there is a danger that tourism will have potentially damaging effects on our rich and diverse cultures and natural resources. Full and transparent environmental impact assessments should be conducted for all major tourism projects. The tourism industry could be a major industry, and thus should receive greater priority at national and provincial levels.

4.6 Upgrading Infrastructure

4.6.1 The link between meeting basic needs through an infrastructural programme and reviving economic growth in manufacturing and other sectors is the essence of the link between reconstruction and development. However, it is more than just providing electricity, water and telecommunications. It is a programme that integrates and upgrades infrastructure at the same time.

4.6.2 The infrastructural programme must ensure an integrated approach to the provision of various services so that we upgrade our infrastructure in a manner that both meets basic needs and enhances new and effective economic activity. This is particularly true in areas of information technology. Upgrading in these areas can facilitate an upgrading of education, health care, recreation and other services, by improving the quality of information available and providing communities throughout the country with access to expertise and usable data.

4.6.3 The use of information technology provides a major challenge in linking basic needs with information highways in innovative ways that improve the capacity of industry to successfully reintegrate into world markets. Southern Africa could lead the way in providing this link so vital to the developing world.

4.6.4 In addition to upgrading infrastructure in existing areas, its extension to all parts of the sub-continent will both break down apartheid and colonial geography, and open up new economic potential in the areas of production and tourism.

4.6.5 **Electrification.** In addition to meeting basic energy and lighting needs for households, specific attention must be paid to making electricity available to micro, small, medium-sized and agricultural enterprises in both urban and rural areas. The benefits of cheap electricity presently enjoyed by large corporations must be extended to all parts of the economy.

4.6.6 **Telecommunications.** Under apartheid, telecommunications were not developed in a manner cognisant of the possibilities for expanding the economy to the lives of all South Africans. As a result, massive inefficiencies and missed opportunities characterise the sector. Information is today considered a commodity of great significance, and South Africa must now catch up in order to take advantage of the changing technological and economic roles that telecommunications can play.

4.6.7 The development of an advanced information network should play a crucial role in facilitating the provision of high-quality services to all the people of South Africa. It must provide a significant advantage to the business sector as it reduces costs and increases productivity, and serves as an integral part of financial services, the commodities market, trade and manufacturing.

4.6.8 The basic infrastructural network must remain within the public sector. Certain value-added services could be licensed within the framework of an overall telecommunications programme. An integrated system of groundline, microwave, fibre-optic and satellite communications must substantially enhance the overall system.

4.6.9 The RDP aims to bring telecommunications closer to all potential users. A telecommunications regulatory authority must be established, which should be separated from policy and operating activities.

4.6.10 The development of telecommunications must be underpinned by a strong telecommunications manufacturing sector. The democratic government must encourage this sector to work closely with the network operators in developing suitable systems for possible export to Africa and other developing areas.

4.6.11 **Transport.** There is an urgent need to develop an integrated and rapid transportation system that links the domestic economy, Southern Africa and world markets. This entails the upgrading of road and rail networks and their extension to the whole area, but also a rapid interface between road, rail, air and sea.

4.6.12 A review of the current situation within all transportation systems must be undertaken in order to assess the capacity of these systems and how they could enhance the development of other sectors of the economy and contribute to the RDP. The structure of the railway network and its operating system was badly distorted by our colonial and apartheid history. A comprehensive review of both the network and operating system is needed to increase their contribution to the RDP. A similar review is required in road freight with particular attention being paid to ownership patterns and barriers to entry. Particular attention must be paid to the regulatory structures of the transportation systems.

4.6.13 A Southern African transportation network enhanced by information networks could play a major role in underpinning the socio-economic reconstruction of the sub-continent.

4.7 Reform of the Financial Sector

4.7.1 The apartheid system severely distorted the South African financial system. A handful of large financial institutions, all linked closely to the dominant conglomerates, centralise most of the country's financial assets. But they prove unable to serve most of the black community, especially women. Nor do they contribute significantly to the development of new sectors of the economy. Small informal-sector institutions meet some of the needs of the black community and micro enterprise. They lack the resources, however, to bring about broad-scale development.

4.7.2 **The regulatory framework.** The democratic government must modify regulations and support innovative financial institutions and instruments which mobilise private domestic savings to help fund the RDP, while not reducing incentives for personal savings. The democratic government must enhance accountability, access and transparency in the financial sector. In cooperation with other stakeholders, it must review both regulations and regulatory system to determine which aspects prove an unnecessary impediment to the RDP, and more generally to greater efficiency in the mobilisation and subsequent allocation of savings. Government must encourage the private sector to cooperate in extending financial services to those who presently do not have access to these services. The establishment of a smoothly functioning and inexpensive payments system, assuring safety of consumer deposits, must be considered a high priority. To improve flexibility in the legal environment, Parliament should establish an oversight committee for the financial sector.

4.7.3 **Prohibition against discrimination.** The democratic government must introduce measures to combat discrimination on the grounds of race, gender, location and other non-economic factors. The democratic government must, in consultation with financial institutions, establish prudent non-discriminatory lending criteria, especially in respect of creditworthiness and collateral; reform the laws on women and banking to ensure equality; forbid blanket bans on mortgage bonds to specific communities ('redlining'); require banks to give their reasons when turning down a loan application; establish community liaison boards; develop simpler forms for contracts and applications; and create an environment which reduces the risk profile of lending to small black-owned enterprises and requires banks to lend a rising share of their assets to small, black-owned enterprise. The law must also require that financial institutions disclose their loans by race and gender; their assets and liabilities by sub-region and sector; their staff by race and gender; the location of their branches and defaults by neighbourhood. To enforce laws against discrimination, the democratic government must establish an ombuds for the financial sector. At the local level, ombuds structures must include community representatives. Where anti-discrimination measures do not generate enough credit for housing, small enterprise and other RDP programmes, the government must provide appropriate kinds of financial support. The democratic government should consider reapplying the Usury Act to small loans (in addition to loans above R6,000, as presently applies), and should enforce the Act more effectively.

4.7.4 **Housing bank and guarantee fund.** The democratic government must establish a Housing Bank to ensure access to wholesale finance for housing projects and programmes. A Guarantee Fund will protect private-sector funds from undue risk. Approximately half the Bank's funds will come from the government in the form of recurrent housing subsidies, in order to ensure affordable bonds.

4.7.5 **Community banking.** Community banks of various types have proven able to finance informal entrepreneurs, especially women. The democratic government must encourage community banking. It must reform regulations to foster the development of community banks while protecting customers. Where possible, government structures at all levels should conduct business with these institutions. The government must encourage the established banks and other financial institutions to help fund the community banks.

4.7.6 **Pension and mutual funds.** Pension and provident funds should be made more accountable to their members, and insurance companies to their contributors. The democratic government must change the law to ensure adequate representation for workers through the trade unions and compulsory contributions by employers, and move towards industry funds.

It must also legislate a transformation of the boards of the Mutual Funds to make them more socially responsible. The RDP must embark on a review of financial institution legislation, regulation and supervision to ensure the protection of pension and provident funds and other forms of savings and investment.

4.7.7 **The Reserve Bank.** The Interim Constitution contains several mechanisms which ensure that the Reserve Bank is both insulated from partisan interference and accountable to the broader goals of development and maintenance of the currency. In addition, the law must change the Act governing the Reserve Bank to ensure a board of directors that can better serve society as a whole. The board must include representatives from the trade unions and civil society. In future, a stronger board of governors should emerge through the appointment of better-qualified individuals. The new constitutional requirement that the board of governors record its decisions, publicise them when feasible, and account to Parliament should help in developing a more professional and credible executive, with greater ability to exercise its mandate than the present board of governors.

4.7.8 The democratic government should immediately increase the resources available in the Reserve Bank and other appropriate agencies for combating illegal capital flight. Furthermore, the democratic government must enter into discussions with holders of wealth in an effort to persuade them of the harmful effects their actions are having on our economy.

4.8 Labour and Worker Rights

4.8.1 Over the years, workers have won many struggles and made many gains in the workplace. The fundamental principle of the RDP is to safeguard these rights and extend them. Organised labour must be empowered to act as a strong force in the reconstruction and development of our country.

4.8.2 There must be equal rights for all workers, embodied in a single set of labour statutes.

4.8.3 **Basic organising rights.** The following rights of workers must be in the Constitution:

4.8.3.1 the right to organise and join trade unions;

4.8.3.2 the right to strike and picket on all economic and social matters, and

4.8.3.3 the right to information from companies and the government.

4.8.4 The Constitution should not prohibit the conclusion of union security agreements, including closed and agency shops. The right to lock out should not be in the Constitution.

4.8.5 **Living wage.** All workers should be entitled to a living wage and humane conditions of employment in a healthy and safe working environment. The interlocking elements of the RDP, in particular the promotion of collective bargaining, minimum wage regulation, affirmative action, education and training, technological development, and provision of services and social security, must all be combined to achieve a living wage for rural and urban workers and reduce wage differentials. The required levels of growth for the successful implementation of the RDP can only be achieved on the basis of living wage policies agreed upon by government, the labour movement and the private sector.

4.8.6 Reconstructing and developing the economy require far-reaching changes in employment patterns and labour market policies. The democratic government must set up institutions and mechanisms to facilitate this process in order to avoid unnecessary hardships while utilising our human resources to their full potential.

4.8.7 **Collective bargaining.** Effective implementation of the RDP requires a system of collective bargaining at national, industrial and workplace level, giving workers a key say in industry decision-making and ensuring that unions are fully involved in designing and overseeing changes at workplace and industry levels.

4.8.8 Industrial bargaining forums or industrial councils must play an important role in the implementation of the RDP. Agreements negotiated in such forums should be extended through legislation to all workplaces in that industry. There must be enhanced jurisdiction for these forums to negotiate:

4.8.8.1 industrial policy including the implementation of the RDP at sectoral level;

4.8.8.2 training and education programmes;

4.8.8.3 job placement programmes in the industry, and

4.8.8.4 job creation programmes.

4.8.9 **Workplace empowerment.** Legislation must facilitate worker participation and decision-making in the world of work. Such legislation must include an obligation on employers to negotiate substantial changes concerning production matters or workplace organisation within a nationally negotiated framework, facilities for organisation and communication with workers on such matters, and the right of shop stewards to attend union meetings and training without loss of pay as well as to address workers.

4.8.10 In addition to the reform of labour law, company and tax law must be amended to ensure that the rights of workers are protected and extended, for example in relation to workers' access to company information.

4.8.11 Instruments of policy such as subsidies, taxes, tariffs, tenders, etc., must all be utilised to encourage stakeholder participation in the RDP and promote worker rights, human resource development and job creation.

4.8.12 Since human resource development is crucial to the successful implementation of the RDP, the democratic government must support programmes to upgrade skills on a broad basis in terms of a national education and training policy negotiated between unions, employers and government ...

4.8.13 **Affirmative action.** Affirmative action measures must be used to end discrimination on the grounds of race and gender, and to address the disparity of power between workers and management, and between urban and rural areas. Those measures must:

4.8.13.1 entail a massive programme of education, training, retraining, adult basic education and recognition of prior learning to overcome the legacy of apartheid;

4.8.13.2 empower not only individuals, but communities and groups, under conditions which promote the collective rights and capacity of workers and their representatives to negotiate workplace issues;

4.8.13.3 establish principles for the hiring and the promotion of workers with similar skills or jobs which will prevent discrimination against people previously disadvantaged by apartheid or gender;

4.8.13.4 accelerate, through collective bargaining programmes, the eradication of discrimination in each and every workplace;

4.8.13.5 provide job security for pregnant women and promote the provision of child care, as discussed in Chapter Three, to further women's equality in employment;

4.8.13.6 ensure that the development of special expertise among South Africans takes priority over the import of outside personnel (this policy should not, however, prejudice foreign investment or cooperation in the Southern African region); and

4.8.13.7 establish legislation and a strong ombuds to monitor and implement affirmative action measures.

4.8.14 Legislation must prohibit sexual harassment, and education programmes must be launched to make workers and employers aware about the issue and about how to lodge complaints.

4.8.15 **International conventions.** The international labour conventions of the International Labour Organisation (ILO) concerning freedom of association, collective bargaining, workplace representation and other fundamental rights must be ratified by the South African government.

4.8.16 **Restructuring of labour market institutions.** The Department of Manpower and labour market institutions related to it, such as the Unemployment Insurance Board and the Workmen's Compensation Board, must be restructured in consultation with the major stakeholders in the tripartite labour market forums, such as the National Manpower Commission.

4.8.17 All of the above, coupled with a democratic political dispensation, improvements in the living standards of workers and a programme of human resource development, will release the resources of the nation's workers and significantly improve productivity in the economy.

4.9 Southern African Regional Policy

4.9.1 In the long run, sustainable reconstruction and development in South Africa requires sustainable reconstruction and development in Southern Africa as a whole. Otherwise, the region will face continued high unemployment and underemployment, leading to labour migration and brain drain to the more industrialised areas. The democratic government must negotiate with neighbouring countries to forge an equitable and mutually beneficial programme of increasing cooperation, coordination and integration appropriate to the conditions of the region. In this context, the RDP must support the goals and ideals of African integration as laid out in the Lagos Plan of Action and the Abuja Declaration.

4.9.2 Whilst South Africa's trade with its neighbours in Southern Africa constitutes a relatively small percentage of its total trade with the world, this trade has been growing rapidly over the past few years. In addition, a significant percentage of South Africa's exports to African countries that are not members of the Southern African Customs Union (SACU) consists of manufactured goods. Various studies have shown that there is a great complementarity between the types of goods imported by Southern African Development Community (SADC) and Preferential Trade Area (PTA) countries and the goods that South Africa is exporting.

4.9.3 However, the current trade pattern between South Africa and the sub-continent is unbalanced, as regional imports from South Africa exceed exports to South Africa by five to one. A democratic government must develop policies in consultation with our neighbours to ensure more balanced trade.

4.9.4 Developing the capacity of our neighbours to export manufactured goods to South African markets requires the democratic government, in consultation with neighbouring states, to encourage and promote industrial development throughout the region. A democratic government must contribute towards the development of regional and industrial strategies for specific sub-sectors, such as mineral beneficiation, auto components and textiles.

4.9.5 A democratic government should also encourage the development of joint, mutually beneficial projects to develop our regional water resources, electricity and energy supply, transport and telecommunications, and agricultural and food production.

4.9.6 One element of regional policy, defended particularly in the call for a Southern African Social Charter by trade unions, is that minimum standards with regard to rights of workers to organise be established across the region as a whole. This will allow a process of greater integration to become one of levelling up rights and conditions of workers, rather than of levelling them down to the lowest prevailing standard.

4.9.7 A democratic government should encourage technical and scientific cooperation with our neighbours to enhance the development of expertise in the region in areas such as agricultural research and development, environmental monitoring and protection, health and other research.

4.9.8 A democratic South African government should apply for membership in SADC and possibly PTA, and should support reforms in SACU to enhance democracy and equity. Within these structures we must enhance our capacity as a region to effectively interact with international financial and trade institutions.

Growth, Employment and Redistribution: A Macroeconomic Strategy

(Published by the Presidency of the Republic of South Africa, 1996)

1. INTRODUCTION

1.1 A Long-run Vision

As South Africa moves toward the next century, we seek:

- a competitive fast-growing economy which creates sufficient jobs for all workseekers;
- a redistribution of income and opportunities in favour of the poor;
- a society in which sound health, education and other services are available to all; and
- an environment in which homes are secure and places of work are productive.

A strategy for rebuilding and restructuring the economy is set out in this document, in keeping with the goals set in the Reconstruction and Development Programme. In the context of this integrated economic strategy, we can successfully confront the related challenges of meeting basic needs, developing human resources, increasing participation in the democratic institutions of civil society and implementing the RDP in all its facets.

1.2 Recent Economic Developments

Against the background of a successful democratic transition, the stagnation that characterised the 1980s has come to an end. Considerable progress has since been made in:

- securing a return to a long-term growth trend in excess of population growth;

- reducing the budget deficit, reforming the tax system and reprioritising public expenditure;
- bringing down inflation and easing the balance of payments constraint;
- opening the economy to international competition and securing access to new markets;
- integrating the civil service and transforming public sector institutions; and
- establishing policy frameworks for delivery of social services.

Notwithstanding these achievements, it has become increasingly evident that job creation, which is a primary source of income redistribution, remains inadequate. It is widely recognised that the present growth trajectory of about 3 per cent per annum:

- fails to reverse the unemployment crisis in the labour market;
- provides inadequate resources for the necessary expansion in social service delivery; and
- yields insufficient progress toward an equitable distribution of income and wealth.

Recent exchange rate developments reinforce these conclusions. In February 1996 a depreciation, which was largely a purchasing power parity correction, occurred. However, the subsequent movements in the foreign exchange market reflected more fundamental economic uncertainties. The depreciation presents both an opportunity and a threat. An uncoordinated response, embroiled in conflict, will cause further crisis and contraction. Linked to an integrated economic strategy, on the other hand, it provides a springboard for enhanced economic activity.

1.3 Points of Departure

Sustained growth on a higher plane requires a transformation towards a competitive outward-oriented economy.

The strategy developed below attains a growth rate of 6 per cent per annum and job creation of 400 000 per annum by the year 2000, concentrating capacity building on meeting the demands of international competitiveness. Several inter-related developments are called for:

- accelerated growth of non-gold exports;
- a brisk expansion in private sector capital formation;
- an acceleration in public sector investment;

- an improvement in the employment intensity of investment and output growth; and
- an increase in infrastructural development and service delivery, making intensive use of labour-based techniques.

The expansion envisaged in the above aggregates is substantial and entails a major transformation in the environment and behaviour of both the private and the public sectors. This must include:

- a competitive platform for a powerful expansion by the tradable goods sector;
- a stable environment for confidence and a profitable surge in private investment;
- a restructured public sector to increase the efficiency of both capital expenditure and service delivery;
- new sectoral and regional emphases in industrial and infrastructural development;
- greater labour market flexibility; and
- enhanced human resource development.

Accompanying the macroeconomic strategy set out below, several appendices provide details and explanatory memoranda. Other coordinated policy programmes, such as the recently announced National Crime Prevention Strategy, complement this framework. Taken together, the Government's approach to development and growth builds a bridge between the present constrained environment and sustainable expansion within an increasingly competitive international context.

1.4 An Integrated Strategy
The core elements of the integrated strategy are:

- a renewed focus on budget reform to strengthen the redistributive thrust of expenditure;
- a faster fiscal deficit reduction programme to contain debt service obligations, counter inflation and free resources for investment;
- an exchange rate policy to keep the real effective rate stable at a competitive level;
- consistent monetary policy to prevent a resurgence of inflation;
- a further step in the gradual relaxation of exchange controls;
- a reduction in tariffs to contain input prices and facilitate industrial

restructuring, compensating partially for the exchange rate depreciation;
- tax incentives to stimulate new investment in competitive and labour-absorbing projects;
- speeding up the restructuring of state assets to optimise investment resources;
- an expansionary infrastructure programme to address service deficiencies and backlogs;
- an appropriately structured flexibility within the collective bargaining system;
- a strengthened levy system to fund training on a scale commensurate with needs;
- an expansion of trade and investment flows in Southern Africa; and
- a commitment to the implementation of stable and coordinated policies.

It is Government's conviction that we have to mobilise all our energy in a new burst of economic activity. This will need to break current constraints and catapult the economy to the higher levels of growth, development and employment needed to provide a better life for all South Africans. We are confident that our social partners will join us in the combined efforts needed to achieve this goal.

2. CRITICAL CONSIDERATIONS: A FRAMEWORK FOR GROWTH

2.1 Present Economic Trends

The trends established over the past two years suggest that the economy is on track for continued, if somewhat slower, growth in exports and investment. Policies are in place to bring the fiscal deficit down steadily and to keep inflation in check. Under these circumstances, detailed simulations, based on diverse econometric models, reach a common conclusion: growth of at best 3 per cent per annum can be expected on average over the next few years. Although this represents a considerable improvement on past performance, it is not a development path which meets the goals South Africans have set for themselves.

Firstly, in the context of 3 per cent growth, and without significant improvements in labour absorption coefficients, it is doubtful whether annual job creation much in excess of 100 000 would be possible over the next five years. The unemployment rate would then rise by some 5 per cent to about 37 per cent in 2000. This estimate takes into account about 20 000 additional jobs created per annum in response to various employment-intensive public expenditure programmes such as land reform, low-cost housing, community water and municipal infrastructure.

Secondly, the scope for increased public spending on social services would be severely limited. Medium-term fiscal projections incorporating a 3 per cent growth scenario, a gradual deficit reduction, the recent public sector wage settlement, and severe cuts (15 per cent) in real spending in several government functions, indicate that there would be sufficient resources to increase real aggregate spending on social and community services by at most 3 per cent per annum, which is barely above the population growth rate. The additional funding available would not cover 15 per cent of current medium-term departmental expansion plans.

Thirdly, the balance of payments remains a structural barrier to accelerated growth. The economy is dependent on imported capital and intermediate goods and, as in the past, the cyclical upswing brings a deterioration in the current account. Whereas this constraint has been eased through capital inflows since the elections in 1994, the lack of sustained long-term capital inflows has made the balance of payments and the economy too reliant on short-term reversible flows and consequently high interest rates.

The recent exchange rate instability presents a further complication. There is a danger of a further capital outflow and a balance of payments crisis. In this scenario growth would be abruptly curtailed and structural adjustment under terms set by international agencies would be unavoidable. Leaving aside this risk, growth forecasts have already been revised downwards by most professional analysts. It is recognised that the burden of the adjustment in the short term will fall on monetary policy and that an economic contraction to reduce import demand is likely.

What options are open to government? An expansionary fiscal strategy could be considered. However, even under the most favourable circumstances, this would only give a short-term boost to growth since it would reproduce the historical pattern of cyclical growth and decline. Increased growth above 3 per cent would be choked off by a rising current account deficit, upward pressure on real wages and curtailment of investment plans. Higher fiscal deficits would also lead to higher inflation and higher interest rates, exacerbating the burden of interest payments on the fiscus. More importantly, in the present climate of instability a fiscal expansion would precipitate a balance of payments crisis. Without attention to more deep-rooted reforms, there is no possibility of sustainable accelerated growth.

2.2 Elements of a Medium-Term Strategy

An integrated medium-term strategy is presented below which provides a broad bridge between the present constrained economic environment and an improved growth and employment performance in the period up to 2000, while strengthening the competitive capacity of the economy in the long term. The core elements of this integrated package are:

- an acceleration of the fiscal reform process, including a tighter short-term fiscal stance to counter inflation, an appropriate medium-term deficit target to eliminate government dissaving, further revision of the tax structure, and a range of budgetary restructuring initiatives to sharpen the redistributive thrust of expenditure and contain costs;
- a further step in the gradual relaxation of exchange controls, the maintenance of monetary policies consistent with continued inflation reduction, and exchange rate management to stabilise the real effective exchange rate at a competitive level;
- a consolidation of trade and industrial policy reforms, incorporating a further lowering of tariffs to compensate for the real depreciation, the introduction of tax incentives for a fixed period to stimulate investment, a campaign to boost small and medium firm development, a strengthening of competition policy, and the development of industrial cluster support programmes, amongst other initiatives;
- the implementation of the public sector asset restructuring programme, including guidelines for the governance, regulation and financing of public corporations, and leading off with the sale of non-strategic assets and the creation of public–private partnerships in transport and telecommunications;
- an expansionary public infrastructure investment programme to provide for more adequate and efficient economic infrastructure services in support of industrial and regional development and to address major backlogs in the provision of municipal and rural services;
- a structured flexibility within the collective bargaining system to support a competitive and more labour-intensive growth path, including greater sensitivity in wage determination to varying capital intensity, skills, regional circumstances and firm size; reduced minimum wage schedules for young trainees, reducing indirect wage costs and increasing the incentives for more shifts, job sharing and greater employment flexibility; and
- a social agreement to facilitate wage and price moderation, underpin accelerated investment and employment, and enhance service delivery.

The measures outlined above are mutually supportive and constitute an integrated strategy to enhance economic growth and employment creation. It is Government's conviction that they will establish a stable and competitive environment for significantly improved export and investment growth.

2.3 Accelerated Growth

The recent depreciation of the rand represents one element in the improved competitiveness which the economy must achieve for higher growth to be sustained. Although higher import prices will impact negatively on importing firms in the short term, the advantages of a lower rand for producers of traded goods for both export and domestic markets represent a crucial window of opportunity over the next few years. It is Government's intention to utilise this opportunity to the fullest. This requires several further adjustments to avoid erosion of the improved trading outlook by macroeconomic imbalances.

In brief, government consumption expenditure should be cut back, private and public sector wage increases kept in check, tariff reform accelerated to compensate for the depreciation, and domestic savings performance improved. These measures will counteract the inflationary impact of the exchange rate adjustment, permit fiscal deficit targets to be reached, establish a climate for continued investor confidence, and facilitate the financing of both private sector investment and accelerated development expenditure.

Drawing on several models of the South African economy, the effects of an integrated economic reform strategy on growth and employment prospects have been tested. Results, bearing in mind the inevitable uncertainties of economic projections, are as follows:

The package will establish a stable platform for a powerful expansionary thrust, with non-gold export growth rising to 10 per cent per annum over the period. Against the background of this expansion and supported by the proposed investment incentives, as well as the integrity of the package as a whole, private sector investment can be expected to continue its strong upward momentum, averaging some 12 per cent growth between 1995 and 2000. Accelerating public sector investment growth, driven by public corporations and local authorities, programmed to reach growth rates of up to 10 per cent per annum by 1998, will complement the demand stimulus of stronger non-gold exports and private investment performance. In the aggregate, these developments are expected to provide sufficient impetus for GDP growth to climb to the targeted 6 per cent by the year 2000.

The danger of an increase in the rate of inflation, reinforced by a wage–price spiral, is a constant threat to the expansion anticipated by the strategy. To contain inflationary pressures requires concerted implementation of complementary stabilisation measures: accelerated tariff liberalisation, sharper deficit reduction, tight monetary policy and, above all, productivity-linked wage increases. Taken together, these measures would hold the inflation rate below the 10 per cent barrier throughout the period, and preserve the competitive advantage of the depreciation.

As a result of the reduction in government consumption expenditure relative to GDP, and the reversal of government dissaving, gross domestic saving is expected to rise from 18 per cent to 22 per cent of GDP. This represents an important basis for the sustainability of the long-run growth path. Gross domestic investment is expected to increase from 20 per cent to nearly 26 per cent of GDP in the year 2000. This requires capital inflows equivalent to almost 4 per cent of GDP. The integrity of this growth strategy is therefore dependent on maintaining a favourable investment climate, in order to attract foreign investment.

Employment projections are sensitive to assumptions regarding real wage growth, easier access to formal job opportunities, and accelerated programmes of small business and small farmer support. A favourable employment response to accelerating growth, reinforced by effective public sector programmes, would see job creation rise to 400 000 per annum by the year 2000. The unemployment rate would then begin to show a visible decline.

There are, in sum, several inter-related aspects of the growth strategy. Departing from the past depreciation of the exchange rate which provides a competitive advantage to exporters, the expected economic expansion will be strengthened if the real value of the currency remains at a stable level. Inflation will not erode competitiveness for the following reasons:

- deficit reduction releases the pressure of the fiscus on the capital market; it also facilitates the accelerated flow of domestic resources into industrial investment and contributes to the overall financial stability of the economy; and
- accelerated tariff reduction compensates for the depreciation and provides an additional buffer against inflation; it also holds imported input prices down and preserves the momentum of restructuring at the firm level.

In addition to maintaining financial stability, job creation is enhanced:

- supply-side industrial measures which replace the general export incentive scheme contribute to industrial competitiveness, investment and job creation;
- public investment to upgrade sustainable economic and municipal infrastructure crowds in private investment and boosts short-term economic performance, while laying the infrastructural foundations for long-term productivity growth;
- wage moderation increases labour demand while lowering inflationary pressures; and
- greater flexibility in the labour market regulatory framework facilitates employment creation while extending basic rights to a broader pool of the workforce.

Responsible monetary policies anchor the competitiveness and stability of the economy in regard to both the domestic value of the rand and its foreign purchasing power, and encourage domestic saving and investment. Finally, the fiscal containment in the package reduces the burden placed on monetary policy.

The policy package is also consistent with long-run sustainable growth on a higher plane:

- tax reforms are aimed at international competitiveness and minimising the distorting effects of taxation on economic behaviour, while preserving the fundamental progressiveness of the overall tax structure;
- trade and industrial policies aim to promote an outward-oriented industrial economy, integrated into the regional and global environment and fully responsive to market trends and opportunities;
- public sector reforms, comprising asset restructuring, budgetary reprioritisation and improved service delivery, underpin social and infrastructural development in both urban and rural areas and contribute to the redistribution of opportunities and income; and
- employment and training policies enhance the growth potential of industry, extend job opportunities to the unemployed, and contribute over time to the redistribution of income.

While recognising that policy-making must remain sensitive to changing circumstances, there is an urgent need to establish firm foundations for this approach to growth and employment creation in the South African economy. The Government's proposals for such a framework are set out in more detail below.

3. FISCAL POLICY

3.1 Recent Fiscal Trends

In response to the unsustainable fiscal situation that had developed by 1992/93, when the overall deficit reached 7.9 per cent of GDP, fiscal policy has been informed by the following goals:

- to cut the overall budget deficit and the level of government dissaving;
- to avoid permanent increases in the overall tax burden;
- to reduce consumption expenditure by general government relative to GDP; and
- to strengthen the general government contribution to gross domestic fixed investment.

Although government dissaving has not yet been eliminated, progress has been made in this respect. The cash-flow adjusted exchequer deficit was reduced to an estimated 5.4 per cent in 1995/96. Consolidated general government tax revenue has increased from 25.6 per cent to 26.8 per cent of GDP between 1992/93 and 1994/95, but still somewhat below the 1989/90 level of 27.1 per cent. At the same time, significant shifts in the allocation of expenditure have been effected in accordance with reconstruction and development priorities.

3.2 A Tighter Fiscal Stance

To remove the domestic savings constraint and benefit from the expansionary impact of the stronger investment and export performance which is envisaged in this strategy, a tighter fiscal policy is necessary. In this way, inflationary pressures will be kept in check and domestic resources will be released for financing capital formation. A lowering of the fiscal deficit target from 4.5 per cent of GDP to 4.0 per cent in the 1997/98 fiscal year is therefore proposed. Two further reductions of 0.5 per cent of GDP in each of the subsequent years would bring the deficit to a satisfactory long-term target of 3.0 per cent of GDP in the fiscal year 1999/00. This, together with the envisaged strengthening of government investment spending, would eliminate government dissaving, currently at 2.5 per cent of GDP.

In order to achieve the new fiscal targets in the 1997/98 budget, the Minister of Finance has initiated a thorough audit of government expenditure, including RDP allocations, to identify those areas in which budgetary cuts can be made without detracting from the priorities and commitments of the Government.

3.3 Public Service Restructuring

The process of administrative restructuring of the public service provided for in the Constitution gathered pace in 1995. With the first phase of the process involving the integration of the public service at national and provincial levels nearing completion, attention is shifting to the longer-term issue of creating a more cost-effective service.

A major step was taken in early 1996 with the devolution to line departments of all career-related personnel functions. The restructured Public Service Commission will retain a research and monitoring role, while the Department of Public Service and Administration will be responsible for broad human resource policy, conditions of service and labour relations.

Careful management of the overall government wage bill is central to the fiscal strategy. In implementing the three-year public service salary adjustment and right-sizing programme, affordability considerations, maintenance of public services and macroeconomic consistency are paramount. Agreement has been reached on the principles of broad-banding and occupational classification.

In order to effect a right-sizing of certain parts of the public service, a voluntary severance package has been introduced. This will be implemented with considerable circumspection in order to limit both the resulting loss of skilled personnel and associated costs to the fiscus.

Successful implementation of the agreement would lead to a real increase in the government wage bill of approximately 2 per cent per annum over the next five years. This, together with strict containment of spending on other goods and services and current transfers, implies a roughly constant level of real recurrent government expenditure and a reduction of 3 percentage points in this aggregate relative to GDP by the year 2000. This would allow an increase in discretionary RDP-related spending on projects of a capital nature of about 8 per cent per year, compared with little more than 2 per cent per year in real terms in the absence of accelerated growth. This represents substantial room for manoeuvre in the developmental dimensions of the budget.

3.4 Budgetary Reform

The budget is the primary vehicle through which access to social services is assured. Nearly half of all government spending is devoted to education, health, welfare, housing and related services. Strengthening of the redistributive thrust of these expenditures remains a fundamental objective of economic policy. Reprioritisation within the health and education budgets, a municipal infrastructure programme, restructuring of the welfare system, land reform and a review of training and small business support policies are amongst the initiatives which aim to address the claims of the poor to a fair package of basic needs. These adjustments are being accompanied by the elimination or scaling down of activities which cannot be provided to all or which could be undertaken effectively by the private sector.

Government recognises the importance of a longer-term fiscal planning framework alongside the annual budgetary process. A multi-year fiscal model has recently been developed which will be updated annually to provide greater clarity regarding public expenditure trends and priorities. It is envisaged that a draft medium-term expenditure model will be available to assist in the preparation of the next budget.

Several budgetary reforms are presently under consideration, including the earlier presentation of budgets to Parliament, the possibility of a switch to an accrual accounting system, a revised basis for reporting assets and liabilities, a restructuring of the accountability of the various departments, and a transformation of the structure of inter-governmental financial relations.

3.5 Revenue Issues

International experience confirms that it is on the expenditure side that the fiscus is most effectively able to contribute to redistribution. It is nonetheless important that the incidence of taxation should remain progressive, while at the same time impacting across a broad base so as to avoid excessive rates. Several further steps in the overhaul of the tax structure, including the rewriting of the Income Tax Act, will be undertaken. A new dispensation for the taxation of retirement funds, higher rates of excise on tobacco products, and improved tax collection will lead to increased revenue on the current income base. This will be partially offset by adjustments to the personal income tax structure with a view to correcting for fiscal drag and reducing the distorting impact of excessive rates of tax.

Recognising the importance of effective tax administration, the new SA Revenue Service has embarked on the upgrading of its revenue and customs and excise offices, including personnel training and modernisation of information systems. This will, in due course, contribute to improved collections and greater fairness of the tax system.

The improvement in economic growth, together with improved tax administration, should lead to a strong increase in tax revenue relative to GDP. This will create considerable scope to effect further reductions in the rates of personal and corporate taxation, while maintaining a ratio of tax to

GDP of about 25 per cent.

In addition, the Department of Finance is reviewing the existing arrangements for the financing of government debt and the management of outstanding debt. The outcome of this process will be the establishment of a fully-fledged Debt Management Office, leading to savings on the interest bill in the medium term. A first step has been taken in this regard with the review of cash management within the public sector.

4. MONETARY AND EXCHANGE RATE POLICY

4.1 Monetary Policy and Inflation

The main objective of monetary policy will continue to be the maintenance of financial stability and the reduction of the inflation rate. Positive real interest rates are a minimum condition for overall financial stability. Low inflation is an important requirement for higher economic growth, the creation of employment opportunities and a more equitable distribution of income.

Inflation reduction has been facilitated by other developments. Trade liberalisation has contributed significantly to the containment of domestic prices, while more moderate wage-setting and improved industrial relations have also played a role in holding cost increases in check.

Monetary policy will also aim to maintain real interest rates at positive levels to encourage savings and investment. However, current levels of interest rates are bound to have negative effects on economic growth. High interest rates hamper the development of the small business sector which is dependent on bank credit and put home ownership out of reach of more people. It is not possible, however, for the Reserve Bank alone to lower interest rates if conditions are not appropriate. Lowering the Bank rate could lead to higher credit demand, higher inflation and, as inflationary expectations take hold, higher long-term interest rates. In addition, such a policy would lead to declining capital inflows, capital flight and higher imports, which all add up to a balance of payments crisis.

What is required is the conditions for lower (but positive) real interest rates. The strategy outlined in this document aims to bring about these conditions. These include sustained lower rates of inflation; a reduction in government dissaving which will reduce pressures on the capital markets; and the attraction of long-term capital inflows, particularly direct investment flows, which will make the capital account less dependent on short-term capital inflows which are attracted by high real interest rates;

the commitment to a stable real exchange rate and higher growth will also reduce the risk premium facing foreign capital inflows and this would then allow for lower real interest rates.

By combating domestic inflation, the monetary authorities will also contribute to stabilising the external value of the rand. Over the long run, low domestic inflation is a prerequisite for greater stability in the average value of the rand against a basket of currencies of major trading partners.

4.2 Exchange Rate Policy

Since mid-February the foreign exchange market has been subjected to intense speculative pressure, causing a substantial real depreciation of the rand. This development to some extent reflects that the rand had become somewhat overvalued in response to a temporary capital surge, but was also the result of increased concerns regarding policy trends and economic prospects. The movements of the exchange rate signal some uncertainty in financial markets, and call for careful policy responses.

In order to maintain the current competitive advantage created by the depreciation of the rand in the first four months of 1996, the objective is to keep the real effective exchange rate of the rand at a competitive level. Although short-term fluctuations may at times be unavoidable, monetary and other policy measures will be geared towards the attainment of long-term real effective exchange rate stability. This will provide the stable environment needed for a concerted expansion of export industries.

Although the exchange rate is primarily market-determined, its value at any moment cannot be considered a true reflection of the underlying value of the rand while exchange controls exist. The

Government has stated repeatedly that it is committed to phasing out controls in a prudent manner. In line with this commitment, the financial rand was abolished in 1995.

In view of the many inherent disadvantages of exchange control, such as the distortion of the price mechanism, the problems encountered in the application of monetary policy, the detrimental effects on inward foreign investment and the large administrative costs, all remaining exchange controls will be dismantled as soon as circumstances are favourable. The gradual approach to the abolition of exchange control is designed to allow the economy to adjust more smoothly to the removal of controls that have been in place for a considerable period.

The current round of exchange control liberalisation is designed as a balanced package which will enhance economic activity. The new measures include the following:

- Policies directed specifically at foreign investors include the relaxation of access to domestic credit. Although a measure of capitalisation from foreign funding is still required, the new regulations will allow for local borrowing capability to be enhanced by doubling the current borrowing limit. In terms of the new regulations, a wholly non-resident-owned entity is able to borrow 100 per cent of shareholders' equity.
- Institutional investors, namely insurance companies, pension funds and unit trusts, may currently obtain foreign assets by way of asset swaps for up to 5 per cent of their total assets, subject to the stipulations of the legal framework within which they operate. This limit will now be increased to 10 per cent.
- Institutional investors will also be allowed foreign currency transfers during 1996 of up to 3 per cent of the net inflow of funds during the 1995 calendar year. Approval for such transfers will be subject to the overall limit of 10 per cent set out above.
- Corporate entities who operate in the export field and also import goods from abroad will be allowed to offset the cost of imports against the proceeds of exports, provided the set-off takes place within a period of 30 days.
- Adjustments to existing exchange control limits and measures designed to effect administrative exchange reform are included in the package.

5. TRADE, INDUSTRIAL AND SMALL ENTERPRISE POLICIES

5.1 Recent Policy Developments

The unreliability of raw material exports in the 1980s persuaded policymakers that the central thrust of trade and industrial policy had to be the pursuit of employment-creating international competitiveness. This entails a shift away from demand-side interventions, such as tariffs and subsidies, which raised prices received by producers, to supply-side measures designed to lower unit costs and expedite progress up the value chain.

While long-term survival strategies have had to be developed for certain sensitive sectors, general progress towards an outward-oriented stance is reflected in a number of achievements:

- replacement of former quantitative restrictions with tariffs;
- rationalisation of the tariff structure by almost halving the number of tariff lines;

- abolition of import surcharges, completed in October 1995;
- phasing down of tariffs, begun in 1995, by on average one-third over five years; and
- phasing out of the general export incentive scheme, to be completed by the end of 1997.

Another critical policy thrust has been the expansion of market access through preferential trade arrangements with industrial countries and pursuit of regional economic integration. In the area of concessionary industrial finance, several schemes have been introduced by the Industrial Development Corporation (IDC), and the Regional Industrial Development Programme (RIDP) has been expanded to include a simplified scheme applicable to smaller enterprises.

The impact of trade restructuring is not easily measured. Many firms have been under intense pressure, compounded by the real appreciation of the exchange rate in 1995. Nevertheless, exports and employment in manufacturing have increased, taking advantage of the international cyclical upswing. The most positive sign, also evident in sectors sensitive to the lowering of trade barriers, has been the significant increase in new foreign and domestic fixed investment in the manufacturing sector.

5.2 Compensating Tariff Reductions

Based on the foundations which have been laid over the past two years, trade and industrial policies will seek to enhance the competitive capacity and employment absorption of manufacturing, alongside continued promotion of tourism as an export sector and appropriate growth-oriented policies in other sectors.

As a result of the real depreciation, a compensating lowering of tariffs is desirable, within the context of an orderly implementation of agreed tariff realignments. The mid-1996 real effective exchange rate is some 12 per cent below the January value, which should permit a significant acceleration of the tariff reductions to which South Africa is committed in terms of World Trade Organisation agreements. These reforms will be structured to lower prices for industrial inputs and low-income households, to avoid job losses in sensitive sectors, and to remove price distortions in domestic markets. The overall effect will be to minimise the negative effects of the depreciation on consumer prices and maximise the positive effects on industrial production. It will also encourage additional investment and job creation in competitive sectors, including priority industries.

5.3 Industrial Support Measures

Industrial innovation support programmes will be enhanced. This includes the incentive provided in terms of the Special Programme for Industrial Innovation, which has had some positive impact on domestic innovation, as well as the matching grants under the Technology and Human Resources for Industry Programme, designed to strengthen the relationship between educational institutions and industry. The technology transfer programme of the Department of Trade and Industry, which serves to police and advise on licensing and royalty agreements, will be converted into an agency dedicated to facilitating access by firms to needed technologies.

Several programmes have already been introduced to promote productivity, such as the IDC's Multi Shift and World Player schemes. A major investigation is now being undertaken under the auspices of Nedlac to develop a programme to encourage the adoption of best-practice work organisation.

To stimulate competitive and labour-absorbing industrial development, an accelerated depreciation scheme will be introduced for all new investments in manufacturing. The tax allowance programme will apply to qualifying plant and equipment which is acquired and brought into use for the first time during the period 1 July 1996 to 31 September 1999. In addition, the current Regional Industrial Development Programme will be replaced by a tax holiday available to completely new pre-approved projects initiated during a window of three years, beginning in the last quarter of 1996. Approved projects will get tax exemptions for a period of time determined by three factors: regional location, job creation and priority industries. The tax holiday, of a maximum of six years, will come into effect as soon as the project becomes liable for tax, and may not be used beyond the tenth year after the initial investment is undertaken.

Closely related are the twelve industrial priority industry investigations as well as the regional industrial locations studies. These major initiatives are intended to identify mechanisms to enhance the competitiveness of selected industrial sub-sectors. While the clusters may be eligible for the proposed tax holiday, specific interventions will also be considered where necessary. These studies involve constant interaction with both owners and workers.

The review of competition policy which is presently under way will be reflected in strengthened new legislation. The main objectives of competition policy are to encourage competition among firms, protect consumers and downstream firms from restrictive practices, and open up new opportunities for investment.

Ongoing efforts to improve the access of South African firms to foreign markets will concentrate on exploring special arrangements with major trading blocs and continuing participation in the multilateral World Trade Organisation process, as well as other initiatives such as the Cairns Group. A further key element of the strategy is the gradual integration of the economies of Southern Africa through the trade and investment protocols of SADC.

The reform of the system of industrial finance is well advanced. The IDC will continue to provide loan finance, equity and credit guarantee facilities, and will adapt its programmes to satisfy new needs. The institutional capacity to support small business is also largely in place. The various regional development corporations, however, still need to be integrated more fully into the new investment promotion effort. Other support institutions such as the Board of Tariffs and Trade, the Competition Board, the South African Bureau of Standards and the National Productivity Institute are also receiving attention to meet the challenge of global competition and employment creation.

5.4 Small and Medium-sized Enterprise Development

The promotion of small, medium and micro enterprises (SMMEs) is a key element in the Government's strategy for employment creation and income generation. Due to obstacles of the past, the SMME sector is severely underdeveloped. A major effort will be made to operationalise and implement the policies outlined in the White Paper on small business promotion. The relevant legislation is under consideration and various programmes and institutions have been established to give effect to the strategy, including:

- the Small Business Centre attached to the Department of Trade and Industry;
- Ntsika Enterprise Promotion Agency to provide non-financial assistance;
- Khula Enterprise Finance Limited for wholesale loans;
- Khula Credit Guarantee Limited for loan guarantees;
- a pre-shipment export finance guarantee facility to expand access to working capital; and
- the Competitiveness Fund for consultancy advice on technology and marketing.

The Simplified Regional Industrial Development programme will be continued in a modified form as a grant programme tailored to the needs of small and medium-sized firms.

6. SOCIAL AND SECTORAL POLICIES

The past two years have witnessed an energetic review of social and sectoral policies in keeping with RDP objectives. Public policies which affect women have come under scrutiny, programmes of action for children have been developed, and a strategy for the disabled has been put forward. Land reform, agricultural development, protection of the environment, programmes in arts and culture, technology enhancement, crime prevention, national defence, urban infrastructure, and housing, water and sanitation, and primary health services are just some of the areas in which detailed analysis and extensive public discussion have led to major policy revision.

This focus of this document is the overall macroeconomic environment. Social and sectoral policy development cannot be outlined comprehensively here, but a few key linkages between growth, redistribution and new policy directions are highlighted below.

6.1 Education

Progress in education shows up consistently in comparative studies as a key determinant of long-run economic performance and income redistribution. Sustained improvements in the quality of public schooling available to the poor and greater equity in the flow of students through secondary and tertiary education are central to the Government's approach. Despite near-universal enrolment in primary education, only some 40 per cent of children currently complete secondary schooling successfully. Inadequate pass rates in science and mathematics are cause for concern.

Reform initiatives under way, aimed at qualitative improvements in the educational system, include restructuring and decentralising of school governance and management, overhauling school curricula, establishing a national qualifications framework, addressing the culture of learning in schools, building and refurbishment of classrooms, rationalising and renewing teacher education, enhancing educational administration, and expanding further education. Suitable norms, together with quality-enhancing rewards, are under review. With spending on education at nearly 7 per cent of GDP, there is a need to contain expenditure through reductions in subsidisation of the more expensive parts of the system and greater private sector involvement in higher education. This will concentrate public resources on enhancing the educational opportunities of historically disadvantaged communities.

6.2 Health and Welfare Services

The systematic restructuring of health services, with a strong emphasis on universal and free access to comprehensive primary care, represents a clear commitment to improving the health conditions of the poor. Within the public health system resources are shifting from tertiary services in metropolitan areas towards overcoming the inadequacies of hospitals and clinics in rural areas and townships.

Partnerships between the state and voluntary organisations centred on developmental welfare services will focus attention on the vulnerable, especially in under-serviced areas, while freeing resources from expensive institutionally-based services. By far the greater part of welfare spending is devoted to social grants, which assist some 3 million elderly or disabled persons or needy children. These transfers play a vital role in poverty alleviation, especially in rural areas. Affordable alternatives to support families and children in need are being investigated.

6.3 Housing, Land Reform and Infrastructure

The implementation of the housing and infrastructure programmes has been slow, with continuous refinements to the policy framework. Since late 1995, an acceleration in housing delivery has been evident. A continuation of this trend will see the provision of housing and related services on a substantial scale. This will have several beneficial distributional effects. Construction is largely labour-intensive and provides jobs and training, while improvements in housing and infrastructure enhance the productivity of labour and the quality of urban life.

Improved water and sanitation is typically the first priority of rural communities. Some 500 projects costing R1.5 billion have been committed. Rapid progress with the supply of water to the 12 million people without adequate access will be a major contribution to poverty relief. These initiatives have been complemented by new policies regarding sanitation systems.

The land reform programme, combining asset redistribution with enhancement of tenure, has an important role in improving the long-term prospects for employment and income generation in the rural economy. Progress has been made to finalising procedures for the rapid release of land and the introduction of a settlement grant. Complementary initiatives include emergent farmer support programmes. As these gain momentum, emphasis will shift to marketing support, appropriate technological interventions and streamlined extension services. Over time, agricultural development associated with land reform will play a key role in improving the distribution of income and economic activity.

7. PUBLIC INVESTMENT AND ASSET RESTRUCTURING

7.1 Investment in Infrastructure

Investment in social and economic infrastructure will play an important role in increasing the productivity of labour and business and thus the achievement of higher growth rates. The National Infrastructure Investment Report indicated that South Africa currently faces a backlog in infrastructure of at least R170 billion, and that innovative financing strategies and careful prioritisation will be needed if sufficient progress is to be made.

This strategy envisages a substantial acceleration in government investment spending, together with improved maintenance and operation of public assets. Higher growth is clearly critical in this regard, as is a thorough restructuring of the responsibilities of relevant public corporations, development finance institutions, and local and provincial authorities.

Public infrastructure needs include domestic and industrial grid electricity and other energy projects; domestic, industrial and agricultural water supplies; sanitation, wastewater and stormwater; roads, railways, airports, harbours and pipelines; telecommunications and postal services; urban housing-related infrastructure; rural development; and hospitals, clinics and educational facilities. Progress in all these areas adds to the quality of life in communities, while simultaneously building productive economic capacity. The provision of basic household infrastructure, in particular, is a relatively low-cost and effective form of public intervention in favour of the poor and consistent with the reduction of income inequalities.

Four basic sources of finance are potentially available: fiscal transfers, concessional finance from multilateral institutions and other international sources, development finance channelled through development finance institutions, and loans raised on commercial terms. The nature of projects, including cost recovery potential and the risks involved, determine the appropriate funding mix.

Recognising the limited capacity of the fiscus, Government is committed to the application of public–private sector partnerships based on cost recovery pricing where this can be practically and fairly effected.

7.2 Corporate Governance and Asset Restructuring

Government has prepared a protocol on corporate governance of all state entities, which includes the following elements:

- formulation of dividend policies, together with clear indications of the objectives and performance appraisal norms for all agencies;

- a revised policy regarding government guarantees;
- appropriate regulatory policies, aimed at ensuring that pricing policies are fair and fully recover operating costs, while also promoting competition or protecting consumers against monopolistic practices; and
- a programme of asset restructuring with respect to the ownership and governance of state entities.

Within the context of government policy and in accordance with the procedures agreed in the National Framework Agreement with organised labour, the process of restructuring state assets is now proceeding. Detailed sectoral consultation, planning and preparation are taking place. The telecommunications sector plans to complete negotiations by September 1996 with a view to finding a strategic equity partner for Telkom and addressing other restructuring issues in this sector. A similar process will unfold in the course of this financial year in other sectors, including minerals and energy, agriculture, forestry and water, leisure and transport. Six significant regional radio stations have been put out to tender for outright sale.

The nature of restructuring, as outlined in the framework agreement, may involve the total sale of the asset, a partial sale to strategic equity partners, or the sale of the asset with government retaining a strategic interest. Work is in progress to address the outstanding issues on the restructuring of the remaining state enterprises. Specific policy issues and further elaboration will be dealt with by the responsible Ministers.

8. EMPLOYMENT, WAGES AND TRAINING

8.1 Present Trends in the Labour Market

South Africa's labour market is extremely fragmented. Employment growth in the formal sector of the economy has stagnated over the past decade and private sector employment has fallen. It is apparent that unregulated low-wage employment has increased significantly since the 1970s, now accounting for an estimated one-third of all job opportunities. In addition, a large pool of unemployed men and women, who earn no income or derive sporadic earnings from informal self-employment, make up about a third of the potential labour force.

Irregular, sub-contracted, outsourced or part-time employment on semi-formal contractual terms is becoming the preferred source of labour for many employers. This is resulting in a growing gap between the wages and benefits in the regulated and unregulated parts of the labour market. Where regulations raise the costs of job creation, employers turn to unregulated forms of employment.

The major development in the primary segment of the labour market over the past two years has been the new Labour Relations Act. This has four key features. It establishes a single industrial relations system for all employees, promotes collective bargaining by providing certain organisational rights for trade unions, establishes new procedures and institutions for resolution of disputes, and provides for workplace forums to facilitate a shift from conflictual employer–employee relations towards joint problem-solving with employee participation. The reduced incidence of industrial unrest in recent years attests to the considerable progress made in this regard.

Present trends in the economy lead to employment growth of 100 000 to 130 000 per year, with unemployment rising to 37 per cent by the year 2000 and an increased casualisation of the labour force. On this trajectory, poorly rewarded employment in survival activities grows nearly twice as fast as formal sector job opportunities. Weakening employment opportunities for the poor imply that income distribution is likely to worsen, impacting particularly severely on the rural poor, young work-seekers and those without education or skills.

8.2 Labour Market Reform Challenges

The fragmented character of the South African labour market, conflictual labour relations and poor productivity have tended to undermine competitiveness and hence investment. Appropriate balances have to be struck in the labour market in respect of job creation, between regions and sectors and between maintaining existing jobs, protecting those in employment, and creating opportunities for new entrants. In a context of approximately 33 per cent unemployment, the challenges are immense.

Government has a responsibility for ensuring that labour market rules are fair and that there are appropriate mechanisms for dispute resolution. Government is also an important employer and the main investor in human resource development in the economy. It influences, through its industrial and other policies, the sectoral growth trend of the economy. Accelerated job creation and improved productivity are direct or indirect goals of a wide range of government policies and programmes, some of which are noted elsewhere in this document.

In this integrated macroeconomic strategy, employment growth accelerates, reaching 409 000 jobs annually in the year 2000 and reversing the upward tendency in the unemployment rate. Over the next five years some 833 000 more jobs are created in the higher growth strategy than would otherwise be possible.

In this strategy there are two broad thrusts relating to labour market policy. The first is the pursuit of regulated flexibility aimed in part at extending the protection and stability afforded by this regulatory framework to an increased numbers of workers. The second is the promotion of continued productivity improvements aimed at bolstering the development of skills across the full spectrum of the workforce in both the formal and non-formal sectors. These points of departure are the basis of Government's labour market policies and will be further elaborated in response to the report of the Comprehensive Labour Market Commission.

The Government will pursue a policy of regulated flexibility in managing the labour market. This entails the regulation of the labour market in a manner that allows for flexible collective bargaining structures, variable application of employment standards, and voice regulation.

The appropriate determination of wages is a critical component of the medium-term macroeconomic strategy. It is a precondition for sustaining the competitive advantage of the currency depreciation, and it is the key to ensuring the maintenance of industrial competitiveness in the longer term. A sudden upsurge in nominal wage demands would either unleash a wage–price spiral that would soon erode any semblance of a real depreciation or force a severe tightening of monetary policy, leading to higher interest rates and economic contraction. It is therefore important that wage and salary increases do not exceed average productivity growth.

Analysis of employment prospects indicates that accelerated job creation can be achieved in broadly three ways. Growth itself could account for about one-third of the increased job creation envisaged under an integrated strategy, some of which would be in informal or other unregulated activities. Government programmes can add a further quarter of the new jobs, mainly through accelerated labour-based infrastructural development and maintenance of public works in urban and rural areas. Some 30 per cent of the increased employment, however, and more than half of the new formal private sector opportunities, will have to arise from institutional reforms in the labour market, employment-enhancing policy shifts, and private sector wage moderation. Stronger growth of more labour-intensive components of industry, facilitated by shifts in industrial policy, is vital. It is these reforms that are needed to bring about the increased responsiveness of labour demand to output growth, and are the essential ingredients of a sustainable, labour-absorbing growth path.

Furthermore, the general direction of economic policy is towards greater openness and competitiveness. The economy will thus become increasingly subject to global forces. The challenge then facing labour market policy is to promote dynamic efficiency, skill enhancement and the expansion of reasonably remunerated employment – while at the same time supporting a labour-intensive growth path which generates jobs for the unemployed, many of whom are unskilled and have never had previous employment. The Government intends to promote collective bargaining while simultaneously pursuing an appropriate balance between productivity enhancement and employment creation.

8.3 A More Flexible Labour Market

Government recognises that industrial agreements which reach across diverse firms, sectors or regions should be sufficiently flexible to avoid job losses and should be extended to non-parties only when this can reasonably be assured. The Minister of Labour's discretion to extend or not to extend agreements should be broadened to permit the Minister to bring labour market considerations into play. Wage agreements must be sensitive to regional labour market conditions, the diversity of skills levels in firms of varying size, location or capital intensity, and the need to foster training opportunities for new entrants to the labour market.

Other labour market policies should be negotiated by labour, business and government constituencies at appropriate levels in terms of a national framework. Reforms consistent with accelerated access of new entrants to employment and training opportunities might include less onerous minimum wage schedules for young trainees, lower indirect wage costs (through a more cost-effective provision of retirement, medical, unemployment and accident benefits), increased incentives for more shifts, job sharing and other measures to support greater employment flexibility. Variations on norms set through collective bargaining must be an integral aspect of a system of regulated flexibility, building on the safeguarding of employment standards and workers' rights implicit in existing policies.

The determination of minimum wages remains, in certain sectors of the economy, to protect the vulnerable and the weak. The approach will not be to set one minimum wage across the whole economy but to determine appropriate standards by sector and area. The determination of these minimum wages must follow proper hearings, investigations and consideration of relevant economic conditions, the potential for employment creation and the alleviation of poverty.

The Department of Labour will encourage, through the mechanisms provided in the Labour Relations, Act, the rationalisation of collective bargaining arrangements to meet the challenges of the new economic environment while recognising the diversity of the domestic labour market.

8.4 Enhancing Productivity

Government also recognises that job creation and improved living standards require a substantially increased commitment by the business sector to industrial investment and productivity-enhancing training. Accelerated investment is a principal thrust of this strategy, and must be promoted across a broad sectoral front, including export-oriented manufacturing and agro-industrial projects, tourism-related industries and improved transport and communication services, and with a particular focus on smaller firms. In many sectors, there is scope for both increased employment and training of the unskilled and improved productivity at higher skill levels.

International indicators show that South African investment in human resource development is inadequate. An enhancement of the level and effectiveness of training across all employment sectors is central to this growth strategy. Training underpins productivity improvement by enhancing human capability – across all labour market segments and product lines – to exploit technological flexibility and add value on competitive terms. Regulated flexibility of the labour market, discussed above, must permit employees to increase their productivity over time. Improved management training, modernisation of work practices, appropriate job grading, and better utilisation of working time are also key aspects of enhanced efficiency.

A refocusing of curricula and the organisation of formal learning are currently in progress under the auspices of the education authorities. Coordination of standards and quality assurance will be the responsibility of the newly established South African Qualifications Authority.

The Department of Labour has embarked on the development of a new human resource development strategy, in partnership with all major stakeholders, which is planned to culminate in new legislation in 1997. Central to this strategy is a new financing mechanism and governance framework which aims to increase the aggregate level of effective investment in training. Towards this end the government is investigating the feasibility of introducing a mandatory levy on payroll. The matter is currently under negotiation with the social partners represented in Nedlac. The strategy includes the following:

- establishment of a tripartite national coordinating council, responsible

for giving strategic direction to human resource development and for building an energetic, coherent national system;
- restructuring of industry training boards to facilitate best-practice training, under industrial management;
- strengthening of the levy-based industrial training financing mechanism;
- appropriately focused funding of training for emergent enterprises and the unemployed;
- an overhaul of the guidance, training, placement and labour market information services of the Department; and
- development of an information and planning capacity to support the national training strategy.

In addition, there will be deliberate campaigns to enrich human resource development programmes within government departments and agencies, aimed at effective service delivery. Management training initiatives are already under way in several key departments.

Government recognises that it has an important role to play in financing education and training activities aimed at the unemployed and the small business sector and in enhancing the quality of technical and vocational education and training. Sustained improvements in the quality of general schooling are also largely the responsibility of the fiscus. Industrial training must remain mainly the responsibility of employers. Government seeks to facilitate the development of financing mechanisms that will enjoy broad support from both the business sector and organised labour.

9. TOWARDS A NATIONAL SOCIAL AGREEMENT

A strong tradition of collective bargaining characterises the South African industrial and social environment. Sectoral and regional agreements are likely to contribute to structuring future growth and development. There is an important role also for a broad national agreement, to create an environment for rapid growth, a brisk investment trend and accelerated delivery of public services based on equity and universal access. The challenge facing the government and its social partners is to ensure that a national agreement underpins rapid growth, job creation, and development.

The immediate objective of the agreement would be to ensure that the recent depreciation of the currency does not translate into a vicious circle of wage and price increases, leading to instability in the financial markets and a decline in competitive advantage. For this reason it is important that wage and salary increases do not rise more than productivity growth. It is equally important that price restraint should be maintained, facilitated through an effective competition policy and continued trade liberalisation.

In the longer term, a broad social agreement might address a wider range of issues related to economic restructuring, income distribution and social policies. Orderly collective bargaining between organised labour and employers must remain the foundation of industrial relations.

For its part, the government commits itself to an accelerated increase in its contribution to social and community living standards. Most of the policy frameworks and institutional systems are now in place to ensure the following:

- the delivery of housing and related services;
- steady improvement in the quality of education;
- universal access to primary health care;
- access to land and agricultural support for emergent farmers;
- electrification of all urban areas and an increasing number of rural communities;
- reliable water supplies and appropriate sanitation infrastructure;
- improved postal and telecommunications services; and
- a broad social security net, comprising social grants and targeted welfare services.

Equally important, the government will provide a combination of real exchange rate management and tax incentives aimed at encouraging private sector investment. For workers, this will give certainty that wage moderation will contribute towards growth, job creation and social benefits. For the business sector, this strategy creates an environment in which investments can be made confidently, competitiveness is enhanced and public policies are clear.

10. POLICY COORDINATION

As a result of political stability and sound policies, economic growth has revived, bringing to an end the stagnation that characterised the 1980s. Our strategy will build firmly on the foundations established since 1994, leading to accelerated growth, increased job creation, and a significantly improved distribution of income and opportunities.

The higher growth path depends in part on attracting foreign direct investment, but also requires a higher domestic saving effort. Greater industrial competitiveness, a tighter fiscal stance, moderation of wage increases, accelerated public investment, efficient service delivery and a major expansion of private investment are integral aspects of the strategy. An exchange rate policy consistent with improved international competitiveness, responsible monetary policies and targeted industrial incentives characterise the new policy environment.

A strong export performance underpins the macroeconomic sustainability of the growth path. Private sector employment creation is reinforced by small business promotion, land reform and emergent farmer support, greater labour market flexibility and labour-based public sector infrastructural development projects.

Accelerated economic growth associated with stronger employment creation is the key to continued progress towards an equitable distribution of income and improved standards of living for all. Employment creation provides a powerful vehicle for redistribution, supported by government housing, water supply and sanitation, health, education, welfare and social security services.

Success in a more open and complex economic environment requires consistent and integrated policies. Timing, sequencing and packaging of reforms are important, as is the clear commitment of social partners to an agreed policy framework. World competitiveness nowadays depends as much on comparative advantage in the public policy arena as it relies on technology, human resources and physical capital.

Government has a clear policy coordination role. There are trade-offs amongst policy options and competing claims by different interest groups which need to be nationally resolved. Whilst institutions have been developed to aid this process, and Government is committed to an open and consultative approach, the ultimate responsibilities for a credible and coherent policy framework lies with Government. As a first step in this process, Government calls for a clear commitment by both business and labour to the broad principles set out in this document.

Within Government, especially in the fields of monetary, fiscal, trade, industrial and labour policies, there is also a critical need for coordination. Inconsistent approaches in any of these areas have the potential to destabilise the credibility of the overall macroeconomic framework. Effective coordination of economic policy at Cabinet level has accordingly been given the highest priority by Government, together with supporting arrangements within key administrations and between Government, the Reserve Bank, the business sector, organised labour and other key constituencies. The strategy set out in this document seeks to remove uncertainty, give clear direction to the economic course on which South Africa is headed, and invite Government's social partners to join in the building of a competitive, fast-growing economy.

Building a National Democratic Society: Strategy and Tactics of the ANC

(Adopted by the 52nd national conference of the ANC, Polokwane, 16–20 December 2007)

I. Introduction

1. South Africa has entered its Second Decade of Freedom with the strengthening of democracy and acceleration of the programme to improve the quality of life of all the people. Steadily, the dark night of white minority political domination is receding into a distant memory.

2. Yet we are only at the beginning of a long journey to a truly united, democratic and prosperous South Africa in which the value of all citizens is measured by their humanity, without regard to race, gender and social status.

3. The achievement of democracy in 1994 marked the birth of our country as an African nation on the southern tip of the continent. It provided South Africans with the opportunity to:
- set up a government based on the will of the people and on people-centred and people-driven principles as part of the process to de-racialise the economy and society at large;
- pursue economic growth, development and redistribution so as to achieve a better life for all;
- strengthen the ANC as a leader in the implementation of a practical programme of social change and a movement rooted among the people;
- build democracy, a culture of human rights and a value system based on human solidarity; and
- work with African and global progressive forces to advance human development in our country, our continent and across the globe.

4. These tasks, which are at the core of the National Democratic Revolution, have to be undertaken in a global environment of contradictory tendencies.

5. The dominance of a capitalist system with minimal regulation presents enormous challenges for social development and for global governance and security.

6. At the same time, programmes of progressive social change are finding pride of place on the agenda of many developing nations and some global institutions. Most African countries have successfully set out to resolve conflict, entrench democracy and reconstruct economies in a manner that benefits the people.

7. This environment provides a basis for the advancement of the National Democratic Revolution (NDR) in our country.

8. However, this cannot be assumed. It depends on the ability of progressive forces to promote the positive elements in both the global and domestic settings and to assert a progressive vision of the world we want to live in.

For the ANC, this also means forging a corps of cadres unwaveringly committed to the cause of change, and the mobilisation of the majority of South Africans to act as one in pursuit of a better life for all.

II. Where We Come From: Streams of an Emergent Nation

9. The South African nation is a product of many streams of history and culture, representing the origins, dispersal and re-integration of humanity over hundreds of thousands of years. Archaeological findings in various parts of the country and the rest of Africa have located South Africa and the continent at large as the cradle of humankind and early forms of human civilisation.

10. From the earliest manifestations of intellectual activity; the settlements of pastoral communities characterised by foundries, artisanship and trade across oceans; colonisation by Europeans; the slave trade and indentured labour – South Africa has emerged as one of the most diverse nations across the globe. This is our collective national heritage which we should continue to research and engage, the better to appreciate who we are as a nation.

11. Besides African inter-communal co-operation and wars of nation-formation, the greatest impact on the evolution of the South African nation-state was made by European colonial settlement. On the one hand, colonialism interrupted internally-driven advancement of indigenous South African communities along the ladder of human development. It resulted in the subjugation of the African population, including the Khoi and the San who were subjected to genocidal campaigns, as well as Indian communities and slaves from Southeast Asia and other areas. On the other

hand, the advanced industrial base of the colonial powers which made such subjugation possible introduced into the South African geographic entity the application of advanced forms of economic production and trade.

12. The South African nation-state is a product of these interactions, characterised between 1652 and 1994 by ongoing and mostly violent conflict between the oppressors and the oppressed. Despite their heroic resistance, the African people were defeated in a series of wars that took place over two-and-half centuries of colonial expansion. Part of this resistance took the form of slave revolts in the Cape Colony and elsewhere. Besides the advanced productive forces at the disposal of the colonial powers, one of the central reasons for the defeat of indigenous communities was division and conflict among these communities themselves.

13. It speaks to South Africa's strategic geographic location that this territory experienced colonial intrusion earlier than most African societies. The discovery of gold and diamonds in the latter half of the 19th century laid the basis for industrialisation, the emergence of more complex links of economic dependence with Europe and North America, and the subjection of the black population to the needs of an emergent colonial capitalism. As a consequence of these and other factors, the colonial designs of the imperial powers were applied more systematically; the European settlers fought intensely among themselves over the territory; and most of these settlers came to characterise South Africa as their home.

14. As such, what emerged in our country was Colonialism of a Special Type, with both the coloniser and the colonised located in a common territory and with a large European settler population. The deal between the descendants of Dutch settlers and the British imperial power at the end of the so-called Anglo-Boer War formalised, in 1910, South Africa's statehood, premised on the political oppression and social subordination and exclusion of the majority of the people.

15. The African National Congress (ANC) was formed in 1912 in part as a response to this deal among the colonisers, as well as the defeat of the Bhambatha Rebellion of 1906 which marked the end of armed resistance against colonial occupation. It was also a product of new forms of African resistance across various parts of the country and the globe.

16. Starting off with petitions to the colonial powers, the ANC over the years developed ever more militant forms of struggle, and finally adopted armed struggle and formed Umkhonto weSizwe in 1961, a year after its banning. Combined with armed actions, the ANC and other resistance movements used international mobilisation, underground organisation and mass mobilisation to challenge colonialism and its apartheid derivative.

In these various terrains of struggle, workers, the rural masses, women, youth, students, the religious community, the intelligentsia, professionals and other sections of society played a critical role. As during the wars of resistance and the anti-slave revolts, they displayed selflessness and heroism that will remain an inspiration to future generations.

17. As a result of generalised mass revolt, a situation was reached in the late 1980s in which the system of white minority domination could no longer be sustained. Yet at the same time, the liberation struggle at the head of which was the ANC had not as yet amassed sufficient strength to overthrow the apartheid regime.

18. Elements within the South African ruling class and its international allies started to weigh the implications of continuing popular revolt – and its culmination in the overthrow of the apartheid regime – on their interests within the country and the region. While it had always accepted the human and material cost of protracted struggle, the ANC had, as a matter of abiding principle, sought a more humane resolution of the conflict without compromising the basic objectives of struggle.

19. Conditions were thus created for a negotiations process which resulted in a settlement underpinned by non-racial democracy, with the first-ever democratic elections held in April 1994.

20. South Africa's colonial experience was based on the intersection of relations of power based on class, race and gender. These social and/or biological features have been used in human history to exclude, to repress and to stymie the progress of individuals and communities.

21. Across the globe, these practices represented and in the main still represent the exercise of raw power as opposed to human compassion; relations based on subjugation as opposed to human solidarity; greed and self-aggrandisement as opposed to shared prosperity; religion and other belief systems used as justification for hatred and war as opposed to spiritual and cultural advancement; and treatment of the world as a theatre for narrow self-interest as opposed to the collective well-being of humanity.

22. Because the struggle against colonialism sought to eliminate most of the manifestations of these iniquitous social relations, it evolved to embrace the best in human civilisation and value systems.

23. While the anti-colonial struggle could easily have been conducted as one against a racial group, it rose above these categories to embrace the principle of non-racialism: to see humanity as one and diversity as a source of strength. While all communities, including the oppressors and the oppressed, evinced patriarchal relations of power, the struggle evolved to appreciate the real and potential role of women, and that their liberation

from patriarchy was and should be an integral part of the new democracy.

24. While in the early years, the liberation movement reflected some characteristics of elitism, it developed over the decades to appreciate the place and role of the working class and the poor both as a critical social force in production and trade and as a militant contingent against apartheid colonialism.

25. As such, the liberation struggle by oppressed communities, even in the midst of bitter confrontation, developed moral values of human compassion and solidarity far beyond the narrow confines of its opposition to the apartheid social system. It represented something good, not just something better than apartheid. It asserted the humanness of the human spirit – the search for societies at peace within and among themselves. It developed to advocate the use of human intelligence to advance collective social comfort and to preserve the endowments of our planet and outer space for the sustenance of current and future generations.

26. In this sense therefore, it is both an honour and a challenge for the ANC to claim the legacy of the liberation struggle, to occupy the high ground of its moral suasion and wield its compass.

III. Vision of Our Collective Effort:
Character of the National Democratic Revolution

27. If the progress we have made since 1994 constitutes only the beginning of a protracted process of change, what is it that we aim for? What kind of society do we seek to create? What is the character of the NDR?

28. Colonialism of a Special Type contained within itself contradictions that could not be resolved through reform. It had to be destroyed. As such, the system we seek to create will stand or fall on the basis of whether it is able to eliminate the main antagonisms of this system.

29. A national democratic society constitutes the ideal state we aspire to as the ANC and the broad democratic movement. It should thus not be confused with tactical positions that the liberation movement may adopt from time to time, taking into account the balance of forces within our country and abroad. Circumstances in which we conduct social transformation will change all the time. And in the process of effecting such transformation, there will be successes and setbacks.

30. The liberation movement should avoid the temptation to crow over such successes in these early years as if we had already achieved our ultimate objective. Nor should we seek to justify mistakes and setbacks as unavoidable, pleading a fixed set of circumstances and thus leading us into

the danger of redefining the ultimate objective.

31. This is where the line should be drawn between strategy – the ultimate goal – and tactics – the methods and actions that respond to changing immediate circumstances. Clearly, at all times we should develop tactics that are suitable for the specific conditions under which we operate. But such tactics should be informed by our commitment to the strategic goal.

32. What does this mean in actual practice?

33. Our definition of Colonialism of a Special Type identifies three interrelated antagonistic contradictions: class, race and patriarchal relations of power. These antagonisms found expression in national oppression based on race; class super-exploitation directed against black workers on the basis of race; and triple oppression of the mass of women based on their race, their class and their gender.

34. The National Democratic Revolution is defined as such precisely because it seeks to abolish this combination of sources of social conflict. It has national and democratic tasks, and it should strive to realise:
- a united state based on the will of all the people, without regard to race, sex, belief, language, ethnicity or geographic location;
- a dignified and improving quality of life among all the people by providing equal rights and opportunities to all citizens; and
- the restoration of the birthright of all South Africans regarding access to land and other resources.

35. The NDR seeks to build a society based on the best in human civilisation in terms of political and human freedoms, socio-economic rights, value systems and identity.

36. Such human civilisation should be reflected, firstly, in the constant improvement of the means to take advantage of our natural environment, turn it to collective human advantage and ensure its regeneration for future use. Secondly, it should find expression in the management of human relations based on political equality and social inclusivity. If there were to be any single measure of the civilising mission of the NDR, it would be how it treats the most vulnerable in our society.

37. One of the most critical acts of the NDR is the creation of a legitimate state which derives its authority from the people, through regular elections and continuing popular participation in the processes of governance. Mobilised around a clear vision of the kind of society we wish to become, the nation should act in partnership – each sector contributing to the realisation of the common good. The means should be put in place for citizens to exercise their human rights, and for the checks and balances

necessary in a law-governed society. The democratic state should also have the organisational and technical capacity to realise its objectives.

38. As with any nation, South Africans will continue to have multiple identities based on class, gender, age, language, geographic location, religion and so on. In a national democratic society, such diversity should feed into an overarching national identity. In its own unique way, South Africa should emerge as a united African nation, adding to the diversity and identity of the continent and humanity at large.

39. The main content of the NDR is the liberation of Africans in particular and blacks in general from political and socio-economic bondage. It means uplifting the quality of life of all South Africans, especially the poor, the majority of whom are African and female. At the same time it has the effect of liberating the white community from the false ideology of racial superiority and the insecurity attached to oppressing others. The hierarchy of disadvantage suffered under apartheid will naturally inform the magnitude of impact of the programmes of change and the attention paid particularly to those who occupied the lowest rungs on the apartheid social ladder.

40. Precisely because patriarchal oppression was embedded in the economic, social, religious, cultural, family and other relations in all communities, its eradication cannot be an assumed consequence of democracy. All manifestations and consequences of patriarchy – from the feminisation of poverty, physical and psychological abuse, undermining of self-confidence, to open and hidden forms of exclusion from positions of authority and power – need to be eliminated. Critical in this regard is the creation of the material and cultural conditions that would allow the abilities of women to flourish and enrich the life of the nation.

41. A nation's success depends also on its ability to encourage, harness and incorporate into its endeavours the creativity, daring and energy of youth. This relates to such issues as access to social and economic opportunities, engendering activism around issues of development and values of community solidarity, and creating the space for youth creativity to flourish.

42. Among the most vulnerable in society are children and the elderly: and a national democratic society should ensure their protection and continuous advancement. Such is the challenge also in relation to people with disability – not merely as a matter of social welfare, but based on the recognition of the right of each individual to dignity and development and of the contribution that each can make to the collective good. In many respects, there is a critical link between the objective condition of children,

the elderly and people with disability and poverty.

43. Implementing these corrective measures requires more than just references to general political rights. A continuing element of democratic transformation should be a systematic programme to correct the historical injustice and affirm those deliberately excluded under apartheid – on the basis of race, class and gender. The need for such affirmative action will decline in the same measure as all centres of power and influence and other critical spheres of social endeavour become broadly representative of the country's demographics. In the process, all inequalities that may persist or arise will need to be addressed.

44. Apartheid colonialism visited such devastating consequences on black communities because it ordered the ownership and control of wealth in such a manner that these communities were deliberately excluded and neglected.

45. Therefore, fundamental to the destruction of apartheid is the eradication of apartheid production relations. This is more than just an issue of social justice. It is also about the fact that these relations had become a brake on the advancement of technology and competitiveness of the economy.

46. A national democratic society should be founded on a thriving economy, the structure of which should reflect the natural endowments of the country and the creativity that a skilled population can offer. It should be an economy in which cutting edge technology, labour-absorbing industrial development, a thriving small business and co-operative sector, utilisation of information and communication technologies, and efficient forms of production and management all combine to ensure national prosperity. This is conditional on ensuring that the brain and brawn of all of society are brought to bear on all economic activity. It requires de-racialisation of ownership and control of wealth, management and the professions.

47. In this regard, such a society will place a high premium on redistribution of land in both urban and rural areas for the benefit of those who were denied access under colonialism. Such access must be provided for a variety of purposes including agriculture, housing, environmental preservation, mining and other economic activity, public utilities and spaces, entertainment and other uses. In order to ensure effective and sustainable land and agrarian reform, effective measures will be put in place to assist 'emergent' and small-scale farmers and co-operatives.

48. A thriving economy in a national democratic society requires as efficient a market as possible, shorn of the racial and gender exclusions that characterised apartheid colonialism, and freed from the barriers to entry

and competition that the economy endured under colonial capitalism. It will also require a state able to use its capacities to direct national development through fiscal redistribution, utilisation of State-owned Enterprises and effective regulation.

49. A national democratic society will have a mixed economy, with state, co-operative and other forms of social ownership, and private capital. The balance between social and private ownership of investment resources will be determined on the balance of evidence in relation to national development needs and the concrete tasks of the NDR at any point in time.

50. In this regard, the state will relate to private owners of investment resources in the context of the national objective to build a better life for all. Through its various capacities the state will encourage socially beneficial conduct on the part of private business. Similarly, through such capacities, it will ensure that these investors are able to make reasonable returns on their investments.

51. Social cohesion in a national democratic society will also depend on the extent to which the rights of those in the lower rungs of the socio-economic ladder are protected. Such a society should proceed from the obvious premise that workers' rights are human rights; and these rights should find expression in law-governed measures to ensure decent jobs, job security and a living wage. Through legislation and other means, the state should manage the environment for fair and balanced relations between employers and employees.

52. Particular attention in such a society should be paid to conditions of the poor in rural areas. This also applies to the life circumstances of such groups as citizens in informal settlements as well as female-headed and single households.

53. A national democratic society should use the redistributive mechanism of the fiscus to provide a safety net for the poor. As such, built into its social policy should be a comprehensive social security system which includes various elements of the social wage such as social grants, free basic services, free education, free health care, subsidised public transport and basic accommodation.

54. A national democratic state should continually implement integrated anti-poverty programmes, ensuring that these programmes address not only social assistance, but also the sustainable integration of all communities into economic activity. This is critical in dealing with poverty in general, but also in addressing the condition of the majority of women.

55. All these measures are important for social cohesion. They should be supported by joint efforts among all sectors of society to strengthen

community organisation and mobilisation around issues pertaining to sport, women's rights, youth interests, the battle against crime and so on. There also should be deliberate collective action to promote a positive role by the institution of the family. The public media also have a critical role to play in promoting social cohesion.

56. Critical elements of a value system based on human solidarity should include pride in social activism and respect for an honest day's work. They should include social dissuasion against conspicuous consumption, ostentation and corruption. This is part of the ideological engagement that should be a permanent feature of the process of change, involving both the state and civil society.

57. Whether such common social decency is achievable under a market-based system with its tendency to reproduce underdevelopment and inequality, in a globalised world, is an issue on which society should continually engage its mind. Concrete practice, rather than mere theory, will help answer this question. What is clear though is that such was the symbiosis between political oppression and the apartheid capitalist system that, if decisive action is not taken to deal with economic subjugation and exclusion, the essence of apartheid will remain, with a few black men and women incorporated into the courtyard of privilege. The old fault-lines will persist, and social stability will be threatened.

58. A national democratic society is, by definition, made up of various classes and strata. The NDR seeks to eradicate the specific relations of production that underpinned the national and gender oppression and super-exploitation of the majority of South Africans. It does not eradicate capitalist relations of production in general. It should therefore be expected that in a national democratic society, class contradictions and class struggle, particularly between the working class and the bourgeoisie, will play themselves out. As such, a national democratic state will be called upon to regulate the environment in which such contradictions manifest themselves, in the interest of national development including fundamental socio-economic transformation.

59. In broad terms, the NDR seeks to ensure that every South African, especially the poor, experiences an improving quality of life. It seeks to build a developmental state shaped by the history and socio-economic dynamics of South African society. Such a state will guide national economic development and mobilise domestic and foreign capital and other social partners to achieve this goal. It will have attributes that include:

- capacity to intervene in the economy in the interest of higher rates of growth and sustainable development;

- effecting sustainable programmes that address challenges of unemployment, poverty and underdevelopment with requisite emphasis on vulnerable groups; and
- mobilising the people as a whole, especially the poor, to act as their own liberators through participatory and representative democracy.

60. The ANC therefore seeks to build democracy with social content. Informed by our own concrete conditions and experiences, this will, in some respects, reflect elements of the best traditions of social democracy, which include: a system which places the needs of the poor and social issues such as health care, education and a social safety net at the top of the national agenda; intense role of the state in economic life; pursuit of full employment; quest for equality; strong partnership with the trade union movement; and promotion of international solidarity.

IV. Progress in Changing Society: Shifting Domestic Balance of Forces

61. How far then have we moved up the road towards a national democratic society? In what ways has the balance of forces changed since the advent of democracy?

62. Our starting point in this regard is that revolutionary democrats shall not find social relations of the new order ripe and ready for harvesting at the point of transfer of power. A national democratic society is a conscious construct, dependent on conscious action by politically advanced sections of society.

63. A mere decade and a few years after the democratic transition in 1994, the liberation movement can claim great progress towards a democratic and prosperous society.

64. But we are not satisfied with the current order of things. Over the years of democratic rule, we have become even more keenly aware that we should not be blinded by form – the fact that blacks are, for the first time, occupying the highest political offices in the land – as distinct from content: the reality that colonial relations in some centres of power, especially the economy, remain largely unchanged.

65. It is possible in national liberation processes to mark time, tinkering with social relations under the veneer of formal political democracy. Yet as with all historical phenomena, to mark time is to move in reverse. The consequence is either gradual regression, with a self-satisfied elite unsighted; or a rapid collapse of social cohesion under the weight of poverty and lawlessness.

66. The political transition of the early 1990s was premised on a few basic principles: firstly, that the outcome of the negotiations process would

not be a compromise between apartheid and democracy but would as rapidly as possible result in democratic majority rule. Secondly, the Interim Constitution prescribed the need for a multi-party government at national and provincial levels. Thirdly, it was considered prudent to ensure orderly management of the exit of senior functionaries of the apartheid state and gradual law-based transformation of state institutions such as the army, the police, intelligence agencies and the judiciary. Fourthly, changes in local government were introduced in stages, with fully-fledged democracy being achieved only in the year 2000.

67. During negotiations, representatives of the previous order sought an outcome that would leave many elements of the apartheid system intact. On the other hand, the liberation movement sued for democratic majority rule as understood throughout the world. The transitional measures were seen by the liberation movement as necessary compromises to ensure the broadest possible legitimacy of the new order and to use the advances made as a beach-head to a truly united, non-racial, non-sexist, democratic and prosperous society.

68. At the point of change of government in 1994, the state was manned at all senior levels by apartheid functionaries; the economy was almost totally in the hands of whites; many of the parties sought constitutional outcomes that would guarantee white privilege; and networks of apartheid and extreme right-wing destabilisation remained burrowed, or had multiple links, within the state. These and other realities impacted on the manner in which the programmes of change were introduced.

69. How has the situation changed since then?

70. South Africa enjoys a system of vibrant multi-party democracy, with a progressive Bill of Rights which recognises political, socio-economic and environmental rights and obligations, and with separation of powers among the executive, the judiciary and the legislatures. Beyond the formal processes of regular elections and legislatures, various forms of legislated and other forums ensure popular participation.

71. The Constitution enjoys the respect of the overwhelming majority of the population, and it is seen as the canvas upon which South Africans' freedom of spirit can find expression. While some within the ranks of those who were privileged under apartheid may harbour ill-feelings towards the process of change and evince racist attitudes, virtually all of them accept that their aims and views should be pursued within the constitutional and legal framework. While pockets of ethnic chauvinism and regionalism still manifest themselves and may take new forms under the new conditions, our society has made massive progress in ensuring a common national identity.

72. We have started to transform state institutions through policy frameworks and practices that guide them as well as improvements in their racial and gender profiles. A state entity has emerged that enjoys such allegiance that only the most fanatical can dare frontally to challenge it. Yet, much more needs to be done further to transform state institutions, and consolidate their legitimacy in the eyes of society.

73. The ANC must continue to exercise maximum vigilance against forces which seek to subvert social transformation. Indeed, there are continuing attempts by forces connected to the old apartheid order and international reaction to undermine the state and to disorganise, weaken and destroy the liberation movement through clandestine means, including all kinds of manipulation within and outside its ranks. In addition, marginalisation and destitution inherited from apartheid and the kind of greed represented by organised crime do create fertile ground for lumpen elements whose actions can have counter-revolutionary implications.

74. The same applies to weaknesses on the part of government across all spheres progressively to fulfil its responsibilities to communities, including service provision and consultations, which can generate upheavals that may be taken advantage of by forces opposed to fundamental change. Further, weaknesses of organisation and political coherence within the ANC and its broad allies can open up space which can be exploited by counter-revolutionary forces.

75. Many short-comings remain in ensuring that all citizens are able in actual practice to exercise their rights; in the efficiency of the state; and in changing mindsets within various state institutions. However, as a broad canvas, the Constitution and the state system provide the requisite wherewithal to implement objectives of the NDR.

76. Since the advent of democracy, a new polity has emerged, with the liberation movement led by the ANC at its head. This movement has gradually mastered the science and art of electoral politics and grown in experience as the leading force in government. This has, however, been accompanied by a declining presence in the mass terrain.

77. The achievement of democracy has opened up critical space for organisations of civil society to flourish. This finds expression in the growth and activism particularly of the labour movement and some community-based and other non-governmental organisations dealing with generic or single-issue campaigns. However, this 'social movement' has manifested contradictory features under democracy. This is partly due to the haemorrhaging of experienced cadreship, and tendencies towards mechanical oppositionism in relation to government or towards an exclusive

focus on narrow self-interest. The question of the role of progressive trade unionism within the state, in relation to broader issues of providing services to citizens, the fight against corruption and revolutionary transformation of the state itself, has not been adequately addressed.

78. While a battery of legislation and programmes has been put in place to transform the socio-economic dynamics of South African society, the changes in this sphere illustrate the distance that still has to be traversed to achieve national democracy.

79. The removal of the glass ceiling of apartheid has created space for many blacks to rise into the middle and upper strata of society. It is in these middle sectors where the greatest dynamism in income mobility is to be found. However, the improvement in black and female ownership and control of wealth and access to management and many professions is still limited, with overall proportions which are inversely related to the country's demographics. This is more starkly reflected in terms of land ownership. As such, while progressive forces have attained political power, economic power remains largely in the hands of the white minority.

80. Even more critically, trends do indicate a persistence of the poverty trap – a form of marginalized Second Economy community excluded from the advanced First Economy mainstream – afflicting mainly black people, especially women.

81. Major improvements have been registered at the turn of the Second Decade of Freedom in terms of the economy's rate of labour-absorption and generation of self-employment. But these have not matched the needs of society. At the same time, while the achievement of macroeconomic balances has released huge resources for social and economic expenditure by government, this has not translated into rates and quality of investment needed to deal with the legacy of apartheid.

82. Combined with this is the restructuring of the economy, which has resulted in higher levels of competitiveness and better access to world markets; but also in the ascendancy of the services sector which requires fewer, skilled jobs. A tendency has also developed in the period since 1994 for the informalisation of jobs, contracting out and utilisation of labour brokers affecting particular sectors of the economy. While the achievement of democracy has resulted in a better regime of workers' rights, this tendency has undermined the quality of jobs, job security and union activism in the affected sectors.

83. The period since 1994 has also seen other macrosocial trends that include:
- rapid rates of migration to areas with better economic potential,

with resultant sprawls of informal settlements in the major cities and towns;
- greater self-assertion by the youth in taking advantage of professions now opened up and opportunities in the arts and other areas, but also marginalisation of millions of young people who do not have the skills required by the economy;
- better gender representation in the legislatures and other organs of state, but also slow progress in the private sector and serious manifestations of poverty and women abuse;
- better advocacy and access in relation to the rights of people with disability, but a huge legacy of marginalisation; and
- greater focus on the rights of children, but still unacceptable levels of child poverty and abuse.

84. The state has massively expanded access to welfare grants; and the social wage includes such elements for the poor as free and compulsory education, free health care, free basic services, and asset provision through the housing and land reform programmes. Steady progress has been made in the battle against crime. However, the reach of such programmes is still constrained by access to information, availability of resources and capacity of the state.

85. The gradual reduction in life expectancy at the turn of the 21st century is a matter of great concern; and it is influenced mainly by the impact of HIV and AIDS. At the same time, we need to address the challenge of crime, particularly unique features such as random violence, disrespect for human life, as well as women and child abuse. These are in part a consequence of social conditions, gender stereotypes and negative value systems such as greed.

86. The legitimacy of the state system is reflected partly in the growing number of South Africans of all colours who view their national identity as the primary form of self-identification. In the middle rungs of the socio-economic ladder, there is much inter-racial acculturation, especially among the youth. But the majority of South Africans still remain separated by a wide chasm of income, skills, assets, spatial settlement patterns and access to opportunities. The majority of the poor are disproportionately black and female.

87. Combined with this chasm and high levels of inequality is a value system within society that encourages greed, crass materialism and conspicuous consumption. These are tendencies that go beyond the necessary spirit of entrepreneurship, ambition, daring, competition and material reward that are inherent to a market-based system and perhaps

to human development in general. Related to this is the fact that the means of ideological discourse are dominated by forces with an outlook that is either ambivalent or hostile to principles of human solidarity. Among the consequences of all this are vacuous media discourse, corruption in state institutions and corporate greed reflected in outrageous executive packages, short-termism in the conduct of business and private sector corruption.

88. Overall, since 1994, the balance of forces has shifted in favour of the forces of change. It provides the basis for speedier implementation of programmes to build a truly democratic and prosperous society. The legal and policy scaffolding for this is essentially in place. Most of society wants this to happen. At least in public discourse, except for a tiny minority, those apprehensive about change express their concerns more in terms of pace and scale rather than substance.

89. The critical questions therefore are: Is society mobilised for faster progress? Does the liberation movement have the cadreship able not only to withstand the pull of negative values, but also to lead society along the road towards a caring nation that a national democratic society should be?

V. Drivers of Change: Motive Forces of the National Democratic Revolution

90. Who then are the drivers of change?

91. The ANC seeks to mobilise all South Africans to contribute to the ongoing transformation of our country. In doing this, we strive to appeal to and foster a common sense of South Africanness and a shared responsibility for our common destiny among all citizens of South Africa, black and white.

92. Yet, any major historical process of social transformation has to be driven by a core of classes and strata that objectively stand to benefit from and have the capacity together to drive such change.

93. It should be emphasised, though, that the mere prospect of objective benefit does not necessarily translate into revolutionary consciousness and resolve to act in the collective interest. Nor does the fact of belonging to either side of the divide remove the possibility of individuals from these classes and strata aligning themselves with the antagonists.

94. It also stands to reason that the extent of receptiveness to ideas of change and commitment to take part in struggle would in broad terms depend on the role in the production process and the depth of subordination and exclusion. In other words, among the classes and strata suing for change, there will be concentric circles or a hierarchy of involvement.

95. Historically, the liberation movement characterised Africans in particular and blacks in general as the motive forces of the NDR. These

communities were, by law, defined outside of the political system except as servants of white minority domination. In class terms, they were made up of workers and the rural poor, the middle strata including small business operators, and real or aspirant capitalists.

96. The liberation movement defined the enemy, on the other hand, as the system of white minority domination with the white community being the beneficiaries and defenders of this system. These in turn were made up of workers, middle strata and capitalists. Monopoly capital was identified as the chief enemy of the NDR. It was also emphasised that apartheid was not in the long-term interest of the white community.

97. More than ten years into democracy, does this still apply? To answer this question we need to examine the strategic objectives of the NDR and changing socio-political dynamics under the new system.

98. As indicated earlier, the character of the NDR – in terms of the social contradictions that it seeks to resolve – remains the same. The progress made since the attainment of democracy is such that we are still some way from the ideal society of national democracy. The ownership and control of wealth and income, the poverty trap, access to opportunity and so on, are all in the main defined, as under apartheid, on the basis of race and gender.

99. As such, the central task in the current period is the eradication of the socio-economic legacy of apartheid; and this will remain so for many years to come. However, the establishment of a government based on the will of the people, progress in the transformation of the state, the codification of rights, and implementation of progressive socio-economic programmes represent a major change in the socio-political environment.

100. Given all these factors, how then do we define the drivers of change today: which are the forces that the ANC relies on to achieve its objectives?

101. To the extent that the socio-economic legacy of apartheid continues to manifest in national terms, to that extent Africans in particular and blacks in general are the motive forces of the NDR. Profound self-interest impels them to act in the collective interest to realise the strategic objectives of the NDR. They are the drivers of reconstruction and development. As in the past when they rose above the politics of race hatred, these communities do carry the responsibility of leading the process of nation-building and reconciliation too. Critical for them to play this role is the defence and consolidation of unity across ethnic and racial divides, to fight racism and tribalism whenever and wherever they rear their ugly head.

102. In class terms, these forces are made up of black workers: employed and unemployed, rural and urban. The early and extensive development of capitalism in South Africa led to the emergence of black workers as the

majority in our society. They are located strategically at the heart of modern production and services. Because of and in addition to this, their sense of organisation and mobilisation locates them as the main motive force and the leader of the process of change.

103. Their tasks in this phase of the NDR include: advancing the struggle for quality jobs and job security; building class and national solidarity among all sectors of workers including casualised, informalised and unemployed workers; ensuring a strategic contribution by public sector workers to the transformation of the state and efficient provision of services to the population; directing the employment of institutional capital in which workers have a large stake towards developmental goals; and leading in the definition of a common vision and in implementing a common programme of action among all the motive forces and the nation as a whole. In addition to leading in mass struggles, the working class will continue to enjoy the confidence of the rest of the motive forces and advance its own interests if it is also able to wield the opportunities and instruments provided by democracy – both economic and political – to advance social transformation.

104. A significant part of the working class in our country is the rural poor, mostly unemployed, landless, engaged in self-employment through survivalist micro-entrepreneurial activity or farm-workers in insecure low-paying jobs. Land dispossession and marginalisation destroyed any semblance of an African peasantry in our country, reducing these rural areas into reserves for cheap labour. In addition to the strategic challenges that face workers in general, these rural masses face tasks that include: taking active part in defining and implementing strategies for rural development; enhancing the struggle for rural workers' rights; advancing the land reform programme; and mobilising for the optimal utilisation of agricultural land and other activities in the agricultural value chain.

105. As part of the motive forces, the black middle strata constitute a critical resource of the NDR. They include the intelligentsia, small business operators and professionals. Besides their varied identification with either of the main classes, these strata – especially the intelligentsia – not only provide professional skills, but also are critical in the determination of culture and value systems. They are called upon to play an active role in the provision of a variety of services to the population; in fostering a culture of searching for new and better ways of doing things; and in promoting progressive intellectual discourse through the media, the arts and other platforms.

106. The achievement of democracy in 1994 has seen the dramatic, if

still exceedingly limited, emergence of the black capitalist group. This group is in most respects a product of democratic change, a direct creation of the NDR. The continued advancement of the revolution, particularly the necessary de-racialisation of ownership and control of wealth and income, is in their objective interest. In this sense they are part of the motive forces, with great potential to play a critical role in changing the structure of the South African economy: developing national forces of production in line with the character of the national democratic society including an extensive manufacturing base, research and development, local economic development, job creation, skills development as well as national and continental economic integration.

107. However, because their rise is dependent in part on co-operation with elements of established white capital, they are susceptible to co-option into serving its narrow interests – and thus developing into a comprador bourgeoisie. Because their advancement is dependent on a variety of interventions and, as with all private capital, on opportunities provided by the state, they are constantly tempted to use corrupt means to advance their personal interests – and thus developing into a parasitic bureaucratic bourgeoisie. The liberation movement must guard against and combat these tendencies.

108. What about the various classes and strata within the white community?

109. Virtually all South Africans pay allegiance to the Constitution. Increasing numbers, including among the whites, entertain a sense of collective belonging to South Africa. It can be argued that most in the white community have come to realise that, indeed, non-racial democracy is in their immediate and long-term interest. This, combined with the social dynamics within the middle strata and acculturation referred to earlier, brings to the fore the question whether merely by dint of being white, this community still can be defined as antagonists of NDR.

110. In terms of practical experiences especially in the private sector, public discourse and voting patterns, it seems that many in the white community still have to realise that the poverty and inequality spawned by apartheid are not in their long-term interest, and that black people are as capable as anyone else to lead and exercise authority in all spheres of life. This derives in part from historical socialisation based on the false ideology of racism, which needs continually to be combated.

111. But, unlike before, when antagonists across the apartheid divide were locked in mortal combat, engagement around issues of transformation in a democracy forms part of legitimate discourse and electoral politics.

Those who continue to resist change within the constitutional framework are opponents in a democratic order. Their political and other organisations are legitimate expressions of a school of thought that should be challenged, but at the same time accepted as part of democratic engagement.

112. It behoves the liberation movement to persist in clarifying the long-term self-interest that the white community shares in ridding our society of the legacy of apartheid. Indeed, formal political democracy including the new human rights regime would be imperilled if conditions of abject poverty and massive inequality persist.

113. In this regard, the liberation movement must lead each of the classes and strata within the black community in narrowing the racial chasm. This applies more so to the working class which, by reaching out across the racial divide within this class, should be the lightning rod to the emergence of inclusive nationhood. But it also does apply in large measure to the middle strata especially the intelligentsia, and the capitalist class.

114. What about the place and role of monopoly capital? There are fundamental areas of divergence between the objectives and value systems of the ANC and those of monopoly capital. In particular, there is much in the nature and behaviour of private monopolies that has the effect of constraining higher rates of growth and skewing development. These include monopoly pricing and other forms of rent-seeking, selfish import parity pricing, barriers to entry in some industries, and a value system based on greed and crass materialism.

115. The approach of the liberation movement to private capital, including monopoly capital, is informed by our understanding of the national democratic society as a system that encourages competition, promotes sustainable labour-absorbing activity, discourages rent-seeking in the form of super-profits arising from monopoly control and other selfish advantages, and so on.

116. The relationship between the national democratic state and private capital in general is one of 'unity and struggle', co-operation and contestation. On the one hand, the democratic state has to create an environment conducive for private investments from which the investors can make reasonable returns, and through which employment and technological progress can be derived. On the other hand, through state-owned enterprises, effective regulation, taxation and other means, the state seeks to ensure redistribution of income, to direct investments into areas which will help national development, to play a central role in providing public goods and broadly to ensure social responsibility. The balance between 'unity' and 'struggle' will be dictated to by the strategic imperatives

of the National Democratic Revolution.

117. As such, the democratic state should have the strategic capacity and the instruments to deal with these negative tendencies, while at the same time mobilising private capital in general to partner it in increasing rates of investment and sustainable job-creation.

118. Across all these class and national permutations women are to be found in their various capacities. As workers they bear the greatest burden of super-exploitation and poverty. As survivalist micro-entrepreneurs, they are called upon to provide use-values to working class communities under unbearable conditions. As middle strata and business-persons, they are compelled to hew their way through the jungle of male-dominated professions and environments. In the home, they carry the burden of nurturing families and are forced to reproduce relations of patriarchy. In challenging these anomalies along with progressive men, women form, in gender terms, the bedrock of the construction of a caring nation.

119. These then are the core, the real and the potential drivers of change in the National Democratic Revolution. Much clearer than before, the concentric circles of united action are taking shape, with black workers at the core and black communities broadly as the motive forces.

120. Unlike before, when white support for non-racial democracy and social transformation was an exception to the rule, large sections within this community accept at least the imperatives of the National Constitution. As such, tapering off towards the outer edges of the concentric circles of drivers of change is the balance of the nation's majority – made up of all races – steadily forging a social compact of common interest.

121. Across these circles the intertwining of black and white interests is taking shape, with the definitions of the past starting to fade. As these circles intertwine and the currents across them flow into one another, so will the objectives of the NDR be reaching maturity. Common interests will increasingly be forged across the racial divide within the various social classes and strata. And so, other defining issues in pursuit of other strategic objectives may become the paramount driving forces for continuing change.

VI. Organisational Leader of Change: Character of the African National Congress

122. Given the vision of a national democratic society and the motive forces of change, what should be the character of the movement to lead social transformation?

123. To carry out the NDR in the current phase requires a progressive national liberation movement which:

- understands the interconnection between political and socio-economic challenges in our society;
- leads the motive forces of the NDR in pursuing their common aspirations and ensuring that their sectoral interests are linked to the strategic objective;
- masters the terrain of electoral contest, utilises political power to advance the objectives of the NDR and wields instruments of state in line with these ideals as reflected in the National Constitution;
- organises and mobilises the motive forces and builds broader partnerships to drive the process of reconstruction and development, nation-building and reconciliation; and
- conducts itself, both in its internal practices and in relation to society at large, in line with the ideals represented by the NDR and acts as a microcosm of the future.

124. The African National Congress is such a movement. Over the years, it led the struggle of the people of South Africa for the achievement of democracy. In turn, during successive elections since 1994, it has resoundingly been returned to office.

125. The primary task of the ANC remains the mobilisation of all the classes and strata that objectively stand to benefit from the cause of social change. The dictum that the people are their own liberators remains as relevant today as it was during the days of anti-apartheid struggle.

126. The dynamics within South African society, resulting in the concentric circles described earlier, impose on the ANC the responsibility to work more intensely among all sectors of the population and to ensure that they join the people's contract to change South Africa for the better. This includes all the class forces from within the white community, each of which can and should make a contribution to the construction of a better society.

127. The vision that the ANC pursues is informed by the morality of caring and human solidarity. The kind of democracy it pursues leans towards the poor; and it recognises the leading role of the working class in the project of social transformation. Recognising the reality of unequal gender relations, and the fact that the majority of the poor are African women, the ANC pursues gender equality in all practical respects.

128. In this context, the ANC is a disciplined force of the left, organised to conduct consistent struggle in pursuit of a caring society in which the well-being of the poor receives focused and consistent attention. In terms of current political discourse, what it seeks to put in place approximates, in many respects, a combination of the best elements of a developmental state and social democracy. In this regard, the ANC contrasts its own positions

with those of:
- national liberation struggles which stalled at the stage of formal political independence and achieved little in terms of changing colonial production relations and social conditions of the poor;
- neo-liberalism which worships the market above all else and advocates rampant unregulated capitalism and a minimalist approach to the role of the state and the public sphere in general; and
- ultra-leftism which advocates voluntaristic adventures including dangerous leaps towards a classless society ignoring the objective tasks in a national democratic revolution.

129. In order for it to exercise its vanguard role, the ANC puts a high premium on the involvement of its cadres in all centres of power. This includes the presence of ANC members and supporters in state institutions. It includes activism in the mass terrain of which structures of civil society are part. It includes the involvement of cadres in the intellectual and ideological terrain to help shape the value systems of society. This requires a cadre policy that encourages creativity in thought and in practice and eschews rigid dogma. In this regard, the ANC has a responsibility to promote progressive traditions within the intellectual community, including institutions such as universities and the media. Playing a vanguard role also means the presence of members and supporters of the ANC in business, the better to reshape production relations in line with the outlook of a national democratic society.

130. The activism of the ANC among the motive forces should be a responsibility of members and leaders alike, informed by a coherent cadre policy that takes into account career-pathing among its activists. And wherever they are to be found, ANC cadres should act as the custodians of the principles of fundamental social change, winning respect among their peers and society at large through their exemplary conduct. They must be informed by values of honesty, hard work, humility, service to the people and respect for the laws of the land.

131. As a multi-class mass movement, the ANC is required to master the science and art of crafting long- and short-term common platforms to ensure that all the motive forces pull in the same direction. We do acknowledge that, at times, the narrow self-interest of a particular class or stratum or group may not necessarily coincide with that of other motive forces. In some instances, as with the working class and the bourgeoisie, these interests may even be contradictory.

132. However, guided by the ideals of the NDR, the ANC has to ensure

that these forces appreciate the common strategic interest. It should strive to manage 'contradictions among the people' in such a manner that they do not undermine the long-term goal of national democratic transformation. In attending to these issues, the ANC should remain steadfast to principle, and guard against attempts by any force to turn it into a hostage of narrow sectoral interest.

133. Our approach to all these responsibilities derives from the understanding that a national democratic society has to be systematically constructed. It is not found ready-made at the point of transfer of political power. Nor can it emerge spontaneously through the agency of the 'hidden hand' of the market. What this means is that members of the ANC should continually improve their capacity – both political and technical – to act as the most advanced elements of society.

134. As such, the ANC cannot conduct itself as an ordinary electoral party. It cannot behave like a shapeless jelly-fish with a political form that is fashioned hither and thither by the multiple contradictory forces of sea-waves. There should be clear value systems that attach to being a member and a leader of the ANC, informed by the strategic objectives that we pursue.

135. In essence, the ANC is faced with two options: either to act as a party of the present, an electoral machine blinded by short-term interest, satisfied with current social reality and merely giving stewardship to its sustenance. Or it can become a party of the future, using political power and harnessing the organisational and intellectual resources of society to attain the vision of a national democratic society.

136. This arises in even bolder relief given the new terrain in which we operate. In actual fact, the world of the ANC changed drastically at the point of the 1994 democratic breakthrough. On the one hand, a new critical instrument of struggle, state power, one of the prime prizes of resistance, was attained. On the other, this instrument of power and status can impact in negative ways on a revolutionary movement.

137. Many leaders and cadres of the movement are found in positions of massive influence in the executive, the legislatures and state institutions. By breaking the glass ceiling of apartheid, the liberation movement opened up enticing opportunities for its cadres in business and the professions. Even within the trade union movement and students', youth, women's and other mass democratic organisations, unprecedented opportunities for individual material gain have opened up. All this creates a problem of 'social distance' between these cadres of the movement and ordinary members and supporters, the majority of whom are working class and poor.

138. Political incumbency also presents a myriad of problems in the

management of relations within the organisation. Patronage, arrogance of power, bureaucratic indifference, corruption and other ills arise, undermining the lofty core values of the organisation: to serve the people!

139. How the ANC negotiates this minefield will determine its future survival as a principled leader of the process of fundamental change, an organisation respected and cherished by the mass of the people for what it represents and how it conducts itself in actual practice. A number of principles need to be observed in dealing with this challenge.

140. Firstly, the critical importance of political power as an instrument to address the ills of colonialism needs to be fully appreciated. In this regard, politics and public service need to be treated as a calling with requisite moral status, in which any of the motive forces can take part, either as a profession or as time-bound service.

141. Secondly, the ANC should give strategic leadership to those of its cadres in institutions of government, through Conferences, Councils and Branch General Meetings. In this respect, it needs to act as the ultimate strategic 'centre of power' for its members.

142. Thirdly, in order to ensure that its strategic mandate is carried out, the ANC needs to strengthen its monitoring and evaluation capacity massively. This will ensure that cadres deployed in various capacities are able to improve their work in meeting set objectives. At the same time, these cadres should have sufficient space to exercise initiative within the strategic mandate rather than being subjected to micro-management.

143. Fourthly, systems of information-sharing within leadership structures and across the organisation should afford those outside of government sufficient data to make strategic interventions. In the same measure, all cadres should apply themselves seriously to governance issues, practically to add strategic value to the work of government.

144. Lastly, in its conduct in relation to the state, the ANC should be guided by its own principles, and act within the framework of the National Constitution and relevant legislation. In this regard, it should manage the state as an organ of the people as a whole rather than a party political instrument.

145. Within the ANC, the Women's League (ANCWL) is tasked with the responsibility of helping the ANC to broaden its mass base, as it champions the aspirations of a section of our society which over the decades, has been oppressed and exploited as 'a nation', as a class and as women. It should continue to be the voice of ANC women members, but it should also be at the cutting edge of the Broad Women's Movement, spearheading gender transformation and the advancement of a women's agenda in all areas of

social endeavour in South Africa.

146. In a similar vein, the ANC Youth League (ANCYL) is a critical tool of South Africa's youth in pursuit of a better life for all. It should continue to function as an organisational and political preparatory school of young activists of our movement, informed by our strategic and tactical positions. The organisational autonomy of the ANCYL always provides organisational vibrancy and the youthful political debate imperative to a revolutionary organisation. It should continually broaden its base and deepen its political and organisational strength. It must strive to galvanise, and place itself at the centre of, the broadest spectrum of youth organisations for reconstruction and development.

147. As part of the process of preserving its values and culture, while adapting them to concrete conditions in which it operates, the ANC places a high premium on the contribution that veterans of the struggle can make. In this regard, the Veterans' League has a central role to play both by force of example and in practical organisational and ideological work within and without the ranks of the broad democratic movement.

148. Historically, the three streams of the national liberation struggle in our country – the revolutionary democratic, the socialist and the trade union movements – have found common cause in pursuit of the objectives of the NDR as commonly understood. This Tripartite Alliance, currently made up of the ANC, the South African Communist Party and the Congress of South African Trade Unions, is therefore not a matter of sentiment, but an organisational expression of the common purpose and unity in action that these forces share, and continue jointly to define and redefine in the course of social transformation. It is a strategic alliance aimed at eliminating the legacy of colonialism in its various manifestations, and not a coalition based on tactical considerations or the subjective mood of the moment. As a leader of the NDR, the ANC will continue to work for strategic unity among all components of this Alliance, in pursuit of a national democratic society.

149. In line with its responsibility to lead the motive forces of change, the ANC will continue to encourage the formation of, and to work within, progressive civil society: organisations of communities, students, youth, women, people with disability, traditional leaders, business and other non-governmental and community-based organisations. It will also continue to reach out to religious and other institutions to ensure common approaches to challenges of transformation. The ANC will conduct such mass work, taking into account the dynamic changes taking place in the social structure and varied lifestyles of South African society.

150. The character and strength of the ANC must continue to reside in

and derive from its mass base. As the leading force in government, the ANC should continually improve its capacity and skill to wield and transform the instruments of power.

VII. The Global Balance: Character of the International Situation

151. The ANC was formed and it evolved as part of progressive forces across the globe in the fight against colonialism, racism, poverty, underdevelopment and gender oppression. It drank and continues to drink from the well of these progressive global experiences. The strategic objectives of our National Democratic Revolution reflect some of the best values in human civilisation.

152. In its conduct of struggle, the ANC takes into account the global balance of forces, the better to help create and take advantage of opportunities for decisive advance and to avoid pitfalls of adventurism. In this regard, we proceed from the understanding that it is the task of revolutionary democrats and humanists everywhere to recognise dangers; but more critically, to identify opportunities in the search of a just, humane and equitable world order – a world with greater security, peace, dialogue and better equilibrium among all nations of the world, rich and poor, big and small.

153. What then is our assessment of the major trends in the world in which we live?

154. Today, the system of capitalism holds sway across the world; and it is underpinned by the unique dominance of one 'hyper-power'. This situation of unipolarity also has secondary multi-polar features reflected in geopolitical blocs among developed and developing countries, and the historical resurgence of China, India, Brazil and Russia as centres of growth and development. These multi-polar features require continuing research and engagement.

155. The world-wide system of capitalism is characterised by globalisation, which has seen impressive advances in the development and utilisation of technology, integration of production and management processes across oceans, massive trade in financial instruments and expansion of trade in goods and services.

156. But beyond this its technical expression, globalisation has also been shaped by the agenda of dominant global forces. These include transnational corporations controlling trillions of rands of humanity's wealth, alliances around one 'hyper-power' whose dominance is reminiscent of empires of a bygone era, and cultural domination reflected in trends towards homogenisation of media content and the arts. A critical consequence of all

this is the undermining of the system of global governance.

157. At the political level, the dominant imperialist powers have historically used various means to assert their geo-political and economic interests. This finds contemporary expression in unilateralism and militarism which have reared their ugly head on a scale hardly witnessed in recent history. In intellectual and policy discourse, notions of empire and benevolent colonialism find respectable articulation. In many respects, the current global balance is evocative of the situation in previous eras of dominant empires and colonialism when brute force was the currency of geo-political intercourse.

158. In a situation in which an exploitative socio-economic system rules the waves, the danger should not be underestimated of widening wars of conquest and other more sophisticated means of subversion in search of resources, markets and geo-political advantage. Indeed, notions of 'pre-emptive wars' and 'regime change' are becoming the political stock-in-trade. This imperils the sovereignty of smaller and weaker nations.

159. Attached to this phenomenon is the assertion of shallow and populist ideologies, such as the so-called 'clash of civilisations', premised on varied expressions of religious fundamentalism, which seek to justify political crusades of blood and gore. By-products of this mindset include racial profiling, the undermining of the rule of law both in domestic and global conduct, and systematic violation of human rights.

160. The growing threat of terrorism on a global scale, conducted by state and non-state agencies alike, forms an indistinguishable part of this phenomenon. Masked as resistance against imperialism or a fight against so-called 'forces of evil', terrorism – which is the deliberate targeting of civilians in violent conflict – is both inhuman and repugnant. Militarism and terrorism feed one another. They are two sides of the same coin.

161. However, these dangers manifest themselves in a period in which humanity is keenly aware of the disastrous consequences of war and the dehumanisation that can result from warped ideologies of race hatred and religious intolerance. Ordinary citizens across the globe are finding various ways of resisting the encroachment of the rapacious licence of empire. Through mass mobilisation and progressive political parties, and through the power of the vote, continuous processes of self-correction do assert themselves.

162. At the socio-economic level, the wonder of technology, including computing, genetics and nano-technology, continues to broaden the horizons of human civilisation and create possibilities that only a few decades ago existed only in the wildest of human imagination. It is the irony

of our age that such possibilities for the resolution of problems of health, environmental degradation as well as poverty and under-development are appropriated for the benefit of a few, and are seen to impress mainly in the shock and awe of war.

163. Technological advancement has created a global economic system that increasingly works as 'a unit in real time on a planetary scale'. The advantages of this are limitless.

164. On the other hand, these opportunities can be abused through financial systems in which paper money begets paper money, with new ingenious ways found to extract so-called shareholder value that has little bearing on actual production. This also creates an environment for a pervasive short-termism that can hold back the development of productive forces. Related to this is the growing tendency to sustain and justify staggering packages and astonishing lifestyles of corporate executives and so-called celebrities, with levels of inequality that are reminiscent of the eras of slavery and feudalism.

165. Globalisation also impels the search for the lowest in human deprivation to locate production and extract maximum returns, with developing countries encouraged to bid one another lower on a catwalk of mutual beggaring. Combined with this is the utilisation of economic power to rip open frontiers of protectionism among the weak, while doing the opposite in developed countries. All these developments and others, such as rapid and unregulated capital flows that include complex derivatives and private equity takeovers, negatively impact on the sovereignty of developing countries.

166. These are some of the fundamental shortcomings of a rampant and poorly regulated market-based system. This system perpetuates under-development and deepens inequality within and among nations, creating what are in fact two global villages. It fuels corruption on a massive scale. It also precipitates migration from poor to rich countries, resulting in a debilitating brain drain and illegal escapes that heighten inter-state tensions. In addition, this system entrenches patriarchy, including the vicious exploitation of female labour, trafficking in women and children, and poor representation of women in global positions of authority.

167. Globalised capitalism has also generated careless exploitation of natural resources, endangering the long-term survival of the human species. The wanton destruction of the environment, the threat to biodiversity and the danger of global warming are all a grave challenge that should receive priority attention. These developments take place in an era in which oil reserves as a non-renewable source of energy are declining at a rapid pace,

and sources of potable water are diminishing relative to social and economic needs. At the same time, food production is not keeping pace with the needs of humanity and food stocks such as fish are being senselessly plundered.

168. Parallel to these short-comings has been the widening access to modern technology and foreign markets across the globe. Nations which organise and position themselves to take advantage of this are advancing at a rapid pace. New economic growth centres are emerging – in Asia – and Africa is poised to join the trend.

169. It is a measure of the changing global economic balance that the fastest-growing regions of the world are located in developing countries. Their share of global production has increased dramatically, with profound implications for global economics and politics. In various parts of the 'developing world', including Latin America, there is a growing assertion of national and collective sovereignty and a progressive developmental agenda. As a consequence, the voice of the South is growing stronger by the day. Both from the point of view of their common historical experiences and common current interests, countries of the South need to strengthen co-operation among themselves. They need to build people-centred and people-driven systems and pool their sovereignty through strategic partnerships.

170. Globalisation also means growing inter-dependence among nations, reflected among others in production and trade, financial flows, environmental challenges, health issues and migration. Further, improved platforms of mass communication help lay bare the advances in human comfort and thus the unfairness of massive global inequality.

171. The global mass movements around these and other issues attest to the impact of these factors on global human consciousness and conscience. Public opinion is steadily turning. Progressive parties, workers' and women's organisations, popular campaigns around local development and environmental issues, associations of professionals and movements of people with disability, indigenous communities, the homeless, the landless and so on, all have resolved to challenge the negative effects of globalisation.

172. It is in part a result of these trends that the United Nations Organisation (UN) has put high on its agenda the notion of human security as encompassing issues of poverty and underdevelopment. Whatever their limitations, initiatives such as the UN Millennium Development Goals, the programme for sustainable development, and the development round in global trade negotiations do reflect the positive impact of a progressive global paradigm. At the same time, the voices calling for democratisation of the UN and other multilateral institutions and the restructuring of the

global exercise of power are growing.

173. South Africa's interests in a complex and unpredictable global environment necessitate the building of capacity for strategic as well as rapid responses to changes in our region, Africa and the world. Within this context, our global strategy for the coming years will remain firmly anchored on the African continent and the developing countries.

174. Africa has the best possibility in this milieu to emerge from an era of political and social decline into a renaissance of hope and social progress. It can on a massive scale turn adversity into opportunity. A new spirit is abroad on the continent, and the people of Africa are determined to use their newly-harnessed energy, pride and self-assertiveness to chart their own course of development and extricate themselves from the lowest rungs of human development.

175. Most of the conflicts on the continent have been resolved. Democracy is spreading. Economic growth is accelerating. And there is a collective determination to turn Africa into one of the centres of rapid industrialisation and social development.

176. While historical experiences of subjugation have much to do with Africa's current position, it is Africans themselves, partnered by others, who can bring about the renaissance of their nations and their continent.

177. The most immediate challenges in this regard consist in the development of infrastructure for economic activity and social services, the deepening of democracy and mass participation, and improved public service. Also crucial are regional integration and assertion of national and collective continental sovereignty in pursuit of a higher trajectory of development and in relation to global partners.

178. The ANC forms part of the global forces – including governments, political parties and civil society organisations in developing and developed countries – campaigning for a humane and equitable world order. In its history it has gained from and contributed to a culture of human solidarity across the globe. It is informed in its international work by values of internationalism, promotion of human rights against all abuses and violations, and support for national liberation. In this regard, the ANC supports the right of all peoples to fight against oppression and tyranny.

179. The ANC will continue to work with other countries and progressive forces to promote the transformation of the global order away from unilateralism and conflict. It will continue to seek a path of hope and human solidarity, to pursue resolution of conflict through dialogue and peaceful means, and to promote mutual friendship among peoples of the world. This we shall do, proceeding from the premise that all nations have a

shared responsibility collectively to improve the human condition.

180. Our standpoint on these matters is both a matter of profound self-interest and an issue about the humanity of our own outlook. We will continue to build and strengthen progressive alliances and networks across the globe, including inter-state, party-to-party and people-to-people relations in Africa and further afield in pursuit of an equitable and humane world order.

VIII. Steps towards the Vision: Programme of National Democratic Transformation

181. What then are the main steps that we need to take, in the programme of the democratic state in the current phase, to bring us closer to the ideal of a national democratic society?

182. The answer to this question is informed by the character of the NDR, actual practical experience since 1994 and our reading of the current balance of forces. In broad terms, our approach is informed by the ideals contained in the Freedom Charter, adopted at the Congress of the People in 1955. The practical measures towards a national democratic society are contained in the Reconstruction and Development Programme (RDP) adopted by the ANC, the Tripartite Alliance and the broad mass democratic movement in the run-up to the first democratic elections. This was further updated and elaborated in election manifestos during subsequent elections.

183. What we outline hereunder are the main emphases in the work of the ANC government in the coming decade.

Constitution and Governance

184. The National Constitution sets out the framework within which to manage social relations. Some of the basic principles include: multi-party democracy; the doctrine and practice of separation of powers in a constitutional democracy; equal human rights and access to opportunity; freedom of speech and of the media; equality of all before the law; respect for the rights of linguistic, religious and cultural communities; social equity and practical corrective action against racial, gender and other forms of discrimination.

185. In order to ensure popular involvement in the processes of change, the ANC will continue to build partnerships across society. Practically, the ANC will strengthen institutions and practices of popular participation and encourage efforts to build an enduring people's contract – for each sector to contribute to the common objective.

186. There will be continuing work to improve the legitimacy of the

democratic state, encourage national identity and the role of the state as an instrument of social cohesion. Informed by this legitimacy, the state will also ensure that its collective national authority as regulator of social relations is respected, in the context of the rule of law.

187. The ANC will consistently improve the role played by legislative organs of government as tribunes of the people, and as platforms to monitor and advance the programme of change. It will continue to promote the transformation of the judiciary and to consolidate the legitimacy of this important arm of the state in a constitutional democracy. Informed by the doctrine of separation of powers, the ANC will encourage mutual respect among the three arms of the state – the legislature, the executive and the judiciary – in dealing with matters of common interest.

Building a Developmental State

188. The first attribute of a developmental state in our conditions should be its strategic orientation: an approach premised on people-centred and people-driven change, and sustained development based on high growth rates, restructuring of the economy and socio-economic inclusion.

189. The second attribute of our developmental state should be its capacity to lead in the definition of a common national agenda and in mobilising all of society to take part in its implementation. Therefore, such a state should have effective systems of interaction with all social partners, and exercise leadership informed by its popular mandate.

190. The third attribute should be the state's organisational capacity: ensuring that its structures and systems facilitate realisation of a set agenda. Thus, issues of macro-organisation of the state will continue to receive attention. These include permutations among policy and implementation organs within each sphere, allocation of responsibilities across the spheres, effective inter-governmental relations and stability of the management system.

191. The fourth attribute should be its technical capacity: the ability to translate broad objectives into programmes and projects and to ensure their implementation. This depends among others on the proper training, orientation and leadership of the public service, and on acquiring and retaining skilled personnel.

192. The ongoing transformation of the state is meant to ensure that these capacities are attained; and the process of identifying weaknesses and correcting them will be intensified. This includes engendering new doctrines, culture and practices as well as ensuring that state institutions reflect the demographics of the country, including appropriate representation of

women and people with disability.

193. This applies to the public service in its totality as well as specialised institutions such as the judiciary, the police, intelligence agencies and the defence force. All these organs should serve the people in an efficient and impartial manner.

Accelerated and Shared Growth

194. Central to the country's economic challenges in the current phase is to build an integrated and growing economy from which all South Africans can benefit.

195. The ANC will continue to strive for macroeconomic balances that support sustainable growth and development. This applies to such indicators as the budget deficit, inflation and interest rates. In other words these balances shall not be treated as things-in-themselves, but as requirements that ensure higher rates of growth, labour-absorption and poverty-reduction.

196. Government action will be guided by an industrial strategy and a corresponding programme which continually identifies and addresses constraints to investment. This will help build an economy that is characterised by high levels of manufacturing activity, modern services, expanding trade, cutting-edge technology and a vibrant small business and co-operative sector. State and private capital as well as resources and capacities in the hands of communities will be mobilised for this purpose. During various periods, specific industries will be identified for concerted joint action by all economic partners. A critical element of this strategy will be a comprehensive programme of land and agrarian reform.

197. To ensure that benefits of growth are shared by all, there will be focus on creating decent jobs and ensuring an improving quality of life for workers. Government will implement programmes to eliminate economic dualism and exclusion. These include skills development, specific attention to industries that lend themselves to involvement by marginalized communities, access to micro-credit and small business assistance, land reform, public works projects and promotion of sustainable livelihoods at community and household levels.

198. The government will intensify broad-based programmes to empower those previously excluded from mainstream economic activity, including women. To ensure balanced and sustainable spatial development, systematic analysis will be conducted of economic potential and incidence of poverty in various geographic areas, and the three spheres of government will integrate their development plans to address these issues.

Macrosocial Tasks: Meeting Social Needs

199. The central objective of social policy should be to preserve and develop human resources and ensure social cohesion.

200. To achieve this objective, the ANC government will continuously improve service to society, through enhanced public infrastructure, efficient systems and requisite personnel. We approach these issues proceeding from the premise that the state has a critical role to play in providing public goods such as health, education, housing, public transport, education and social security.

201. The ANC will implement a comprehensive social security system which brings together initiatives such as free basic services for the poor, passenger transport subsidy, social grants, expansion of the asset base of the poor through housing, small business and land reform programmes as well as private retirement savings, unemployment and accident insurance, and medical aids.

202. Government will align and integrate the various programmes – economic and social – directed at eradicating poverty with the aim of ensuring effectiveness and better monitoring and evaluation. Given the reality of feminisation of poverty, central focus in this regard will be paid to the conditions of women, especially in rural, 'township' and informal settlements.

203. Central to the preservation of human resources is the issue of the nation's health profile and causes of death. The ANC government will strive to massively reduce cases of TB, diabetes, malnutrition, maternal deaths and malaria, as well as violent crime and road accidents. Over and above this, the impact of the pandemic of HIV and AIDS requires a massive joint effort of the state and all sectors of society so as to reverse and finally eradicate it. Government will intensify its implementation of the comprehensive strategy against this pandemic and mobilise all sectors and all citizens to play their role.

204. The ANC government will implement a comprehensive human development strategy which includes: improvement of the general education system; intensification of education in mathematics and natural sciences; promotion of social sciences that help build social cohesion; expansion of the nation's artisanship base; improving throughput and research in the universities; and an effective adult basic education programme.

205. Specific programmes of redress such as land restitution and follow-up to the recommendations of the Truth and Reconciliation Commission will continue.

Building Social Cohesion: Promoting Values of a Caring Society

206. The government led by the ANC will consolidate partnerships across society to strengthen social cohesion and ensure that our nation achieves the values of a caring society, inspired by the traits of human compassion which informed our struggle against colonialism. Indeed, the need to build co-operation among all South Africans applies more so to matters of spiritual sustenance such as beliefs and moral values, which are as communal as they are profoundly personal.

207. This we shall do, proceeding from the understanding that comprehensive social transformation entails changing the material conditions of all South Africans for the better, but also ensuring that we forge a nation inspired by values of human solidarity. It is the combination of these factors that describes the civilisation of national democracy that we seek to build.

208. Liberation also means engendering freedom of the human spirit to search for better ways of doing things, to express oneself freely and to enjoy the creative endeavours of humanity. But, informed by the precepts of the country's Constitution, including the Bill of Rights, we do recognise that attached to individual freedom is individual responsibility; attached to collective freedom is collective responsibility.

209. We will work with all sectors of society to promote an overarching South African identity, recognising the diversity of the country's people. We will promote pride in our heritage including geographic and place names, our African identity and our common humanity as global citizens.

210. In this regard, we shall ensure that the content of the education system encourages the inculcation of these values while at the same time promoting critical thought.

211. In promoting intellectual discourse, media freedom and diversity of views, the ANC will encourage appreciation by the media fraternity and the intelligentsia as a whole of the role that they can play in promoting human solidarity and a caring society. The same applies to the arts including music, the oral and written word, crafts, theatre and film.

212. The ANC government will encourage development and promotion of languages used by South Africans. Traditions, religious expressions and other belief systems which are consistent with the values of the country's Constitution form a critical part of the nation's collective resource in the promotion of humane values. In this regard, we will seek to emphasise that which is common and good.

213. By encouraging a positive role for the institution of the family and community, youth involvement in a variety of social endeavours, patriotism

and civic responsibility, community activism, sporting and other social activities, we will seek to promote healthy lifestyles, moral integrity and role models informed by human compassion, generosity, incorruptibility and accountability.

214. While encouraging individual initiative, drive and entrepreneurship, we shall also promote appreciation of the responsibility on the part of those who command political, social, material and other forms of power towards poor and vulnerable sectors of society. In this regard, we will fight against all manifestations of racism, super-exploitation, patriarchy, ethnic chauvinism, religious and political intolerance, and abuse of women and children; discourage greed and the arrogant display of wealth; and campaign against the abuse of drugs and alcohol.

215. Central in this endeavour will be the mobilisation of all South Africans to strengthen the nation's moral fibre informed by the ideals of human compassion and solidarity.

Safety and Security

216. The national struggle for freedom was the critical over-arching vehicle to bring about peace, security and stability to our society. In dealing with issues of crime, the ANC proceeds from the premise that a rising quality of life also means improvement in the safety and security of citizens in their homes and environs where they live, work and engage in extramural activity.

217. Three principles are critical in addressing the challenge of crime, especially its uniquely random and violent nature in our country.

218. The first of these is that the battle against crime cannot be separated from the war on want. In the main, incidents of contact crime such as murder, grievous bodily harm and rape occur among acquaintances in poor communities where living and entertainment environments do not allow for decent family and social life.

219. Secondly, specific mindsets and historical conditions drive elements of the crime problem. These are the proliferation of firearms in the hands of civilians, greed and conspicuous consumption, the psychology of patriarchal power relations, and attitudes towards weaker members of society, especially children.

220. Thirdly, the networks of crime have grown in their reach and sophistication across national boundaries. These include syndicates that deal with money laundering, human smuggling as well as drug trafficking and abuse.

221. The overall programme of national democratic transformation

will gradually eliminate some of the conditions that breed social crime. So shall our contribution to creating an environment of peace, stability, economic growth and social development in Southern Africa and the rest of the continent.

222. Critically, focus must be placed on mobilising society to make life difficult for criminals in our midst. This should include an overhaul of gender and family relations and intolerance of abuse within communities. The transformation of institutions dealing with crime, including integrated efficiency, is also critical. This applies to management, expansion of personnel, utilisation of latest technology, enhanced intelligence capacity, commitment to work with the people and eradication of corruption within the 'criminal justice system'. It also applies to the efficient regulation of the private security industry to ensure that its various capacities, integrity of its recruitment practices and employees' conditions of service are in line with the requirements of what is otherwise an important part of our nation's security establishment.

223. Government will continue to expand and deepen co-operation among law-enforcement agencies in the region and further afield. At the same time we will enhance our systems of border control and improve the capacity of our defence force and intelligence agencies to secure the integrity of our nation-state. We will continue to pay attention to any remaining networks from apartheid's 'dirty war', some of which are an integral part of the criminal networks.

IX. Conclusion

224. Contained in this outline of our Strategy and Tactics is the ANC's assessment of the environment in which we live and the immediate and long-term tasks that we face. It is our collective view of the theory of the South African revolution.

225. During the First Decade of Freedom, we were able to consolidate and deepen our democratic system and introduce critical programmes for social transformation. The progress we have made is commendable; and the decisive actions in the early years of the Second Decade of Freedom hold out the promise of faster progress towards our ideals. But we are only at the beginning of a protracted process of change.

226. The ANC celebrates the end of the first century of its existence wielding political power – a critical platform to improve the quality of life of South Africans and contribute to building a better world. The strategic task remains the same. But the environment in which it has to be pursued has changed significantly for the better.

227. In this phase of national democratic transformation, the ANC commits itself to intensifying its work around the five pillars of social transformation:
- the state,
- the economy,
- organisational work,
- ideological struggle, and
- international work.

224. We will undertake these tasks conscious of our responsibility as one of the battalions of the global army for progressive social change, a disciplined force of the left.

225. The ANC is confident that South Africans will persist in building an enduring national partnership further to change our country for the better. Working together with them, we shall spare neither strength nor courage, until the strategic objective has been attained.

226. The struggle continues!